EU Electronic Communications Law

Robert SK Bell
BA (Nottm) LLM (UCL), Partner, Nabarro Nathanson

Neil Ray
LLB (LSE), Solicitor, Nabarro Nathanson

RICHMOND

EU Electronic Communications Law

Published by:
Richmond Law & Tax Ltd
12-14 Hill Rise
Richmond TW10 6UA
United Kingdom
Tel. +44 (0) 20 8614 7650
Fax +44 (0) 20 8614 7651
info@richmondlawtax.com
www.richmondlawtax.com

ISBN 1-904501-22-2

British Library Cataloguing in Publication Data
A catalogue record for this publication is available from the British Library

Cover design by Bill Anderson Associates
Printed and bound by Antony Rowe Ltd

Table of Contents

Table of Cases

Table of Legislation

1

OVERVIEW OF THE PREVIOUS EU REGULATORY FRAMEWORK

A. INTRODUCTION

With the arrival of the full liberalisation of telecommunications in the majority of the Member States of the European Union on 1 January 1998, a ten-year process of harmonisation and liberalisation was completed.[1] In the period since then, the European telecoms market has undergone something of a revolution. New players have come on to the market offering innovative new services, improved quality and the prices of many services have fallen in real terms. Mobile communications and online services, notably via the Internet, are seeing continued strong growth, as telephone companies compete with each other to offer new combined fixed and mobile service packages, cheaper second phone lines, together with new pricing formulae and new ways of paying for services.

These developments are crucial to permit Europe to participate fully in the benefits of the Information Society. Telecoms liberalisation is the cornerstone of Europe's transition, lowering the price of communicating, encouraging innovation and investment in new services and networks as well as contributing to improved competitiveness and increased employment.

But the transition from a world of incumbent monopolist telecoms to a fully competitive one has not been easy. To effect this difficult transition, detailed rules have been necessary. The application of those rules has had to be carefully monitored and enforced. So the Commission's work was not complete once 1 January 1998 had arrived. Resources had been focused on scrutinising the implementation and practical application of the EU regulatory framework in the Member States, with a number of legal actions being launched where problems arose in national transposition of the measures making up the 1998 Reform Package.

The National Telecommunications regulators (hereinafter referred to as National Regulatory Authorities (NRAs)), which were established in all Member States, were also set a range of tasks by the EU regulatory framework, from the grant of new mobile and fixed network licences, to approving interconnection prices and agreements; policing prices charged to customers for changing operators, and dealing with the allocation of numbers to new market players. National competition authorities (in some

---

1 Transposition of the relevant harmonisation Directives was not fully in place in Portugal, Luxembourg, Italy, Greece and Belgium at that time.

cases one and the same) were also occupied with scrutinising the new telecoms market.

Up until 1980, telecommunications in the EU was characterised by a series of national public monopolies, often run in conjunction with postal services. This began to change in the early 1980s, with privatisation and the introduction of limited competition in some Member States. This development was primarily driven by the increasing application of information technology in the telecommunications sector, which offered the potential to revolutionise the industry. In 1987, the Commission issued a Green Paper[2] in which it proposed a twin-track approach: the introduction of more competition in the telecommunications market; and a higher degree of harmonisation in order to maximise the opportunities offered by a single EC market. The Green Paper was the first step in a ten-year process that culminated in the liberalisation of all telecommunications services and networks by 1 January 1998. There were three key strategies which the Commission adopted to open the market:

(a) progressive liberalisation of a former monopoly sector;

(b) accompanying harmonisation measures;

(c) competition rules.

Each will be discussed in turn below.

1. Progressive liberalisation of a former monopoly sector

The mechanism chosen to liberalise telecoms in the EU was a series of EU Directives based on Article 86 (ex 90) of the EC Treaty. Article 86 gives the Commission power to require the removal of special or exclusive rights granted to undertakings by Member States where other Treaty rules are broken as a result. In the telecoms sector, the Commission considered that giving certain public enterprises special and exclusive rights to produce telecommunications equipment, or to provide telecommunications services and operate networks, breached the EC competition and free movement rules. The various Directives abolished these rights, requiring Member States to permit the provision of competing services. However, there remains no requirement for privatisation of former State controlled monopolists.

A series of Directives was adopted which gradually opened up the market:

(a) In 1988, the Commission adopted a Directive[3] removing all special and exclusive rights to import, market, connect, bring into service and

---

2 Green Paper on the convergence of the telecommunications, media and information technology sectors and the implications for Regulation COM(87)290.
3 Commission Directive 88/301/EEC ([1988] OJ L131/73) on competition in the markets in telecommunications terminal equipment.

maintain telecommunications *terminal equipment* in the Member States.

(b) In 1990, the 'Services Directive'[4] required the abolition of special and exclusive rights over public telecommunications services (but not networks) except the provision of voice telephony services. This covered value-added telecommunications services targeted at business customers, and opened up the provision of communications for businesses or within so-called 'closed user groups' (eg, private branch exchanges – PBXs) to competition.

Subsequent liberalisation was introduced by amending this latter Directive to expand the scope of the activities in the liberalised area.

(1) By 1 January 1993, liberalisation was extended to the provision of data services to the public.

(2) By mid-1993, the Commission had carried out a broad public consultation which led to political commitments from the Council and European Parliament to accept the full liberalisation of telecoms services from 1 January 1998 (subject to possible transitional periods for certain countries). The Council extended this agreement to telecoms networks in the autumn of 1994.

(3) In 1994, the provision of satellite services and satellite equipment was liberalised.

(4) 1995 saw the first steps to liberalise networks with the Cable Directive,[5] which required Member States to allow cable TV networks to be used to offer telecommunications services which were open to competition. (At the time, that opened the possibility of using those networks for corporate and closed user group voice and data services, for value-added services and for the provision of public data services.)

(5) Also in 1996, the Mobile Directive[6] required the removal by 1998 of certain restrictions on the way in which mobile networks were operated (ie, allowing operators to build their own infrastructure or microwave links, rather than relying on the networks provided by the national fixed network operator. This meant they could directly interconnect with mobile or fixed networks in other Member States, rather than having to interconnect via the incumbent operator in their

---

4 The Services Directive: Commission Directive 90/388/EEC ([1990] OJ L192/10) on competition in the markets for telecommunications services.
5 The Cable Directive: Commission Directive 95/51/EC ([1995] OJ L256/49), amending Directive 90/388/EEC with regard to the abolition of the restrictions on the use of cable television networks for the provision of already liberalised telecommunications services.
6 The Mobile Directive: Commission Directive 96/2/EC ([1996] OJ L20/59), amending Directive 90/388/EEC with regard to mobile and personal communications.

home State). There was also a requirement to license DCS 1800 systems[7] in every Member State from 1998.

(6) Finally, in 1996, the Full Competition Directive[8] provided for the early liberalisation of alternative telecoms networks from July 1996, and set the deadline of 1 January 1998 for full liberalisation as well as a mechanism for requesting additional transitional periods. It opened up the market for directory information to full competition, and set out a range of provisions addressing licensing, Universal Service, interconnection, and numbering, which established basic regulatory principles derived from the competition rules.

(7) A further Article 86 Directive[9] was adopted in July 1999. This followed the detailed review of the issue of cable network ownership by telecoms operators and of the restrictions imposed on telecoms operators which prevented them from offering broadcasting services over the telecoms networks. The Directive dealt only with the issue of joint ownership of cable and terrestrial networks by incumbent operators, and required Member States to ensure the structural separation of the cable business. This provision required separation, but not divestiture, of the cable business.

2. Accompanying harmonisation measures

The above-mentioned liberalisation Directives were complemented by a series of harmonising Directives adopted by the Council and European Parliament under Article 95 (ex 100a, internal market), Article 47 (ex 57) and Article 55 (ex 66, freedom to provide services). The aim of these measures was to put in place detailed harmonised regulation to ensure that the aims and principles set out in the Article 86 Directives were upheld across the EU.

The 1990 Framework Directive[10] established the principle of Open Network Provision (ONP) (ie, open access to publicly available telecommunications networks and services, according to harmonised conditions). It set a timetable for legislative action, identifying the need for a series of harmonisation Directives and Recommendations. It also

7 Digital Cellular System 1800 is a personal communications network consisting of GSM (Global System for Mobile Communications) or digital cellular system operating in the GHz band.

8 The Full Competition Directive: Commission Directive 96/19/EC ([1996] OJ L74/13), amending Commission Directive 90/388/EEC regarding the implementation of full competition in telecommunications markets.

9 Commission Directive 99/64/EC ([1999] OJ L175/39), amending Directive 90/388/EEC in order to ensure that telecommunications networks and cable TV networks owned by a single operator are separate legal entities.

10 Council Directive 90/387/EEC of 28 June 1990 ([1990] OJ L192/1) on the establishment of the internal market for telecommunications services through the implementation of open network provision.

established the 'ONP Committee' composed of delegates of the Member States and chaired by the Commission, with both consultative and regulatory powers. The Committee assisted the Commission on matters relating to the legislative programme.

A further Directive, on the application of ONP to leased lines,[11] was adopted by the Council in June 1992 and aimed to ensure the availability throughout the Union of a minimum set of analogue and digital leased lines with harmonised technical characteristics. Leased lines were vital to the early development of competition, since they were the only means by which new entrants could compete with the incumbent.

The Directive on the application of ONP to voice telephony services was adopted by the European Parliament and Council in December 1995.[12] The aims of the ONP Voice Telephony Directive were to ensure the availability throughout the Community of good quality telephone services, and to define the services available to all users, in the context of Universal Service.

In 1995, the Commission's Green Paper on Liberalisation of Infrastructure Part II[13] pointed to the need to adapt the existing ONP Directives to a competitive environment and to develop a further specific Directive on Interconnection. Together with the Licensing Directive, these measures made up the so-called '1998 package' of legislation which was established in time for the opening of the EU telecoms market on 1 January 1998.

3. Competition rules

Alongside the detailed sector-specific legislation, European competition law was applied to telecoms as it had been to all other sectors of the economy. Since a liberalised telecoms market was a relatively new phenomenon, the Commission published Guidelines on the application of EC competition law in the telecoms sector. These guidelines sought to clarify, specifically in relation to telecoms, what sort of behaviour was likely to fall foul of the competition rules (Articles 81 and 82 of the Treaty). The Commission also issued a Notice on the Application of Competition Rules to Access Agreements[14]. These agreements were considered vital if new entrant operators were to be able to reach end-users served exclusively by an

---

11 Council Directive 92/44/EEC of 5 June 1992 ([1992] OJ L165/27) on the application of open network provision to leased lines.

12 Directive 98/10/EC of the European Parliament and of the Council of 26 February 1998 ([1998] OJ L101/41) on the application of open network provision (ONP) to voice telephony and on universal service for telecommunications in a competitive environment.

13 European Parliament Resolution of 19 May 1995 on the Green Paper on the liberalisation of telecommunications infrastructure and cable television networks Part II: A common approach to the provision of infrastructure for telecommunications in the European Union (A4-0111/95; [1995] OJ C151/479).

14 Notice on the application of the competition rules to access agreements in the telecommunications sector; Framework, Relevant Markets and Principles ([1998] OJ C265/1).

incumbent's network. The Commission considered that the control incumbents had over access to end-users could prove a source of competition problems. The Notice therefore set out the access principles which stem from EC competition law; defined the interplay between competition law and the telecoms regulatory framework; and explained how the competition rules would be applied in a consistent way across the various sectors involved.

B. MAIN THEMES

1. Significant Market Power

The concept of 'Significant Market Power' (SMP) was an important one in the ONP regulatory framework.[15] Operators with such power were subject to additional regulatory obligations, such as the requirement to offer cost-oriented interconnection rates, or to meet all reasonable requests for access to their network. Generally, there was a presumption that SMP existed where an operator, whether fixed or mobile, was judged by the NRA to have 25 per cent or more in the relevant market, though the NRA could determine that an operator had SMP with less than 25 per cent of the market, or indeed that it did not, even if the operator had more than 25 per cent.[16] Apart from determining the relevant market, existence of SMP was determined on a range of other factors: the organisation's ability to influence market conditions; its turnover relative to the size of the market; its control of the means of access to end-users; its access to financial resources and its experience in providing products and services in the market. All incumbent operators were judged to possess SMP in the fixed public telephone market.

In the case of mobile operators, the Interconnection Directive[17] required that cost-oriented interconnection pricing would only apply where the operator had SMP on the national market for interconnection (ie, fixed and mobile).

2. Fixed/mobile

Just as there was differentiation in the level of regulation applying to individual players depending on their market power, there was also differentiation between sectors. One major theme which ran through all

---

15 Council Directive 90/387/EEC of 28 June 1990 ([1990] OJ 192/1) on the establishment of the internal market for telecommunications services through the implementation of open network provision.

16 The definition of 'Significant Market Power' was set out in Art 4(3) of Directive 97/33/EC of the European Parliament and of the Council of 30 June 1997 ([1997] OJ L199/32) on interconnection in telecommunications with regard to ensuring universal service and interoperability through application of the principles of Open Network Provision (ONP).

17 Directive 97/33/EC ([1997] OJ L199/32).

the legislation was the principle that rules for the fixed sector were stricter than those for the mobile sector. The reason for this was primarily historical: the mobile sector, as a relatively new technology, had always been subject to some degree of competition. Therefore the obligations which applied were less onerous.

3. Open Network Provision

As has been earlier stated, the regulatory framework for telecommunications had been based on the concept of Open Network Provision (ONP). This established the need for harmonised conditions of access to public networks and services according to defined principles of objectivity, transparency and non-discrimination. These principles applied to the actions of both regulators and market players and set the basis for fair and even-handed regulation and commercial conduct in a liberalised telecoms market.

One example of this was the requirement in the Interconnection Directive[18] that operators apply similar interconnection terms and conditions to all operators offering similar services (including their own activities and those of subsidiaries and partners). Another less obvious example was the need for greater transparency than might be appropriate in more traditional markets because, in the transition from a monopoly to a liberalised environment, effective competition could require more information to be in the public domain because of the strong position enjoyed by incumbent operators. The Interconnection Directive therefore contained a requirement for interconnection agreements to be made available by the NRA to all interested parties.

4. Pricing principles

In a fully competitive market, market forces and the commercial process set prices rather than regulators. However, in the transition to full and effective competition where these forces might not be sufficiently strong, Community legislation in the telecoms sector contained two pricing principles which departed from this principle.

First, the requirement for cost-oriented tariffs applied in a wide range of areas to operators to be notified to the Commission as having SMP (as defined in Community law). This requirement applied, inter alia, to interconnection charges, the provision of leased lines, the provision of special network access and voice telephony services.

Given the importance of interconnection charges in securing strong competition in a newly liberalised market, guidelines to assist NRAs in determining whether interconnection charges were cost-oriented or not

18 Directive 97/33/EC ([1997] OJ L199/32).

were set out in the Commission Recommendation on interconnection pricing.

Secondly, a requirement for affordability existed in the Voice Telephony Directive[19] in relation to the provision of Universal Service as defined in Community law. Affordability was for each Member State to define in the light of the different priorities which existed for consumers in different Member States and the differing standards of living.

5. Subsidiarity

As in all Community legislation, subsidiarity is an important consideration in the EC regulatory framework in telecoms. The regulatory framework at Community level established a set of minimum requirements which Member States were obliged to implement and enforce. But the means of implementation was left to each Member State to decide according to its own requirements and national legal system. Day-to-day management and enforcement of the regulatory framework was the responsibility of the NRAs of each Member State. Licences were granted exclusively at national level, and NRAs decided whether particular services in their territory should be subject to general authorisations or individual licences, within the overall framework established by the Licensing Directive.[20] So Member States had a good deal of freedom to regulate their own national telecommunications market according to specific national conditions.

Moreover, in certain areas, it was possible for Member States to impose additional national requirements on operators, for example in the area of mandatory service provision. The EC regulatory framework introduced the concept of Universal Service, ie, a set of minimum services which had to be available to all. EC legislation gave NRAs discretion to establish a Universal Service fund to compensate the Universal Service operator if it considered that the cost of providing those services outweighed the benefits of being a Universal Service operator.

It was open to a Member State to set additional obligations on operators as part of Universal Service in its territory. An example of one such additional obligation was the requirement in Belgium for the provision of ISDN-based Internet access for all schools. But where a Member State does so, such obligations could not be funded via a Universal Service funding mechanism. Normally, this meant that any costs associated with such obligations had to be met either by the operator(s) concerned or directly by

19 Directive 98/10/EC of the European Parliament and of the Council of 26 February 1998 ([1998] OJ L101/41) on the application of open network provision (ONP) to voice telephony and on universal service for telecommunications in a competitive environment.
20 The Licensing Directive: Directive 97/13/EC of the European Parliament and of the Council of 10 April 1997 ([1997] OJ L117/15) on a common framework for general authorisations and individual licences in the field of telecommunications services.

the State. They would also have to be consistent with the Treaty rules, and in particular, the competition rules relating to State aid.

In other areas, EC legislation did not allow Member States to go further. For example, the Licensing Directive[21] set out an exhaustive list of conditions which could be applied to licences. Member States were not permitted to impose any other conditions on licences, and the Commission took action against certain Member States which had done so.

C. MAIN PROVISIONS

Some of the key provisions of the 1998 package and liberalisation Directives are set out below.

1. National Regulatory Authorities

The responsibility for implementing and enforcing the EC telecoms regulatory framework rested primarily with the National Regulatory Authorities (NRAs). In this sense, the proper functioning of the legislation relied on NRAs carrying out their tasks effectively. Member States were therefore required to ensure that NRAs had sufficient resources to do so. The regulatory package also required Member States to ensure that the historic regulatory functions of the public monopolies were vested in independent bodies, and that where national governments retained some degree of ownership or control over organisations providing telecommunications networks and/or services, the regulatory function was structurally separate from activities associated with ownership or control.

2. Licensing

Speedy, transparent and effective licensing of communications services and networks is essential to the proper functioning of a vigorous, competitive internal market in electronic communications. The previous framework set out a series of principles (non-discrimination, transparency, proportionality and objectivity) for the granting of authorisations and licences. The framework distinguished between general authorisations (eg, class licences) and individual licences, and sought to restrict the use of the latter (administratively heavier) procedure to certain prescribed cases (in general terms, use of frequency, numbers, rights of way, SMP operators, Universal Service, and voice telephony). The framework also required that there was no limitation on the number of licences granted, except where this was unavoidable (ie, where the available frequency for a service imposed a limit on the number of licensees). As has been mentioned earlier, licences were granted by Member States; there was no mechanism to grant licences at European level, though there were provisions for the

21 Directive 97/13/EC ([1997] OJ L117/15).

harmonisation of licensing conditions across the EU and the development of a one-stop-shopping procedure.[22]

3. Interconnection

An interconnection framework is central to the successful development of a competitive telecoms market, because new entrants have to rely on the networks of incumbent operators to deliver, transit or terminate traffic from or to their customers. Regulation at EU level started from the premise that interconnection was primarily a matter for commercial negotiation. But it was a key policy objective of regulation that there should be end-to-end interoperability for telecoms services in the EU. Therefore, in general terms, the regulatory framework ensured that operators had a basic right and obligation to negotiate interconnection. In the absence of such a framework, there would be little incentive for incumbent operators to conclude interconnect arrangements with new entrants, or they would only do so on terms which reflected their natural advantages in terms of market position and information. As has been mentioned above, operators with SMP had an obligation to agree interconnection terms, and to meet all reasonable requests for access to their network.

4. Universal Service

The political importance of ensuring a defined level of service at an affordable price for all users is widely recognised. In a monopoly environment, service came from a single operator and lower charges for connection, line rentals and local calls could be subsidised out of the higher revenues generated by long-distance and international call charges. As liberalisation approached, a number of Member States as well as consumer and other organisations were concerned about the ability of market forces on their own to deliver Universal Service in a competitive environment. EU regulation therefore defined Universal Service at European level and provided for mechanisms for sharing any costs associated with its provision amongst market players (so-called Universal Service funding schemes), where this was considered necessary by the NRA. As has been mentioned above, Member States were free to extend the definition of

---

22 The one-stop-shopping (OSS) procedure for licences was set up by the European Telecommunications Office (ETO). The ETO was established by the Member States and was charged with facilitating the provision of certain liberalised services across the Member States through the OSS procedure. The ETO has subsequently been integrated with its sister office – the European Radiocommunications Office (ERO). The OSS procedure consists of: (a) a single ERO point of contact for service providers; (b) information on licensing procedures in the Member States; (c) a single application form in English, common to all Member States; (d) a single document summarising the results of the procedure, with any licences granted by different NRAs attached; and (e) a procedure where an answer is given to the service provider in no more than nine weeks.

Universal Service at national level if they so wished, but they were not permitted to fund such provision via contributions from market players.

5. International aspects

The EU's trade relations with third countries in respect of telecommunications are principally governed by the GATS Fourth Protocol on Basic Telecommunications Services which came into force in February 1998. The Protocol covers all telecommunications services sub-sectors: local, long-distance and international, irrespective of whether they consist of the transport of sound, data, images or any combinations thereof. Generally, the commitments made by WTO countries on basic telecommunications include all possible technological means of transmission: cable, radio or satellites. The commitments cover market access and national treatment, and are mostly phased-in: the dates for liberalisation of services such as public voice telephony vary from 1998 to 2011.

Forty-eight WTO Members, including the EC and its Member States, also undertook commitments on regulatory principles on the basis of the so-called Reference paper, which addresses issues such as interconnection, anti-competitive practices, licensing conditions, scarce resources, Universal Service and independence of the regulatory authorities. They aim to underpin market access and national treatment commitments made by WTO Members.

6. European standardisation

A key part of telecoms liberalisation and the creation of a European single market is European standardisation. To this end, one of the first steps in telecommunications policy was the establishment of the European Telecommunications Standards Institute (ETSI) in 1988. The ONP framework[23] made provision for standards developed by ETSI to be published in the Official Journal and their use encouraged by Member States. Similarly, in the field of telecoms terminal equipment, ETSI has been given mandates by the Commission to develop standards. European standardisation and ETSI in particular have also played a vital role in the development of mobile and wireless communications, for example in the development of the GSM standard.

---

23 Council Directive 90/387/EEC ([1990] OJ L192/1).

D. THE FUTURE OF TELECOMS REGULATION AT EU LEVEL

The 1998 package of Directives was successful in creating the conditions for vigorous competition in the European telecoms market. But for the Commission, much work remained to be done to build on this success.

The telecoms sector was undergoing a period of immense technological and market change. This was evidenced by the public consultation that the Commission launched in December 1997 on implications of the phenomenon of convergence of the telecommunications, broadcasting and IT sectors for regulation of electronic communications in the next century. The results of that consultation demonstrated that convergence was reshaping the communications market, and would have enormous consequences for society in terms of economic development, job creation and cultural identities. One key message from that consultation was the need for horizontal regulation across the converged sectors, which implied equivalent treatment of all transport network infrastructure and associated services, irrespective of the types of services carried. Rules pertaining to sectors concerned would need to be reviewed to examine whether they would be relevant in the light of convergence or whether some rules would hamper growth.

The Commission was obliged by the previous framework to undertake a Review by the end of 1999 to examine what provisions of the regulatory framework would need to be adapted in the light of market developments, evolution of technology and changes in consumer demand. The goal of this Review was to clarify and simplify the regulatory framework so as to be able to build on the achievements of the then current framework and create a regime that would be able to adapt quickly and flexibly to developments in technology and market structure.

The Commission issued a Communication on the Review, which launched a public consultation on certain key policy issues towards the end of 1999. In the light of this public consultation, the Commission produced proposals to amend the framework during 2000.

2
OBJECTIVES OF THE NEW REGULATORY FRAMEWORK

A. INTRODUCTION

The telecommunications sector was liberalised in most Member States of the European Union on 1 January 1998, so that competing operators were able to enter all parts of the telecoms market[24]. This completed a ten-year process of harmonisation and liberalisation begun in 1990.

By unleashing the forces of competition, EU telecoms policy has had a major impact on the development of the market, contributing to the emergence of a strong communications sector in Europe, and allowing consumers and business users to take advantage of greater choice, lower prices and innovative services and applications.

The application of the EU's regulatory framework for telecommunications has substantially enhanced the EU's global competitiveness, and has also created a world class communications industry; an essential pre-condition for Europe's transition to an Information Society. Information Society industries already contribute around 15 per cent to growth of the EU's Gross Domestic Product and create one out of every four new jobs in the European economy.

But in a sector that is as dynamic as telecommunications, regulatory policy cannot stand still. New communications services and in particular the development of the Internet have been revolutionising the way people communicate and do business. This revolution has been driven by the convergence of the telecommunications, media and information technology sectors. The EU has had to ensure that its regulatory policies remain effective in increasing competition, facilitating the provision of innovative new services and driving down prices, for the benefit of all consumers.

Experience so far has demonstrated that the regulatory framework can best sustain and drive forward these developments by encouraging effective and vigorous competition at all levels of the market, while at the same time safeguarding key public interests. The previous regulatory framework for telecommunications had achieved this balance, but its very success in promoting competition and innovation meant a new framework was required.

---

24 Portugal and Greece benefited from derogations until 1 January 2000 and 31 December 2000 respectively.

B. TECHNOLOGICAL AND MARKET DEVELOPMENTS

It was for these reasons that the European Commission launched a review of the current telecoms framework in its consultation document, the 1999 Communications Review, published in November 1999. The aims of the Review were five-fold:

(a) to promote more effective competition;

(b) to react to technological and market developments;

(c) to remove unnecessary regulation and simplify associated administrative procedures;

(d) to strengthen the internal market; and

(e) to protect consumers.

It drew on the key messages of a series of consultations, reports and independent studies, in particular the Communication on the Convergence of the Telecommunications, Media and Information Technology Sectors,[25] the Communication on the consultation on the Radio Spectrum Green Paper,[26] the report on the development of the market for Digital Television in the European Union,[27] and the fifth report on the Implementation of the Telecom Regulatory Package.[28]

The starting point of the Review was that the communications sector was characterised by technological and market developments taking place at an unprecedented speed. These developments are discussed below.

The *convergence* of the telecommunications, IT and media sectors was reshaping the communications market and required a more horizontal approach to regulation. The fact that all communications networks, whether telecoms, cable TV or satellite and terrestrial broadcast, can carry any form of digital information (voice, image or data) meant that regulatory policy could no longer distinguish between different communications infrastructure. It was essential therefore that any new framework treat all transport network infrastructure and associated services in an equivalent manner, irrespective of the types of services carried.

The *globalisation* of technologies and markets had accelerated in scope and intensity, raising technical, commercial, and legal issues which

25 Communication to the European Parliament, the Council, the Economic and Social Committee and the Committee of the Regions on the Convergence of the Telecommunications, Media and Information Technology Sectors and Implications for Regulation, COM(99)108.

26 Communication from the Commission: Next Steps in Radio Spectrum Policy - Results of the Public Consultation on the Green Paper, COM(99)538 of 10 November 1999.

27 Commission Communication on the development of digital television in the European Union, COM(99)540.

28 Commission Communication on the fifth report on the implementation of the telecommunications regulatory package, COM(99)537.

required global solutions. Organisations at intergovernmental and private sector levels had been mobilised into working towards common approaches within a variety of formal and cooperative frameworks.

Considerable concentration in the industry brought about profound changes in the nature of the telecommunications industry and relationships between key players. These changes had created firms which were driving the implementation of pan-European and global services, built on new and expanded infrastructures.

The *Internet* continued to a large extent to overturn traditional market structures, by providing a common platform for the delivery of a wide range of services. The Internet blurs the distinction between voice and data transmission services, revolutionises traditional pricing models for communications services, and challenges existing regulatory structures. In Europe, the Internet has been experiencing a continued expansion, in terms of the number of users and the volume of traffic. This growth will be fuelled by implementation of the next generation of Internet protocols that will facilitate the delivery of voice, data and video over the Internet with agreed levels of quality of service.

C. IMPROVEMENTS IN PROCESSING, ACCESS AND BASIC TRANSMISSION TECHNOLOGIES

In particular, wave division multiplexing on optical fibres and digital subscriber loop (xDSL) technologies in local access networks are reducing the cost and increasing the capacity of communications infrastructure. Computing power is doubling every 18 months, transmission capacity every 12 months. Previous uneconomic applications will therefore become commonplace as communications costs fall.

Wireless applications are increasingly entering all segments of the market. The mobile sector continues to experience strong growth, likely to be further strengthened by the introduction of third generation systems. Competition in local access markets will be strengthened by the development of wireless broadband local loop technology. Meanwhile, the race to develop new systems offering global mobility has given new impetus to the growth of the satellite sector, with the development both of narrowband personal communications services and 'Internet in the sky' broadband multimedia communications.

Software re-configurable technologies are enabling operators and service providers to easily tailor their services to meet the specific local market requirements. Software re-configuration is providing flexibility and innovation in the fixed as well as mobile networks, by permitting dynamic re-configuration of access points, terminal and network resources. This is having profound implications for manufacturers, operators (eg, dynamic allocation of resources, active networks, security, quality of service, service providers, eg time-to-market), users (eg transparency and portability of services), as well as regulators and standardisation bodies (eg, terminal type approval).

The development of technologies within the media sector, in particular digital television (DTV), is providing a wide range of innovative services for both pay TV subscribers and free-to-air viewers. These include transactional 'on demand' services and other new services such as digital teletext, Internet and e-commerce.

The new regulatory framework therefore had to address the emerging shortcomings of the current framework for telecommunications, and take into account the market and technological developments described above. It had to reinforce competition in all market segments, particularly at local level. In particular, it has been designed to cater for new, dynamic and largely unpredictable markets with many more players than today. Finally, it aims to ensure a light regulatory approach for new service markets, while ensuring that dominant players do not abuse their market power.

D. POLICY OBJECTIVES

It cannot be forecast with certainty how all the above trends will shape the market over the coming decade. While the underlying technological trends are relatively well understood, the new products and services that will exploit this technology will have to compete for acceptance in the marketplace, and it is by no means clear which ones will emerge as 'winners'. Regulators and market players alike face uncertainty as they look towards the future convergent environment.

Regulators therefore need to have very clear objectives including those of public interest and a set of general-purpose regulatory 'tools' if they are to succeed in stimulating and sustaining a market that remains vigorously competitive and meets users' and consumers' needs, while at the same time protecting consumers' rights.

The review of the regulatory framework for communications took the form of a Communication from the Commission of the European Parliament to the Council of Ministers, the Economic and Social Committee and the Committee of the Regions. This Communication[29] presented a review of the European Union's regulation in the sphere of telecommunications and proposed the following series of high level policy

29 Communication from the Commission to the European Parliament, the Council, the Economic and Social Committee and the Committee of the Regions on a new framework for electronic communications infrastructure and associated services: infrastructure, transmission and access, COM(99) 539.

objectives for national regulators to follow in this new regulatory framework.

(1) To promote an open and competitive European market for communications services, as the means of:

- providing EU consumers and businesses with the best deal in terms of low prices, high quality and maximum value for money;

- ensuring that competition is not distorted in a complex and converging market;

- offering choice and variety of innovative services in response to user needs.

(2) To benefit the European citizen, by:

- ensuring that all citizens have affordable access to a Universal Service specified at European level, and access to a wide range of communications services;

- protecting consumers in their dealings with suppliers, in particular by ensuring the availability of simple and inexpensive dispute resolution procedures;

- ensuring a high level of data protection and privacy for citizens;

- requiring transparency of the tariffs and conditions for using communications services, in order to allow users to make informed choices;

- addressing the special needs of specific social groups, in particular disabled users.

(3) To consolidate the internal market in a converging environment, by:

- removing remaining obstacles to the provision of communications networks and services at European level;

- ensuring that, in similar circumstances, there is no discrimination in the treatment of companies across the EU;

- ensuring the effective management of scarce resources, in particular radio spectrum;

- encouraging the establishment and development of trans-European networks and the seamless interoperability of pan-European services.

Safeguarding Community interests in international negotiations is also an important objective for the Commission and Member States in this sector. Liberalisation of public telecommunications networks and services in 1998 as a result of the GATS/WTO agreement has been clearly beneficial to the Community. The Community has stated that it will continue to press for extension of this agreement to other countries in the forthcoming WTO negotiations to ensure that electronic commerce and the Internet can develop at a global level.

E. REGULATORY PRINCIPLES

The Communication[30] proposed five principles that would underpin the new regulatory framework and govern regulatory action at Community and national level.

1. The first principle
Regulation should be based on clearly defined policy objectives fostering economic growth and competitiveness thereby promoting employment and ensuring objectives of general interest where they are not satisfied by market forces.

The main policy objectives for the sector are described above. However, competition and a free market cannot meet all the policy objectives and the new regulatory framework will therefore continue with a combination of sector specific legislation, horizontal legislation and application of the competition rules.

2. The second principle
Regulation should be kept to the minimum necessary to meet those policy objectives.

An unduly restrictive regulatory system risks acting as a brake on investment or may fail to stimulate sustainable investment. Many of the previous regulatory framework provisions addressed the need to create a competitive market, for example by requiring incumbent operators to meet all requests for access to and interconnection with its network.

Once a competitive market is effectively established, many of these provisions should no longer be necessary and it will therefore be sufficient to rely mainly on the application of the competition rules of the Treaty. The new framework therefore will have built-in mechanisms whereby certain basic rules are reviewed periodically to assess whether they are still necessary.

Wherever possible, the new framework will rely on existing horizontal regulation rather than sector-specific legislation. New regulation at EU level will be proposed only where absolutely essential, for example where there is market failure to meet a particular public interest objective.

Market players will be encouraged to take self-regulatory initiatives, for example to develop codes of practice in those areas where a common approach is necessary, so as to minimise the need for formal regulation.

---

30 See para [60], note 1.

3. The third principle

Regulation should further enhance legal certainty in a dynamic market.

The regulatory framework will continue to offer legal certainty to market players to allow them to make investment decisions. The new regulatory framework has recognised the importance of being capable of adapting flexibly to market developments if it is to remain effective in meeting its objectives. Detailed rules quickly become obsolescent, necessitating frequent changes in regulation thereby undermining legal certainty.

The new framework therefore will set out basic rules, principles and objectives, and supplement these with non-binding measures such as Recommendations. In this context, it has been important to establish the right mechanisms to coordinate interpretation of these rules by regulators across the EU. The strength, independence and effectiveness of NRAs is recognised as essential to the success of implementation of this model, as well as the availability of timely and transparent decision-making processes.

4. The fourth principle

Regulation should aim to be technologically neutral.

Technological neutrality means that legislation will define the objectives to be achieved, and should neither impose, nor discriminate in favour of, the use of a particular type of technology to achieve those objectives. The previous legislative framework was not technologically neutral. Different rules applied, for example, to services provided over mobile and fixed networks, and to access to frequencies for telecoms and broadcasting networks. As has been mentioned earlier, convergence, whether between broadcasting and telecommunications or between fixed and mobile telephony, allows the same service to be delivered over networks which to date have been regulated differently.

As far as possible therefore, regulation of communications services will not differentiate between technologies over which such services are delivered. Regulation that is based on specific technology can quickly become outdated, and may lead to inefficient investment by market players. This principle does not mean that all communications infrastructure should be regulated in an identical manner. Some rules are specific to certain types of network: for example, 'wireless' networks are subject to rules on frequency allocation and usage; 'wired' networks are subject to rules about rights of way and digging up streets.

But it does mean that the provision of services should be regulated in a homogenous way whatever the communications infrastructure on which they are carried, whether telecoms networks or broadcasting networks, so that the regulatory framework does not distort competition. There will continue to be instances, eg, investigations under competition law, where different networks could constitute separate markets and regulatory measures will be needed to be taken on the basis of specific network or product technologies. However, the principle of technological neutrality will not be used as a means to introduce more restrictive rules in any market.

5. The fifth principle

Regulation may be agreed globally regionally or nationally but should be enforced as closely as is practicable to the activities being regulated.

Increasingly, communications is a global market. Regulation will therefore increasingly be agreed at global level, for example in such fields as electronic commerce and spectrum management for global services. The EU aims to continue to pursue international solutions, consisting of principles and guidelines on industry codes of practice self-regulation, interoperable technological solutions, and legal rules where needed. The global nature of convergence demands flexible international cooperation mechanisms.

Enhanced international cooperation will require flexible regulatory instruments whose scope will not be territorially confined, even though the sanction mechanisms for such rules would retain a territorial component. Experience in the EU has demonstrated that effective enforcement of legal measures is best when closest to the activities regulated.

This implies the following lines of approach:

(a) Primary responsibility for achieving objectives set out in sector-specific Community legislation will rest with the independent national regulators, who are best placed to take account of the different levels of competition and market development in the Member States.

(b) The natural counterpart of such delegation is greater coordination of Member States' actions, in order to avoid fragmentation of the internal market; market operators are entitled to an environment in which pan-European services can be deployed without encountering significant regulatory differences in different Member States.

(c) This requires closer Commission monitoring and quality assessment activities to ensure consistent and effective implementation of regulation at national level. Experience with the previous legislative framework for telecommunications (which is quite detailed) shows that the way in which Community legislation is implemented at national level has a major impact on the actual level of competition in a market.

(d) In addition, this approach emphasises the need for transparency and impartiality in the conduct of public authorities, coupled with effective dispute-settlement mechanisms, so that the fundamental economic and civil rights of citizens, economic operators and investors are protected.

F. THE DESIGN OF THE FUTURE REGULATORY FRAMEWORK

The Communication proposed that the future regulatory framework should cover all communications infrastructure and services associated with that infrastructure. In other words, the new framework would apply to to satellite networks, fixed and mobile terrestrial networks (whether circuit or packet switched), cable TV networks and other networks used for radio and television broadcasting, as well as to services such as Application Program Interfaces, which control access to services. However, the new framework would not cover services carried over that infrastrucure, eg, services providing broadcasting content.

The Communication also contained a large number of specific proposals. Among the most important were the following.

1. Licensing and authorisations: deregulating market access

The Communication noted that the current framework for telecommunications allowed Member States to insist on the use of individual licences (authorisations specific to an individual operator and requiring the operator to seek an explicit authorisation from a regulator before beginning operations). The Communication argued that this degree of control on market entry had created administrative barriers which in some cases appeared to be disproportionate. It had also contributed to large variations in authorisation regimes across the EU, which were holding back innovation, competition and the provision of pan-European services.

The Communication proposed that the new framework should require operators providing communications services to be licensed using general authorisations (ie, no requirement for explicit authorisation by a regulator before providing services). Specific authorisations would remain necessary for the use of radio spectrum and numbering resources. This deregulated, harmonised framework would reduce the current variation in licence regimes for telecommunications across the EU.

2. Access and interconnection

The Communication proposed that the new framework should establish common principles for regulation of access and interconnection across all communications infrastructure. This would ensure new entrants could compete effectively against dominant operators whatever the transmission medium and would mean that any new competition bottlenecks could be dealt with effectively as they arose. In particular, it was proposed to build in flexible mechanisms to reduce regulatory intervention as competition increased and respond to a rapidly changing market.

3. Universal Service

The Communication recalled the Commission's commitment to ensuring affordable access for all to communications services necessary for participation in the Information Society, in particular in order to avoid the emergence of a 'digital divide' between the 'info-rich' and the 'info-poor'. Universal Service was crucial in this regard because it guaranteed a minimum set of services to which all were entitled at an affordable price.

The Communication concluded that it was essential that consideration of whether additional services should be included in an extended scope of Universal Service had to combine an analysis of the demand for and availability of the service with an assessment of its social and economic desirability. Otherwise there was a risk of distortion of competition and an unfair cross-subsidy[31] by the majority of consumers to higher bandwidth users (generally businesses and 'early adopters'). The Communication therefore proposed to maintain at this stage the current definition and scope of Universal Service, but ensure that procedures for periodic review were put in place to allow Universal Service to keep pace with market and technological change.

4. Competition in the local loop

The Communication called for urgent action to increase competition in the local loop (the line between the local exchange and the subscriber's premises). It noted that incumbent operators still dominated the market for provision of communications services at local level, despite growing use of new and existing alternative infrastructure (eg, cable TV or wireless local loop networks) by new entrants to compete with the incumbent.

The Communication announced the Commission's intention to use Recommendations and, in specific cases, its powers under the competition rules of the Treaty to encourage local loop unbundling throughout the EU.

5. Consistent regulatory action at EU level

The Communication argued that inconsistent application of certain provisions of telecommunications legislation was hindering the development of effective competition and the deployment of pan-European services. The Communication rejected calls for the establishment of a European Regulatory Authority for communications services at this stage.

---

31 Cross-subsidisation occurs where an undertaking uses revenue from one market to subsidise losses in another market. Where an undertaking uses revenues from a market where it is dominant, it may be unfair and there may be a breach of the Chapter II prohibition: Competition Act 1998, Chapter II.

But it called for cooperation between the Commission and national regulators to be urgently improved. It was proposed to create a High Level Communications Group of National Regulatory Authorities and the Commission, in which these types of problems could be discussed and solutions found on the basis of rules agreed at Community level. Where necessary, these solutions would be backed up by legal measures adopted by the Commission under its executive powers, with the assistance of a new Communications Committee. This Committee would replace the two current committees in the area of telecommunications.

G. THE CONSULTATION

Recognising that the policy issues at stake were vital for Europe, the Commission sought the views of interested parties on the policy positions proposed in the Communication over a three-month period running up to 15 February 2000. More than 200 responses were received, from a wide range of interests inside and outside the EU. A list of respondents can be found in the Annex to this Communication. In addition, over 550 people attended a two-day public hearing held by the Commission on 25 and 26 January 2000. On the basis of the comments received in the course of the consultation, the Commission proceeded to draw up proposals for legislation. At the end of April, DG Information Society published for consultation five working documents which summarised the key issues that it considered should form the basis of the proposed legislation. It held a public hearing in May 2000 on the working documents and received over 100 further contributions from interested parties, commenting on the content of the working documents.

H. THE EIGHT PROPOSED LEGAL MEASURES

The Commission then issued on 12 July 2000 eight proposed legal measures that would replace the 20 existing regulatory measures and make up the new electronic communications regulatory framework. The measures are as follows:

(a) the Framework Directive;[32]

(b) the Access and Interconnection Directive;[33]

---

32 Framework Directive 2002/21/EC ([2002] OJ L108/33) (implemented by the Communications Act 2003).

33 Access and Interconnection Directive 2002/19/EC ([2002] OJ L108/7) (implemented by the Communications Act 2003).

(c) the Authorisation Directive;[34]

(d) the Users' Rights and Universal Service Directive;[35]

(e) the Data Protection Directive;[36]

(f) the Local Loop Unbundling Regulation;[37]

(g) a Decision on Community Radio Spectrum (the Radio Spectrum Decision); and

(h) a draft Competition Directive.

The Framework Directive[38] is the Directive on a common regulatory framework for electronic communications networks and services. The Framework Directive is the cornerstone of the new regulatory framework, containing the common provisions that underlie the other measures in the new framework. Key provisions are as follows:

(a) It sets out the enlarged scope of the new framework, covering all forms of electronic communications networks and electronic communications services.

(b) It contains the new definition of undertaking with Significant Market Power (SMP), on whom regulatory obligations can be placed to guarantee effective competition. The new definition is based on the competition law concept of dominance.

(c) It sets out duties of national regulators, establishes a right of appeal against regulatory decisions, and lays down procedures for dispute resolution.

(d) It obliges regulators to consult widely on all their important decisions. It also seeks to introduce a 'single market reflex' via a transparency mechanism. This has two important provisions: (i) it obliges regulators to consult other national regulators on proposed measures before they are adopted; and (ii) it allows the Commission to require a National Regulatory Authority (NRA) to amend or withdraw a draft measure in certain circumstances. All this is aimed at ensuring consistent implementation throughout the EU.

(e) It sets out rules for management of frequency and numbers, as well as certain provisions governing rights of way.

34 Authorisation Directive 2002/20/EC ([2002] OJ L108/21) (implemented by the Communications Act 2003).
35 Users' Rights and Universal Service Directive 2002/22/EC ([2002] OJ L108/51) (implemented by the Communications Act 2003).
36 Draft Data Protection Directive ([2002] OJ L201/37) (due to be implemented by 31 October 2003).
37 Regulation 2887/2000/EC ([2000] OJ L336/4) on unbundled access to the local loop.
38 Framework Directive 2002/21/EC ([2002] OJ L108/33).

(f) Finally, it establishes the Communications Committee and the High Level Communication Group of national regulators that will assist the Commission in ensuring that the new framework is really effective on the ground.

The Access and Interconnection Directive[39] is the Directive on access to and interconnection of electronic communications networks and associated facilities. This Directive provides a pro-competitive and harmonised framework to stimulate competing network infrastructures and interoperability of services, while ensuring that bottlenecks in the market do not constrain the emergence and growth of innovative services that benefit users and consumers. Key provisions are as follows:

(a) It maintains the 'primary interconnectivity rule', according to which all operators have both the right and the obligation to negotiate interconnection.

(b) It specifies a set of regulatory obligations (including non-discrimination, cost-oriented pricing, access to specific network elements) that regulators can impose on specific operators to guarantee fair competition.

(c) It provides continuity with the existing framework by maintaining existing obligations, but requiring regulators to review them against the new framework once it is in force.

(d) It maintains existing obligations on providers of conditional access systems to offer access to their facilities on fair, reasonable and non-discriminatory terms.

The Directive on the Authorisation of Electronic Communications Networks and Services[1] aims to simplify administrative controls on market access for operators, which is still subject to a great deal of red tape in many Member States. In particular, it:

(a) requires the use of general authorisations for all electronic communications networks and services (with separate rights of use for spectrum and numbers);

(b) limits and harmonises conditions that can be imposed on authorisations to the minimum necessary;

(c) limits administrative charges strictly to administrative costs and exempts small enterprises from such charges;

(d) simplifies procedures, including the information regulators can request when verifying compliance with authorisation conditions;

---

39 Access and Interconnection Directive 2002/19/EC ([2002] OJ L108/7).

(e) strengthens the internal market, by ensuring that operators do not face widely divergent licence regimes or fees when they enter each Member State.

The proposed Directive on Universal Service and users' rights relating to electronic communications networks and services[40] sets out the rights of users and consumers in the field of electronic communications networks and services, including the level of Universal Service. Key provisions are as follows:

(a) to adapt and modernise existing measures on Universal Service so as to define the scope of this service, the rights of users and the measures for compensating providers of the service without distorting competition;

(b) to create a process for reviewing the scope of Universal Service obligations;

(c) to lay down specific users and consumers rights, eg, on contracts, quality of service, transparency of information, etc;

(d) to allow NRAs to take measures to safeguard the interests of users and consumers, eg, in relation to retail price regulation;

(e) to extend the obligation for number portability to mobile networks;

(f) to recognise and codify the right of Member States to impose proportionate 'must carry' obligations on network operators to meet legitimate public policy considerations;

(g) to underpin the industry's efforts to ensure interoperability of consumer digital television equipment;

(h) to ensure the availability of leased lines in the EU until competition in these services develops;

(i) a requirement for caller-location information to be made available to authorities handling calls to the European emergency number 112, where technically feasible;

(j) a requirement for operators to handle calls to numbers using the new code 388 for Europe-wide services.

The Directive on the Processing of Personal Data and the Protection of Privacy in the Electronic Communications Sector[41] updates the current Directive to ensure it is technologically neutral and to extend its scope to all

40 Users' Rights and Universal Service Directive 2002/22/EC ([2002] OJ L108/51).
41 Draft Data Protection Directive ([2002] OJ L201/37).

electronic communications networks and services. Key changes are as follows:

(a) creating a possibility for operators to undertake further processing of traffic data for the purpose of value added services with the consent of the subscriber or user;

(b) ensuring that location data available to mobile operators may only be used with the consent of the subscriber, and providing subscribers and users with a simple means to temporarily deny processing of their location data;

(c) giving subscribers the right to determine whether they are listed in a public directory and what personal data appears in such a directory;

(d) prohibiting 'spam' (unsolicited commercial emails) except where subscribers have 'opted in', ie, they have indicated that they want to receive such emails for direct marketing purposes.

The local access network remains one of the least competitive segments of the liberalised telecommunications market. It is therefore essential to enable new entrants to get access to these local loops and upgrade them to provide higher speed Internet services. The Regulation on unbundled access to the local loop[42] provides a legal basis to enforce unbundled access to local loops of operators having SMP by 31 December 2000. Key provisions are as follows:

(a) Incumbent operators are required to provide competitors with unbundled access to their local copper loops (both on the basis of exclusive use and of shared use) on fair, reasonable and non-discriminatory terms. This includes the right for competitors to have access on the same terms as those offered to the operators themselves or their associated companies.

(b) Physical access must be granted at any technically feasible point on the copper loop. It also includes the right for the new entrant to co-locate its own network equipment with that of the incumbent.

(c) The price for unbundled access to the local loop must be cost-oriented, so long as competition is not sufficient to prevent excessive pricing.

(d) Operators must publish a reference offer for unbundled access to local loop, including prices, terms and conditions.

42 Regulation 2887/2000/EC ([2000] OJ L336/4) on unbundled access to the local loop. This Regulation came into force on 1 January 2001. Notified operators were to publish from 31 December 2000, and keep updated, a reference offer for unbundled access to their local loops and related facilities. They were also, from 31 December 2000, to meet reasonable requests from beneficiaries for unbundled access to their local loops and related facilities, under transparent, fair and non-discriminatory conditions.

The Radio Spectrum Decision establishes a policy and legal framework in the Community in order to achieve the harmonisation of the use of the radio spectrum. It proposes to:

(a) establish a policy forum which, on the basis of technological, market and regulatory developments and after consultation of relevant spectrum user communities, would advise the Commission on the use of radio spectrum in EU policy areas of a commercial and non-commercial nature;

(b) establish a legal framework which would allow the Commission to grant mandates to the European Conference of Postal and Telecommunications Administrations (CEPT) and to secure implementation by the Member States of measures aimed at the harmonised availability and use of radio spectrum for EU policies;

(c) ensure EU wide transparency through coordinated and timely provision of information relating to radio spectrum use so that investment and policy decisions can be made;

(d) safeguard EU interests in international negotiations on radio spectrum by ensuring that common positions are adopted to reach EU policy objectives.

The Competition Directive consolidates all the specifically competition orientated provisions of the previous regime and replaces Commission Directive 90/388/EEC and its provisions as amended. It also introduces further amendments in the areas of: exclusive and special rights for electronic communications networks and electronic communications services; vertically integrated public undertakings; rights of use of frequencies; directory services; Universal Service obligations; satellites; and cable television networks.

The package constitutes a substantial simplification and consolidation of previous legislation with approximately 20 legal measures reduced to five Directives and one Regulation. These six proposals and the Radio Spectrum Decision[43] were adopted jointly by the European Parliament and the Council under Article 251 of the EC Treaty on 7 March 2002. The Competition Directive's provisions were adopted by the Commission under Article 86(3) on 16 September 2002. Each of the Directives will be discussed in detail in the following chapters.

---

43 Decision 676/2002/EC of the European Parliament and of the Council on a regulatory framework for radio spectrum policy in the European Community ([2002] OJ L249/21).

I. THE ROLE OF COMPETITION LAW

As competition becomes fully established, ex-ante rules take a backseat and the focus of concern migrates to the behaviour of market players, so competition rules will be of increasing importance in this sector. The Commission intends to increase its surveillance of the sector in order to avoid incumbent operators extending their strong or dominant position throughout the converged markets, when sector specific rules designed to ensure competition are relaxed. The Commission has already launched a Sector Inquiry[44] under its competition law powers to assess whether the current situation with respect to leased line tariffs, local telephone tariffs and mobile telephone (GSM/DCS-1800) roaming results from a violation of the competition rules or from a lack of competitive structure in the market place.

When deciding whether to handle complaints or open own initiative cases, the Commission will take into account the powers that NRAs have to deal with the relevant matters. An essential element in this evaluation is the extent to which an NRA is in a position to provide an effective remedy for an infringement of Article 81 or Article 82. However, this may prove difficult, for example, in cases involving cross-border elements.

---

44 European Commission Sector Inquiry on the Competitive Provision of Leased Lines in EU Telecoms Markets, Public Hearing, Brussels, 22 September 2000.

3
THE FRAMEWORK DIRECTIVE

A. INTRODUCTION

The convergence of the telecommunications, media and information technology sectors has led to the adoption of a single regulatory framework covering all transmission networks and services. The new regulatory framework aims to maximise growth in the electronic communications market and provide the platform for building 'eEurope'.

The previous telecoms-related Article 94 (ex 100) Directives were transposed and implemented by Member States in a disparate manner. There was little harmonisation in the implementation of the various measures. Many Member State governments or NRAs imposed additional restrictions and rules further limiting the compatibility and cost-effectiveness of networks and services offered across the single market.

Therefore, the strengthening of the single market and the creation of an Europe-wide Information Society is now envisaged through harmonising the implementation of European Directives in all Member States. The Framework Directive is very important in this regard, as it aims to significantly enhance the harmonisation of electronic communications regulation across Europe.

The Framework Directive establishes a harmonised framework for the regulation of electronic communications services, electronic communications networks, associated facilities and associated services across the EU. It sets out the roles of the Member States' national regulatory authorities and establishes a set of procedures to ensure the harmonised application of the regulatory framework throughout the European Union. It is the 'umbrella' under which the four specific Directives function[45]. The Framework Directive is accompanied by four specific Directives and one competition Directive. Together, these six Directives replace 26 Directives that made up the prior regulatory

---

45 The four Specific Directives are as follows:
– Directive 2002/20/EC of the European Parliament and of the Council of 7 March 2000 ([2002] OJ L108/21) on the authorisation of electronic communications networks and services;
– Directive 2002/19/EC of the European Parliament and of the Council of 7 March 2000 ([2002] OJ L108/7) on access to, and interconnection of, electronic communications networks and services;
– Directive 2002/22/EC of the European Parliament and of the Council of 7 March 2000 ([2002] OJ L108/51) on universal service and users' rights relating to electronic communications networks and services;
– Directive 2002/58/EC of the European Parliament and of the Council of 12 July 2002 ([2002] OJ 201/37) on the processing of personal data and the protection of privacy in the electronic communications sector.

framework. The only Directive under the old framework that survives is the 1999 'RTTE' Directive[46].

B. DEFINITIONS

The Framework Directive[47] defines 'electronic communications service' as a service: (a) normally provided for remuneration; (b) which consists wholly or mainly in the conveyance of signals; (c) on electronic communications networks.

The Framework Directive defines 'electronic communications network' as: (a) transmission systems and, where applicable, switching or routing equipment; (b) that permit the conveyance of signals; (c) by wire, radio, optical or other electromagnetic means. Each definition contains a list of examples of services or facilities that are included or excluded from the definition.

Electronic communications services include: (a) telecommunications services; (b) transmission services in networks used for broadcasting. But they exclude: (a) services providing or exercising editorial control over content transmitted using electronic communications networks and services such as web-based content, financial services and broadcasting content; (b) Information Society services which do not consist wholly or mainly in the conveyance of signals on electronic communications networks.

Electronic communications include: (a) satellite networks; (b) fixed (circuit and packet switched, including Internet) and mobile terrestrial networks; (c) electricity cable networks, to the extent that they are used for the purpose of transmitting signals; (d) networks used for radio and television broadcasting and cable TV networks.

All of the above types of networks are covered, irrespective of the content of the information conveyed. The Competition Directive adds to this list by indicating that 'fibre networks which enable third parties, using their own switching or routing equipment, to convey signals' should also be included in the definition of electronic communications networks.[48]

The Framework Directive includes within its scope 'associated facilities' and associated services. 'Associated facilities' are defined as:

(a) facilities associated with an electronic communications network and/or an electronic communications service;

---

46 Directive 1999/5/EC of the European Parliament and Council of 9 March 1999 ([1999] OJ L91/10) on radio equipment and telecommunications terminal equipment at the mutual recognition of their conformity.

47 Framework Directive 2002/21/EC ([2002] OJ L108/33).

48 Directive 2002/77/EC ([2002] OJ L249/21), recital 7.

(b) which enable and/or support the provision of services via that network and/or service.

Associated facilities includes conditional access systems and electronic program guides. 'Associated services' is not defined.

C. EXCLUSIONS

1. Information Society services

Most Information Society services fall outside the new framework. Article 1 of the Transparency Directive[49] defines 'Information Society services' as, 'Any service normally provided for remuneration, at a distance, by electronic means and at the individual request of a recipient of services'.

Radio broadcasting, television broadcasting services and teletext services are not 'information society services' because they are not supplied 'at the individual request of a recipient of services'.[50] Voice telephony, telefax and telex services are not considered 'information society services' because they are not provided by electronic processing inventory systems.[51]

The Framework Directive states that most information society services do not qualify as electronic communications services (and fall outside the new Framework) because they 'do not consist wholly or mainly in the conveyance of signals on electronic communications networks'.[52] The Framework Directive then specifies that voice telephony services and email services are covered by the Framework Directive.

The Framework Directive also states that a bundle of services will fall, in many cases, both under rules on content and rules on electronic communications services. The Framework Directive gives the examples of an ISP that offers both electronic communications services, such as Internet access, and content services, such as web-based content.

---

49 Directive 98/34/EC of the European Parliament and the Council of 22 June 1998 laying down a procedure for the provision of information in the field of technical standards and regulations and of rules of Information Society services ([1998] OJ L204/37), as amended by Directive 98/48/EC ([1998] OJ L217/18).
50 Framework Directive 2002/21/EC ([2002] OJ L108/33), Annex V.
51 Ibid.
52 Framework Directive 2002/21/EC ([2002] OJ L108/33), recital 10.
53 Council Directive 89/552/EC ([1989] OJ L331/51) on the coordination of certain provisions laid down by law, regulation or administrative action in Member States concerning broadcasting activities.

---

2. Broadcasting services content

Broadcasting services in the editorial and content sense fall outside the Framework. Article 1 of the Television Without Frontiers Directive[53] defines television broadcasting as follows:

> the initial transmission by wire or over the air, including that by satellite, in encoded or unencoded form, of television programmes intended for reception by the public. It includes the communication of programmes between undertakings with a view to their being relayed to the public. It does not include communication services providing items of information or other messages on individual demand such as telecopying, electronic data banks, and other similar services.

The definition of 'television broadcasting' includes services consisting mainly or exclusively of the conveyance of signals over electronic communications networks. The Framework Directive makes clear, however, that it does not mean to exclude 'television broadcasting' from its scope of application, only the content of television broadcasting. Television broadcasting is therefore covered, and by the Television Without Frontiers Directive as regards the editorial content of the programme.

3. National security

The new framework does not affect law enforcement or national defence activities.[54] Rules on wiretaps, interception of emails, retention of data for law enforcement purposes and encryption will continue to be governed by the national law of each Member State. These rules fall outside the new Directives.

The Framework Directive covers all satellite and terrestrial networks, including both fixed and wireless (ie, the public switched telephone network, networks using Internet Protocol (IP), cable TV, mobile and terrestrial broadcast networks). However, the Framework Directive does not cover services such as broadcast content, or electronic commerce services.

---

53 Council Directive 89/552/EC ([1989] OJ L331/51) on the coordination of certain provisions laid down by law, regulation or administrative action in Member States concerning broadcasting activities.
54 Framework Directive 2002/21/EC ([2002] OJ L108/33), recital 7.

Telecommunications terminal equipment is also not within the scope of the Framework Directive[55].

D. NATIONAL REGULATORY AUTHORITIES

The primary responsibility for implementing the new framework will rely, as in the previous framework, on the National Regulatory Authorities (NRAs) in the 15 EU Member States. NRAs are seen as best placed to assess the specific conditions in their national markets, and the measures required to address them.

The Framework Directive establishes a more flexible set of rules at Community level, and gives NRAs a large degree of flexibility to choose the tools most appropriate to deal with regulatory concerns as they arise. But as a counterweight to this increased flexibility, the Framework Directive seeks to improve cooperation between NRAs, and between the European Commission and the NRAs, in a transparent manner, to ensure the consistent application throughout the EU of the provisions of the legislation. Requirements for consultation and for cooperation between NRAs and other national authorities (in particular national competition authorities) are also more detailed compared to the current framework, as are the provisions on appeal.

The relevant provisions are contained in Chapter II of the Framework Directive, entitled 'National Regulatory Authorities' (NRAs), which contains Articles 3 to 7. These Articles set out the NRAs' areas of responsibility and their obligations to facilitate various operational procedures.

1. Establishment

The Framework Directive states how NRAs must be constituted. For example, Member States are obliged to guarantee the independence[56] of the NRAs to ensure that they are able to make impartial decisions. For those Member States[57] who retain ownership interests or control of companies providing electronic communications networks and/or services,

---

55 The Framework Directive 2002/21/EC ([2002] OJ L108/33) does not cover the content of services such as broadcasting content, financial services and certain information society services. Ibid, Art 1(3) states that Member States are free to regulate such content and audio-visual policy in order, for example, to promote cultural and linguistic diversity and media pluralism. Member States are also free to legislate to safeguard national security interests, and allow the investigation, detection and prosecution of criminal offences, including obligations (which must be specific and proportional) applicable to providers of electronic communications services. The Directive also does not cover equipment within the scope of Directive 1999/5/EC but does cover consumer equipment used for digital television.

56 Independent means that NRAs must be legally distinct and functionally independent of all those companies providing electronic communications network, equipment or services.

57 For example, France and its 'golden shares' in France Telecom.

they must put in place effective structural separation between the NRA and the commercial activities of those companies.

Member States must also ensure that NRAs are provided with all the necessary resources. Historically, many NRAs had suffered from large staff turnover, lack of sector knowledge and poor finances. However, the Framework Directive emphasises that Member States should provide NRAs with the staffing, expertise and finances necessary for carrying out their regulatory functions.

Member States must ensure that the roles of national NRAs are clearly defined and published, especially if certain assigned tasks are the responsibility of other government institutions,[58] for example, in the areas of competition law and consumer law.[59] These government institutions must cooperate closely together and are permitted to exchange confidential information submitted to them.

2. Right of appeal

Member States are obliged to put in place effective procedures which allow aggrieved undertakings to challenge the decision of an NRA. The appeal must be available to any user or supplier of electronic communications networks or services who is 'affected' by the decision.[60] Although this language would appear to give a right of appeal to an entity that is not directly subject to an NRA decision, for example, a decision involving a mobile operator giving rise to an appeal by another mobile operator adversely affected by the decision, in accordance with using recitals as an aid to integration, the provision should be interpreted in accordance with recital 12 of the Framework Directive which contains a narrower definition. Recital 12 states that only a 'party who is the subject of a decision' will have the right of appeal.

The appeal body may be a court or another independent body. It must have the appropriate expertise to decide any contested decisions. It must be able to consider the merits of the case, rather than just the procedure that was followed. Decisions of the NRA are binding pending the outcome of any appeal decision. And all appeal decisions are subject to review by the European Courts.

---

58 The new regulatory framework covers not only traditional telecommunications services but also broadcasting networks and services. Member States may therefore have to rethink the roles and structures of their existing regulatory bodies. For example, in the UK, a new regulator, OFCOM, is being established to be responsible for all communications – both traditional telecommunications and audiovisual broadcasting.

59 Framework Directive, Art 3(6) also obligates Member States to notify to the Commission the various government bodies that will be responsible for the implementation of the various obligations contained in the Directives.

60 Framework Directive, Art 4(1).

3. Exchanges of information

Supply of information to NRAs: The Framework Directive requires that entities providing electronic communications network or services comply with information requests from the NRAs.[61] The NRAs' information requests must be proportionate to the performance of the regulators' tasks under the Framework Directive, and must include reasons for the request.

Supply of information to the Commission: NRAs, in turn, must comply with reasoned information requests from the Commission.[62] The Commission's requests must also be proportionate to the performance of the Commission's tasks and it must make the information it receives available to NRAs in the other Member States (unless the NRA providing the information makes an explicit or reasoned request to the contrary).

Supply of information from an NRA to other NRAs: Following a reasoned request, each NRA must also make the information it receives available to other NRAs, either in the same country or in another Member States. The Commission and NRAs must ensure that the confidentiality of information they receive (eg, business secrets and other confidential information) is maintained.

Supply of information to the Communications Committee:[63] The Commission must provide the Communications Committee with details of the outcome of regular consultations with operators, service providers, users, consumers, manufacturers, trade unions, third countries and international organisations.[64] The Committee is aimed at fostering an exchange of information between Member States, and between Member States and the Commission.[65]

Information regarding application of the Directives: Member States must publish information on the application of the Directives, and make such information available to the Commission (who in turn will make it available to the Communications Committee).[66] Finally, for transparency purposes, NRAs must publish such information as would contribute to an open and competitive market.[67] NRAs must publish rules for obtaining access to any such information.[68]

---

61 Framework Directive, Art 5(1).

62 Framework Directive, Art 5(2).

63 The Communications Committee consists of representatives of the Member States and is chaired by the Commission. In practice, the Member States send representatives of their respective Ministries of Telecommunications and/or Broadcasting. The Communications Committee sets up its own rules of operation in accordance with the Comitology Decision under Art 5.

64 Framework Directive, Art 23(1).

65 Ibid, Art 23(2).

66 Framework Directive, Art 24(1).

67 Framework Directive, Art 5(4).

68 Framework Directive, Art 5(5).

Consultation and transparency mechanism: NRAs are placed under an obligation in Article 6 of the Framework Directive to consult whenever they take decisions affecting third parties. NRAs must give interested parties a reasonable period to comment on draft measures that will have a significant impact on a relevant market. NRAs must publish their consultation procedures and establish a single information point through which all current consultations can be accessed. The responses to the consultation process should be made publicly available subject to any confidential information submitted by interested parties.

4. Consolidating the internal market for electronic communications

In order to ensure the consistent application of the new Directives in all Member States and to the extent that NRA measures affect trade between Member States, NRAs are required under Article 7 to submit draft decisions on:

(a) the designation of undertakings with Significant Market Power on particular markets; and

(b) the definition of individual markets that differ from those defined in the Commission Recommendation to the Commission and the other Member States' NRAs.

The Commission and the other NRAs have one month to comment on the draft measures. The NRA is under an obligation to take 'the utmost account' of comments made by the other NRAs and the Commission but can still adopt its own draft measures except as described below.

If the Commission considers that a draft measure would create a barrier to the single market or harbours serious doubts as to its compatibility with EU law, then the Commission can insist that the draft measure not be adopted for a further two months. During this period, the Commission may ask the NRA to withdraw the draft measure. However, its decisions must be detailed and accompanied with an objective analysis as to why the draft measure should not be adopted and specific proposals for amending the draft measure. Only in exceptional circumstances can Member States derogate from this procedure, for example, when required to safeguard competition or protect the interests of users, but can only adopt proportionate and provisional measures. Any attempt by an NRA to make such decisions permanent are subject to the consultation process above and Commission approval[69].

---

69 This procedure is without prejudice to the notification procedure provided for in Directive 98/34/EC and the Commission's prerogatives under the Treaty in respect of infringements of Community law.

5. Policy objectives and regulatory principles

Chapter III of the Framework Directive sets out the tasks of the NRAs. Article 8, in particular, requires NRAs to follow a defined set of objectives and principles set out in paras 2, 3 and 4 which are aimed to contribute to the fulfilment of broader Community policies in the promotion of culture, employment, the environment, social cohesion and town and country planning. NRAs are also required to take 'the utmost account of the desirability of making regulations technologically neutral'. Simply, NRAs cannot impose on or discriminate against particular types of technology.[70]

Article 8(2) lists how NRAs can promote competition in the provision of electronic communications networks, electronic communications services and associated facilities[71] and services by, inter alia:

(a) ensuring that users, including disabled users, derive maximum benefit in terms of choice, price and quality;

(b) ensuring that there is no distortion or restriction of competition in the electronic communications sector;

(c) encouraging efficient investment in infrastructure, and promoting innovation; and

(d) encouraging efficient use and ensuring the effective management of radio frequencies and numbering resources.

Article 8(3) lists how NRAs can contribute to the development of the internal market by, inter alia:

(a) removing remaining obstacles to the provision of electronic communications networks, associated facilities and services at European level;

(b) encouraging the establishment and development of trans-European networks and the interoperability of pan-European services, and end-to-end connectivity;

(c) ensuring that, in similar circumstances, there is no discrimination in the treatment of undertakings providing electronic communications networks and services; and

(d) cooperating with each other and with the Commission in a transparent manner to ensure the development of consistent

---

70 However, this does not prevent Member States from taking proportionate action to promote specific services when it is justified, for example, where Member States wish to encourage the adoption of digital television as a way of increasing spectrum efficiency.
71 This is defined in Framework Directive, Art 2(e), and means 'those facilities associated with an electronic communications network and/or an electronic communications service which enable and/or support the provision of services via that network and/or service. It includes conditional access systems and electronic program guides'.

regulatory practice and the consistent application of this [Framework] Directive [and the other adopted Directives].

Article 8(4) lists how NRAs can promote the interests of EU citizens by, inter alia:

(a) ensuring all citizens have access to a Universal Service;[72]

(b) ensuring a high level of protection for consumers in their dealings with suppliers, in particular by ensuring the availability of simple and inexpensive dispute resolution procedures carried out by a body that is independent of the parties involved;

(c) contributing to ensuring a high level of protection of personal data and privacy;

(d) promoting the provision of clear information, in particular requiring transparency of tariffs and conditions for using publicly available electronic communications services;

(e) addressing the needs of specific social groups, in particular disabled users; and

(f) ensuring that the integrity and security of public communications networks are maintained.

E. MANAGEMENT OF RADIO FREQUENCIES FOR ELECTRONIC COMMUNICATIONS SERVICES

Article 9 sets out a number of obligations related to allocation and assignment of radio spectrum. Given the importance of radio frequencies to the development of radio-based communications services, the Framework Directive provides that their allocation must be according to objective, transparent, non-discriminatory and proportionate criteria[73]. Member States are also obliged to seek ways to promote the harmonised use of radio frequencies in accordance with Decision 676/2002/EC (Radio Spectrum Decision).[74]

The Framework Directive also introduces a right for NRAs to permit the trading of frequency assignments subject to certain safeguards. Any transfer by an undertaking of its radio frequencies must be notified to the NRA responsible for spectrum assignment and must take place in

---

72 As specified in Directive 2002/22/EC.
73 Framework Directive, Art 9(1). Member States can also take into account the democratic, social, linguistic and cultural interests related to the use of the frequency.
74 The Radio Spectrum Decision 676/2002 ([2002] OJ L108/1) establishes a framework for harmonisation of radio frequencies and action taken under the Framework Directive is intended to facilitate the work under that Decision.

accordance with pre-published procedures. NRAs must ensure that competition in the marketplace is not distorted as a result of any such assignment of radio frequency.[75]

1. Numbering

Article 10 sets out the obligations in respect of national numbering plans. In particular, the Framework Directive requires NRAs to ensure sufficient numbers exist for all public providers of electronic communications services[76]. Assignment of numbering resources must be based on transparent, objective and non-discriminatory criteria[77]. However, Member States are allowed to use competitive or comparative selection procedures for the assignment of radio frequencies and numbers which have 'exceptional economic value'[78].

The Commission, using its executive powers, may implement measures where there is a need for harmonisation of numbering resources in the Community to support the development of pan-European services. Member States are also obliged to coordinate their positions within international organisations and forums in discussions on the global interoperability of services and issues relating to the numbering, naming and addressing of electronic communications networks and services[79].

2. Rights of way

Article 11 covers the grant of rights of way to public and private electronic communication networks[80]. NRAs must have procedures[81] which are timely, non-discriminatory and transparent[82] when dealing with applications for the granting of rights to install facilities on, over, or under public or private property. Where public or local authorities maintain an ownership or control interest in undertakings operating electronic communications networks, there must be an effective structural separation between the grant of these rights and the undertaking's commercial activities. There must also be an effective and independent appeal against decisions not to grant the rights requested.

75 Where radio frequency use has been harmonised through the Radio Spectrum Decision or any other Community measure, the transfer cannot result in the change of use of that radio frequency.

76 The Framework Directive does not establish any new areas of responsibility for NRAs in the field of Internet naming and addressing.

77 Framework Directive, Art 9(3) provides that national numbering plans are subject only to limitations imposed on grounds of national security.

78 In administering such schemes, NRAs must take into account the provisions of ibid, Art 8.

79 Framework Directive, Art 10(5).

80 The provisions are without prejudice to national provisions governing the expropriation or use of property, and the normal exercise of property rights.

81 The procedures can differ depending on whether the applicant is providing public communications networks or operates a private network.

82 Conditions attached to the grant of the rights must also be transparent and non-discriminatory.

3. Co-location and facility-sharing

To the extent that undertakings enjoy the right to install facilities on public or private property, Article 12 obliges NRAs to encourage the sharing of these facilities on the land. It specifically refers to town planning, public health and environmental benefits[83] and encourages NRAs to promote the adoption of voluntary agreements between companies. However, where undertakings are deprived of access to viable alternatives, Member States may impose compulsory facility- or property-sharing after full public consultation. Any sharing or coordination arrangements can include rules for apportioning the costs of the facility or property sharing.

4. Accounting separation and financial reports

Entities enjoying special or exclusive rights in other fields (such as water or electricity) must either:

(a) maintain separate accounts for their electronic communications activities as if those activities were carried out by a legally independent company; or

(b) implement full structural separation.[84]

The choice is left to Member States. Member States may opt out of this requirement for companies having a revenue of less than 58 million in electronic communications services.

F. UNDERTAKINGS WITH SIGNIFICANT MARKET POWER

The approach underlying the Framework Directive is to regulate where there is not effective competition. In that case, certain specific obligations will fall on those operators which have Significant Market Power (SMP) and are operating on particular markets where competition is not effective. The first step for regulators is therefore to identify those markets where competition is not effective, and secondly to designate which operator(s) have SMP on those markets.

Under the previous regulatory framework, regulated markets were pre-defined in the legislation on the basis of what type of service was being provided (eg, fixed telephony). Moreover, the SMP designation was based on a 25 per cent market share threshold, though NRAs have some flexibility to deviate from this. Now that similar services can be provided

---

83 For example, the Directive states that where mobile operators are required to share towers or masts, such mandated sharing can lead to a reduction in the maximum transmitted power levels allowed for each operator for public health reasons, but may in turn require operators to install more transmission sites to ensure national coverage.

84 Framework Directive, Art 13(1).

over a variety of different technological platforms, the current framework has become too inflexible.

The Framework Directive acknowledges the need to maintain ex-ante obligations in certain circumstances in order to maintain the development of a competitive market. Historically, the definition of SMP in Directive 97/33/EC of the European Parliament and of the Council of 30 June 1997, on interconnection in telecommunications with regard to ensuring Universal Service and interoperability through application of the principles of Open Network Provision (ONP),[85] has proved effective in the initial stages of market opening as the threshold for ex-ante obligations, but this has been adapted to the more complex and dynamic markets. For this reason, the definition used in this Directive is equivalent to the concept of dominance as defined in the case law of the Court of Justice and the Court of First Instance of the European Communities:

> An undertaking shall be deemed to have significant market power if, either individually or jointly with others, it enjoys a position equivalent to dominance, that is to say a position of economic strength affording it the power to behave to an appreciable extent independently of competitors, customers and ultimately consumers.[86]

NRAs will have to follow the Guidelines on market analysis and the assessment of market power published by the Commission under Article 15. The new definition of SMP is unlikely to change the regulatory status of the incumbent fixed-line operators in each country. For example, BT, Deutsche Telecom, France Telecom, Telefonica and Telecom Italia are likely to continue to be deemed SMP operators for most services in their home markets. The most significant change will be for European mobile network operators. Three or four operators normally share the market in most Member States, with no single operators controlling more than 50 per cent of the market. No operator will therefore have SMP status in contrast to the previous regime where an operator with 25 per cent market share would be deemed as holding SMP and subject to specific conditions. The Framework Directive states that two or more undertakings can be found to enjoy a joint dominant position if there are structural or other links between them and also where the structure of the relevant market is conducive to coordinated effects, for example, it encourages parallel or aligned anti-competitive behaviour on the market. The criteria used in making such assessments are found in Annex II which is extracted in the following paragraph.

> Two or more undertakings can be found to be in a joint dominant position within the meaning of Article 14 if, even in the absence of

---

85 [1997] OJ L199/32, as amended by Directive 98/61/EC ([1998] OJ L268/37).
86 Framework Directive 2002/21/EC ([2002] OJ L108/33), Art 14(2), which uses terminology from Case 27/76 United Brands v EC Commission [1978] ECR 207, [1978] CMCR 429.

structural or other links between them, they operate in a market the structure of which is considered to be conducive to coordinated effects. Without prejudice to the case law of the Court of Justice on joint dominance, this is likely to be the case where the market satisfies a number of appropriate characteristics, in particular in terms of market concentration, transparency and other characteristics mentioned below:

– mature market;

– stagnant or moderate growth on the demand side;

– low elasticity of demand;

– homogeneous product;

– similar cost structures;

– similar market shares;

– lack of technical innovation, mature technology;

– absence of excess capacity;

– high barriers to entry;

– lack of countervailing buying power;

– lack of potential competition;

– various kind of informal or other links between the undertakings concerned;

– retaliatory mechanisms;

– lack or reduced scope for price competition.

The above is a non-exhaustive and non-cumulative list. The list is only intended to illustrate the sorts of evidence that could be used to support claims concerning the existence of joint dominance.

The Framework Directive also recognises the possible leveraging of SMP held in one market into a closely related market which would strengthen the overall market position of an undertaking. In such cases, an undertaking may also be regarded as holding SMP on the closely related market[87].

G. MARKET DEFINITION PROCEDURE

Ex-ante obligations will only be imposed in markets where there is no effective competition, namely, those markets where there are one or more undertakings with SMP, and where national and EC competition law remedies are considered insufficient to solve the problem. The

87 Framework Directive 2002/21/EC ([2002] OJ L108/33), Art 14(3).

Commission[88] is charged with the responsibility of adopting a Recommendation on Relevant Product and Service Markets which will define product and service markets (in accordance with the principles of competition law)[89] within the electronic communications sector which may justify the imposition of regulatory obligations contained in this and the other Directives. A list of the markets included in the final Commission Recommendation[90] is extracted below.

1. Markets referred to in Directive 2002/22/EC (Universal Services Directive).

Article 16 – Markets defined under the former regulatory framework, where obligations should be reviewed.

– The provision of connection to and use of the public telephone network at fixed locations.

– The provision of leased lines to end-users.

2. Markets referred to in Directive 2002/19/EC (Access Directive).

Article 7 – Markets defined under the former regulatory framework, where obligations should be reviewed.

– Interconnection (Directive 97/33/EC).

– Call origination in the fixed public telephone network.

– Call termination in the fixed public telephone network.

– Transit services in the fixed public telephone network.

– Call origination on public mobile telephone networks.

– Call termination on public mobile telephone networks.

– Leased line interconnection (interconnection of part circuits).

– Network access and special network access (Directive 97/33/EC, Directive 98/10/EC).

– Access to the fixed public telephone network, including unbundled access to the local loop.

– Access to public mobile telephone networks, including carrier selection.

– Wholesale leased line capacity (Directive 92/44/EEC).

– Wholesale provision of leased line capacity to other suppliers of electronic communications networks or services.

88 After public consultation and consultation with the NRAs.
89 And without prejudice to markets that may be defined in specific competition law cases.
90 Commission Recommendation of 11/02/03 on relevant product and service markets within the electronic communications sector susceptible to ex-ante regulation in accordance with Directive 2002/21/EC of the European Parliament and of the Council on a common regulatory framework for electronic communication networks and services, C(2003)497.

3. Markets referred to in Regulation 2887/2000.

– Services provided over unbundled (twisted metallic pair) loops.

4. Additional markets.

The national market for international roaming services on public mobile telephone networks.

The Commission is also responsible for drawing up guidelines for NRAs to follow in assessing whether competition is effective in a given market and in assessing SMP. In its guidelines, the Commission must address the issue of newly emerging markets where the de facto market leader is likely to have a substantial market share but where it may be inappropriate to impose specific obligations.

NRAs must take 'utmost' account of the Recommendation and the Guidelines in defining relevant national markets.[91] In particular, the Framework Directive states that NRAs are also required to include an analysis as to whether an individual market is prospectively competitive and whether therefore the lack of effective competition will be merely transitory.

H. MARKET ANALYSIS PROCEDURE

Following the publication of the Commission's Recommendation, NRAs are required to carry out their analysis of the relevant markets in accordance with the Commission's Guidelines. If NRAs conclude that a market is effectively competitive, they cannot impose any specific conditions on undertakings in that market. In the case of existing ex-ante regulation, NRAs must remove any specific conditions placed on individual undertakings in that market. There is an assumption that, over time, obligations will be removed as competition increases in the relevant markets.

Where NRAs conclude that a relevant market is not effectively competitive, they must determine those undertakings with SMP and can impose (or maintain if they already exist) specific conditions.[92]

As a transitional measure, NRAs will be able to maintain the conditions imposed under national law and referred to in Article 7 of the Access Directive and Article 16 of the Universal Service Directive until the relevant

91 Where there are transnational markets, NRAs are obliged to cooperate with each other and the Commission may, in accordance with the procedure laid down in Art 22(3), adopt a Decision identifying transnational markets.

92 In the case of transnational markets, NRAs must jointly carry out market analysis and decide on the imposition, maintenance or amendment of any specific conditions.

NRA has completed its market analysis review.[93] Similarly, fixed public telephone network operators designated as having SMP by their national NRA will continue to be considered as 'notified operators' for the purposes of Regulation 2887/2000 until the relevant NRA has completed its market analysis review accordingly.

I. EUROPEAN REGULATORS GROUP

The Commission has set up an advisory group of the independent NRAs on electronic communications networks and services, the 'European Regulators Group for Electronic Communications Networks and Services'.[94] The Group is composed of the heads of each relevant NRA in each Member State or their representatives. The Commission is also represented and provides the secretariat to the Group.

The role of the Group is to advise and assist the Commission in consolidating the internal market for electronic communications networks and services. It will provide a very useful mechanism for encouraging cooperation and coordination of NRAs. It will help to ensure the consistent application, in all Member States, of the provisions set out in this Directive and the specific Directives, in particular in areas where national law implementing Community law gives NRAs considerable discretionary powers in application of the relevant rules.

J. STANDARDISATION

Standardisation remains a primarily market-driven process under the Framework Directive[95]. However, the possibility exists for the implementation of selected standards to be made mandatory. Under Article 17(1), the Commission, using the procedure referred to in Article 22(2), can draw up and publish in the Official Journal of the European Communities a list of standards and/or specifications which will serve as a basis for encouraging the harmonised provision of electronic communications networks, electronic communications services and associated facilities and services.

---

93 Framework Directive 2002/21/EC ([2002] OJ L108/33), Art 27(1).
94 Commission Decision 2002/627/EC ([2002] OJ L200/38) establishing the European Regulators Group for Electronic Communications Networks and Services.
95 Standardisation procedures under this Directive are without prejudice to the provisions of Directive 1999/5/EC, Council Directive 73/23/EEC of 19 February 1973 on the harmonisation of the laws of Member States relating to electrical equipment designed for use within certain voltage limits, and Council Directive 89/336/EEC of 3 May 1989 on the approximation of the laws of the Member States relating to electromagnetic compatibility.

Following consultation of the Committee established by Directive 98/34/EC,[96] the Commission may also request that standards be drawn up by the European Standards Organisations (European Committee for Standardisation (CEN),[97] European Committee for Electrotechnical Standardisation (CENELEC),[98] and European Telecommunications Standards Institute (ETSI)).[99]

Member States are obliged to encourage the use of these standards and/or specifications for the provision of services, technical interfaces and/or network functions, to the extent that they are necessary for the interoperability of services and they promote consumer choice. To the extent that there are standards and/or specifications not published by the Commission, Member States are obliged to encourage the implementation of standards and specifications adopted by the European Standards Organisations.

Member States are also committed to promote future international standards and/or recommendations adopted by the International Telecommunications Union (ITU), the International Organisation for Standardisation (ISO) and the International Electrotechnical Commission (IEC).[100]

One important issue is how far a Member State has the possibility to make implementation of standards compulsory. In this regard, national measures concerning electronic communications services or associated facilities which are not telecommunications services fall within the scope of the Transparency Directive 98/34/EC, modified by Directive 98/48/EC.

---

96 Also, acting under the procedure referred to in Framework Directive, Art 22(2).

97 Based in Brussels, Belgium, the European Committee for Standardisation (CEN) is responsible for standardisation in areas other than the electrotechnical and telecommunications fields. In relation to information and communications technologies, CEN has created the Information Society Standardisation System (CEN/ISSS). In addition to the traditional CEN Technical Committees, this makes use of open workshops, which are standards committees created whenever there is an identified need for consensus. They are open to all interested parties and their deliverables are published by CEN as CEN Workshop Agreements (CWAs).

98 Based in Brussels, Belgium, the European Committee for Electrotechnical Standardisation (CENELEC) is officially responsible for standardisation in the electrotechnical field. Its members have been working together in the interests of European harmonisation since the 1950s, creating both voluntary and harmonised standards. CENELEC works with 35,000 technical experts from 22 European countries.

99 Based in Sophia Antipolis, France, the European Telecommunications Standards Institute (ETSI) is officially responsible for standardisation in telecommunications, broadcasting and certain aspects of information technology within Europe. As such, it also plays a major role in global standardisation. ETSI unites almost 800 members from 56 countries inside and outside Europe, including manufacturers, network operators, administrations, service providers, research bodies and users.

100 Where international standards exist, Member States must encourage the European Standards Organisations to use them, in whole or in part, as a basis for standards they develop unless such standards would be 'ineffective'.

Making implementation of a standard compulsory within a Member State can create obstacles to the free movement of goods and services within the internal market, in breach of Articles 28 and 49 of the EC Treaty.[101]

If the interoperability of services in one or more Member States is hampered by the failure to implement the standards and/or specifications listed by the Commission, then the Commission can mandate the use of the specific standard and/or specification. It must publish a notice in the Official Journal of the European Communities and invite public comment by all interested parties. The Commission, acting in accordance with the procedure referred to in Article 22(3), will then make implementation of the relevant standards compulsory by making reference to them as compulsory standards in the list of standards and/or specifications published in the Official Journal of the European Communities.

Similarly, the Commission may remove standards and/or specifications referred to in its list if the Commission considers that they no longer meet consumers' needs or are hampering technological development and they no longer contribute to the provision of a harmonised electronic communications service.

K. INTEROPERABILITY OF DIGITAL TELEVISION SERVICES

Interoperability is essential in digital television. Interactive television is a relatively new area but there are a number of application program interfaces (APIs) in the market, and little attention was initially paid to interoperability. Interoperability must be able to evolve hand-in-hand with market developments in the future and is recognised as an essential element for consumer choice and for broadcasters wanting to distribute interactive applications on different platforms. This was the political concern when the Framework Directive was being adopted.

---

101 There is a relevant case concerning Directive 95/47/EC on the application of standards for the transmission of television signals, where a Member State sought to go beyond the standardisation requirements of the Directive and to require use of a particular standard. The Commission took the view that if a Member State were to mandate a standard that was not required by the provision of this Directive, such a measure would create a barrier to the operation of the single market. The Commission decision considered that the proposed measure would constitute a measure having equivalent effect to a quantitative restriction, in violation of Art 28 of the EC Treaty, as well as an obstacle to the free movement of services in breach of Art 49 of the Treaty. In the framework of Notification 2000/394/A, the Commission issued a detailed opinion on the basis of Directive 98/34/EC. The notified measure aimed to impose the obligatory use of the common interface system at the expense of the 'simulcrypt' system for achieving interoperability between conditional access systems.

The Framework Directive seeks to promote the interoperability of consumer digital interactive television services and equipment on the basis of 'the free flow of information, media pluralism and cultural diversity'.

Member States are encouraged to persuade digital interactive television platform operators to implement an open API[102] which conforms to standards or specifications adopted by a European Standards Organisation. Migration from existing APIs to new open APIs will be encouraged through, for example, Memoranda of Understanding between all relevant market players. Open APIs are intended to facilitate interoperability[103] and full functionality of content on enhanced digital television equipment. The efficiency of the receiving equipment and the need to protect it from malicious attacks, for example from viruses, can be taken into account.

The Commission can mandate the necessary standards[104] and/or specifications if it feels that the necessary level of interoperability and freedom of choice of users has not materialised. In accordance with Article 18(3) , the Commission will within one year after the date of application of the new framework (ie, June 2004) examine whether interoperability and freedom of choice for users have been adequately achieved in the Member States. It is envisaged that the Commission will issue a consultation document on digital interactive TV in late 2003/early 2004 to seek comments on:

(a) whether interoperability and freedom of choice for users have been achieved in the Member States;

(b) if not, whether mandatory implementation of one or more standards would achieve these objectives, and if so by whom;

(c) whether MHP is a suitable candidate to be so mandated.

The Commission may subsequently take action in accordance with the procedure in Article 17(3) and (4).

L. HARMONISATION PROCEDURES

The Framework Directive also states two procedures concerned with harmonisation of the single market. The first, in Article 19(1), relates to the production of Commission guidance (eg, Recommendations), which aims to increase harmonisation of implementation of specific obligations in the

---

102 Which is defined in Framework Directive, Art 2(p), and means 'the software interfaces between applications, made available by broadcasters or service providers, and the resources in the enhanced digital television equipment for digital television and radio services'.

103 Ie, the portability of interactive content between delivery mechanisms.

104 The Commission is encouraging the voluntary application of the multi-media home platform standard, MHP, which it feels satisfies the needs of interoperability in this field.

new regulatory framework. It re-emphasises the importance of NRAs following the advice contained in Commission guidance and requires NRAs on those occasions where it diverges from the Commission's Recommendations to give a reasoned explanation. The second procedure contained in Article 19(2) allows the Commission to propose binding harmonisation measures using comitology procedures where it considers that the divergence of national measures constitute a barrier to the single market.

M. DISPUTE RESOLUTION

Disputes regularly arise between undertakings in competitive markets. Market forces lead to these being sometimes resolved either through commercial negotiation or by some form of arbitration. Alternatively, the undertakings decide not to do business with each other. No issues of consumer detriment or public policy arise in these types of situation. However, the presence of operators with large market power and the existence of public policy reasons for specific obligations on certain operators means that market mechanisms may not always work effectively and/or that there will be a major welfare loss from a failure to agree. Regulation is therefore needed to ensure that this does not occur.

NRAs previously had a duty to resolve a wide range of disputes and were bound by the duty in the previous Interconnection Directive to take steps to resolve disputes in six months. The Framework Directives reduces this deadline. In the event of disputes,[105] for example, on obligations for access and interconnection or as to the means of transferring subscriber lists, an aggrieved party that has negotiated in good faith but failed to reach agreement will still be able to ask the NRA to resolve the dispute. But NRAs will be under an obligation to reach a final decision within four months.

However, NRAs may refuse to resolve a dispute submitted to it for adjudication if they feel that there are other, better alternative dispute mechanisms. The success of ADR depends on the incentives of the parties involved to reach a solution but practical considerations such as the numbers of operators involved in a dispute also influences the suitability of ADR as a dispute resolution mechanism.

But if the dispute fails to be resolved within an initial four-month period, the NRA, at the request of either party, will have to resolve the dispute within a further four-month period. Dispute resolution by the NRA will not preclude either party from bringing its claim before the courts.[106]

---

105 Namely those between undertakings in the same Member State in an area covered by this Directive or the specific Directives.
106 Framework Directive, Art 20(5).

The Directive provides for a mechanism involving cross-border disputes.[107] When a cross-border dispute arises, the NRAs of the relevant countries must resolve the dispute together. In such cases, the four-month time limit no longer applies. The Framework Directive does not describe how NRAs should proceed to resolve a cross-border dispute jointly. NRAs – perhaps in the context of the European Regulations Group – will have to develop joint dispute resolution procedures to be used in the case of cross-border disputes. Joint proceedings could give rise to a number of potential procedural problems, such as the language of the proceedings and relevant appeal mechanisms.

N. THE COMMUNICATIONS COMMITTEE

The Framework Directive establishes the Communications Committee.[108] It consists of representatives of the Member States and is chaired by the Commission. The Framework Directive requires the Commission to seek the Committee's opinion before vetoing the decision of a NRA (as outlined above). In such cases, the Committee's view is only advisory. Its opinion is also advisory on recommended technical standards drawn up by the Commission,[109] or Recommendations to Member States intended to facilitate harmonised application of the Directives.[110]

However, for compulsory technical standards,[111] pan-European decisions,[112] or decisions identifying transitional markets,[113] the Commission must take account of the Committee's position before implementing the measure. Otherwise the matter must be referred to the European Council and European Parliament.[114]

The Communications Committee sets up its own rules of operation in accordance with the 'Comitology Decision'.[115] It will assume the role previously filled by the ONP and Licensing Committees established under the old framework. The Commission must keep the Communications Committee informed of the outcome of consultations with operators,

---

107 Framework Directive, Art 21(2).
108 This Communications Committee replaces the 'ONP Committee' instituted by Directive 90/387/EEC, Art 9 and the Licensing Committee instituted by Directive 97/13/EC of the European Parliament and of the Council of 10 April 1997 on a common framework for general authorisations and individual licences in the field of telecommunications services, Art 14.
109 Framework Directive, Art 17(1).
110 Ibid, Art 19(1).
111 Framework Directive, Art 17(4).
112 Ibid, arts 10(4), 19(2).
113 Framework Directive, Art 15(4).
114 Comitology Decision 1999/468/EC, Art 5 ([1999] OJ L184/23).
115 Comitology Decision 1999/468/EC ([1999] OJ L184/23), Art 7.

service providers, consumers, users, manufacturers, trade unions, third countries and international organisations.[116]

If the Directives are not transposed by 24 July 2003, the Commission may initiate infringement proceedings against the infringing Member State(s). Also, if the provisions in the Directives are sufficiently clear, unconditional and unambiguous, private parties could enforce its provisions in their national courts.

O. REVIEW PROCEDURES

Within the lifetime of this and the specific Directives, the European Union will be enlarged. The regulatory framework must therefore be adaptable to cope with different stages of development and maturity of competition in the communications market. New technology may also enable the utilisation of new network architectures and innovative services. However, exploitation of the full benefits of such networks and services may be limited by restrictions imposed by NRAs to the disadvantage of end-users, and the European economy.

The Commission is therefore placed under an obligation to periodically review the provisions of this Framework Directive with a view to determining whether modifications should be made in the light of changing technological or market developments. The first review must be completed by 25 July 2006.

---

116 Framework Directive, Art 23(1).

4
LICENSING AND AUTHORISATION

A. INTRODUCTION

Administratively efficient, transparent and effective licensing of communications services and networks is essential to the proper functioning of a vigorous, competitive internal market in communications. Licensing can become a barrier to market entry where it is characterised by delays, inconsistency and unnecessarily burdensome regulations and administrative procedures.

Following the liberalisation of telecoms markets within the European Union, most Member States continued to require some form of licence or authorisation from companies wishing to offer telecommunications services or operate networks in their territory. Attention at an EU level has therefore focused on developing a common framework for these licences and for the procedures according to which they are granted in order to facilitate the development of a single market in telecoms.

However, licences are still granted by Member States. Current legislation does not contain a mechanism to grant licences at European level covering more than one Member State, though there are provisions for the harmonisation of licensing conditions across the EU and the development of a one-stop-shopping procedure. But Member States are required to facilitate the provision of telecoms services between Member States.

B. BACKGROUND

The new Authorisation Directive[117] is intended to replace Directive 97/13/EC on a common framework for general authorisations and individual licences in the field of telecommunications services which was adopted by the European Parliament and by the Council on 10 April 1997 and had to be implemented by 1 January 1998.[118]

The key elements of that Directive were the prohibition of any limitation in the number of new entrants (except to the extent required to ensure an efficient use of radio frequencies), priority given to general authorisations, as opposed to individual licences, and the definition of

117 Authorisation Directive 2001/20/EC ([2002] OJ L108/21).
118 Directive 97/13/EC of the European Parliament and of the Council of 10 April 1997 ([1997] OJ L117/15) on a common framework for general authorisations and individual licences in the field of telecommunications services.

harmonised principles, including an exhaustive list of licensing conditions. However, the Commission's Fifth Report on the Implementation of the Telecommunications Regulatory Package expressed serious concern about the way in which the Directive had been implemented within the Community.

The Commission Communication on the results of the public consultation on the 1999 Communications Review and Orientations for the new Regulatory Framework (COM(2000)239) revealed strong support for significant further harmonisation and simplification of national authorisation rules.

C. AIMS AND OBJECTIVES

In line with the policy objectives and principles of the new regulatory framework, the new Authorisation Directive therefore revises the existing authorisation and licensing regimes and is based on the need to stimulate a dynamic, competitive market for communications services, to consolidate the internal market in a converging environment, to restrict regulation to the necessary minimum and to aim at technological neutrality and accommodate converging markets.

Three studies conducted by the European Telecommunications Office[119] under mandates by the European Commission[120] made clear that in the Community today there is no harmonised approach to authorising market entry for communications service providers but a patchwork of 15 national regimes which are widely divergent in their basic approach and specific detail.

Licence categories created by Member States vary from only two to no less than 18, each with their own conditions, procedures, charges and fees attached. To sustain the segmentation created, Member States require many different kinds of information from service providers ranging from nothing at all under the lightest regime, to 49 items under one of the heaviest licensing schemes. As a consequence, the regulatory workload involved in managing the authorisation and licensing regime varies from relatively light to extremely heavy with the result that administrative charges imposed on operators are zero in some Member States and excessive in others.

As the simpler regimes have demonstrated, there is no objective justification for splitting up authorisations in to so many service categories

119 The European Telecommunications Office was created in 1994 to oversee number and licensing issues for all European connections and merged with the European Radiocommunications Office in January 2001.
120 Categories of authorisations, information required for verification, fees, published at www.eto.dk.

and this approach will therefore be abandoned. While some Member States have shown that light regimes are feasible, workable and successful, the previous Licensing Directive did not prevent other Member States from developing rather heavy-handed market access regulation. This was not in line with the policy objective of stimulating the development of a competitive and dynamic market in communications services nor did it take account of convergence between services, networks and technologies. Adjustment at the level of the EU regulatory framework was therefore required.

Moreover, although in today's economic reality, markets of communications services are still fragmented along traditional national borders, the development of pan-European services is picking up and must be encouraged actively. Clearly, the existing divergence of regulatory regime does nothing to help the process.

An efficient and effectively functioning single European market can therefore be achieved by rigorously simplifying existing national regimes using the lightest existing regimes as a model. If procedures and conditions for authorising electronic communication services are reduced to what is strictly necessary, a single European authorisation or mutual recognition of authorisations would not seem to be needed to allow and support the development of a dynamic and competitive internal market.

Article 1(1) therefore confirms the aim of the Authorisation Directive as being to 'implement an internal market in electronic communications networks and services through the harmonisation and simplification of authorisation rules and conditions in order to facilitate their provision throughout the Community'. The Authorisation Directive covers authorisation of all electronic communications networks and services whether they are provided to the public or not.[121]

D. DEFINITIONS

Article 2 of the Authorisation Directive contains only two definitions, which are used throughout the Authorisation Directive, and referred to in the following paragraphs.

'General authorisation' refers to the legal framework established by the Member State ensuring rights for the provision of electronic communications networks or services and laying down sector specific obligations that may apply to all or to specific types of electronic communications networks and services, in accordance with the Authorisation Directive.

---

121 Authorisation Directive 2002/20/EC ([2002] OJ L108/21), Art 1(2).

'Harmful interference' refers to interference which endangers the functioning of a radionavigation service or of other safety services or which otherwise seriously degrades, obstructs or repeatedly interrupts a radiocommunications service operating in accordance with the applicable Community or national regulations.

E. INDIVIDUAL LICENCES AND GENERAL AUTHORISATIONS

Although the previous Authorisation Directive gave priority to general authorisations,[122] it still left a wide margin to Member States for the use of individual licences. A majority of Member States made ample use of this margin to the extent that individual licences became the rule rather than the exception in most national regimes. This made entry into the national market cumbersome and created a barrier to the development of cross-border services.

In spite of common rules on procedures for licensing, operators considered previous formalities at national level as unnecessarily cumbersome. Some Member States imposed cumbersome requirements for information to be provided prior to market entry. Compliance with all conditions had to be proven in advance of service provision. There was no objective need for such extensive prior verification of compliance with licensing conditions, and the lighter national regulatory regimes which have proved their effectiveness in practice have been followed as a model in this respect.

The present Authorisation Directive attempts to create the least onerous authorisation system possible for the provision of electronic communications networks and services which should stimulate the development of new electronic communications services and pan-European communications networks and services and allow service providers and consumers to benefit from the economies of scale of the single market.

It aims to create a legal framework to ensure the freedom to provide electronic communications networks and services.[123] Article 3(1) of the Authorisation Directive therefore obliges Member States to ensure the freedom to provide electronic communications networks and services and

---

122 'General authorisation' is defined as a legal framework established by a Member State ensuring rights for the provision of electronic communications networks or services and laying down sector specific obligations that may apply to all or to specific types of electronic communications networks and services.
123 Subject only to the conditions laid out in the Directive and any restrictions in conformity with Art 46(1) of the Treaty, in particular, measures regarding public policy, public security and public health.

not prevent undertakings from providing electronic communications networks and services.[124]

These aims are therefore achieved in Article 3(2) by the general authorisation of all electronic communications networks and services without requiring any explicit decision or administrative act by the National Regulatory Authority (NRA) and by limiting any procedural requirements to the provision of simple notification only.[125]

The notification will be merely a declaration[126] to the NRA of the intention to commence the provision of electronic communication networks or services and the submission of the minimal information which is required to allow the NRA to keep a register or list of providers of electronic communications networks and services.

This information will therefore state the name of the provider and ask for details such as the provider's registration number, the provider's contact person, the provider's address, a short description of the network or service, and the estimated date for starting the activity.

Filing a declaration is an admission that an entity is a provider of electronic communications networks or services. An entity providing electronic communications networks or services without having filed a declaration will be operating illegally, it could be sectioned and prevented from conducting business – this would apply to providers who clearly fall within the definition. For borderline cases, NRAs would require the entity concerned to file a declaration.

Licence authorisations will continue to cover only individual Member States, and the fact that an operator or service provider is authorised in one Member State does not remove the need to be authorised in other EU Member States for the right to provide services there. During the public consultation there was some demand for the creation of a single European licence for electronic communications services or mutual recognition of authorisations. In particular, the satellite industry, cross-border by nature, pleaded the case of a more far-reaching harmonisation of authorisation regimes.

As originally drafted, the Authorisation Directive envisaged a simplification of national authorisation regimes to dismantle all significant obstacles to the single European market, and the possible introduction of harmonisation measures regarding conditions, procedures or fees through a comitology procedure where necessary. However, the final adopted text took the approach that advocated the achievement of an effective internal market through a significant simplification of national regimes.

---

124 Authorisation Directive 2002/20/EC ([2002] OJ L108/21), Art 3(1).

125 Without prejudice to the specific obligations referred to in the Authorisation Directive 2002/20/EC ([2002] OJ L108/21), Art 6(2) or rights of use referred to in ibid, Art 5.

126 Notification can be made either by a legal or natural person.

F. MINIMUM LIST OF RIGHTS DERIVED FROM THE GENERAL AUTHORISATION

Filing a declaration affords several rights that can be of particular value to a network or service provider:

(a) the right to apply for rights of way over public, and in some cases private, property;[127]

(b) the right to request access to network elements of operations holding Significant Market Power (SMP);[128]

(c) the right to request access to network elements of operators holding SMP;

(d) the right to be designated as a Universal Service provider.[129]

Filing a declaration may also help in obtaining frequency usage rights and numbering usage rights.

G. CONDITIONS ATTACHED TO GENERAL AUTHORISATIONS

Network or service providers that have filed a declaration will automatically be bound by standard licence conditions. The Authorisation Directive contains an Annex of standard licence conditions that Member States may impose. Member States cannot go beyond what is contained in the list.[130]

(a) Universal Service: The provider may be required to contribute to universal funding where applicable.

(b) Administrative charges: The provider must pay administrative charges associated with the general authorisation.

(c) Interoperability: The provider must ensure interoperability of its network and/or services to the extent required by the Access Directive. If the provider operates a publicly available network, the provider must negotiate interconnection with other providers of publicly available networks or services.

(d) Connectivity: The provider must ensure access by end-users to numbers from the national numbering plan. This is to ensure universal connectivity, meaning that the operator must interconnect

127 Authorisation Directive, Art 4(1)(b).
128 Ibid, 4(2)(a).
129 Authorisation Directive, Art 4(2)(b).
130 Authorisation Directive, Art 6(1).

with another operator capable of completing calls to all subscribers in the country, either directly or via other interconnections.

(e) Local land use restrictions: The provider must comply with town and country planning requirements 'as well as requirements and conditions linked to co-location, and facility sharing in conformity with the [Framework] Directive and including, where applicable, any financial or technical guidelines necessary to ensure the proper execution of infrastructure works'.

(f) 'Must carry': Where applicable, the operator may be required to carry certain mandatory audiovisual programmes.

(g) Data protection: The provider must apply data protection rules, and ensure security of its public network against unauthorised access, as required by the Communications Data Protection Directive.

(h) Consumer protection: The provider must apply consumer protection rules as required by the Universal Service Directive.

(i) Illegal content: The authorisation may include restrictions in relation to the transmission of 'illegal content' as permitted under the Electronic Commerce Directive, and 'harmful content' as contemplated by the Television Without Frontiers Directive.

(j) Providing information: The authorisation may require the operator to provide information to its NRA.

(k) National security: The authorisation may contain provisions requiring operators to enable the police authorities to intercept communications in conformity with the Communications Data Protection Directive and national rules on criminal investigations. The authorisation may impose usage restrictions and priorities during major disasters.

(l) Radio interference and health: The authorisation may include provisions in radio interference, and protection of human health against exposure to electromagnetic fields. This provision will enable Member States to implement measures to comply with Council Recommendation 1999/519/EC. [131]

(m) Standards: The authorisation may include provisions to ensure compliance with standards and/or specifications.

(n) Access obligations: The authorisation may include access obligations that apply to non-SMP operators. These obligations include, for operators of publicly available networks, the obligation to negotiate interconnection with other operators of publicly available

---

131 Recommendation 1999/519/EC of the Council on 12 July 1999 ([1999] OJ L199/59) on the limitation of exposure of the general policy to electromagnetic fields (0hz to 300GHz).

networks; for providers of conditional access services, the obligations include the requirement to offer services to all broadcasters on a non-discriminatory basis.

(o) Maintenance and network integrity: The authorisation may include provisions regarding the maintenance and integrity of the networks.

H. RIGHTS OF USE FOR RADIO FREQUENCIES AND NUMBERS

A general authorisation does not give an operator the right to the radio frequencies. For radio frequencies, the Authorisation Directive sets up a system of individual permits (referred to as 'grants of individual rights of use') that Member States must use when allocating spectrum.

The Authorisation Directive states that Member States 'shall, where possible, in particular where the risk of harmful interference is negligible, not make the use of radio frequencies subject to the grant of individual rights of use'.[132]

However, in practice, Member States may feel inclined to maintain the requirement for individual permits for most kinds of frequency use, even where the risk of interference is slight.

1. Who may obtain rights of use?
The Authorisation Directive instructs Member States to grant individual rights of use of frequency to any 'provider' or 'user' (ie, a provider of content) of electronic communications network or services.[133] Although the purpose of the new framework is to separate the regulation of transmission networks from rules or 'content', the Authorisation Directive acknowledges that frequency will in some cases be linked to content. The Authorisation Directive confirms that rights to use spectrum should be granted according to 'objective, transparent and non-discriminatory criteria, taking into account the democratic, social, linguistic and cultural interests related to the use of frequency'. When granting spectrum to such broadcasters, Member States need only 'pursue general interest objectives in conformity with community law'.[134] The allocation of frequencies to broadcasting may then be based on cultural policy. The licensing of frequency usage rights therefore marries the worlds of telecoms and media regulation.

---

132 Authorisation Directive, Art 5(1).
133 Authorisation Directive, Art 5(2).
134 Ibid, Art 5(2).

2. How are frequency rights granted?

Each Member State is free to set up its own system for allocating rights to use frequency, as long as the system does not violate any of the Directive's principles.

3. Procedures and criteria

National procedures must be 'open, transparent and non-discriminatory'. However, as stated above, Member States, when allocating spectrum to providers of radio or television broadcast program services, can take into account democratic, social, linguistic and cultural interests. The language suggests that when Member States fix objective, transparent and non-discriminatory selection criteria for television or radio content broadcasters, Member States may include cultural interests among those selection criteria.

4. Transferability

Member States must specify whether the usage rights are transferable or not. The transferability of spectrum is discussed below.

5. Appropriate duration

The duration of the grant must be 'appropriate for the service concerned'.[135] This principle suggests that the grant should not be shorter than the minimum time needed for the provider to recoup its investments, and should also take into account the difficulty of moving the spectrum user to another frequency band if needed.

6. Number of grants

The numbers cannot be limited 'except where this is necessary to ensure the efficient use of radio frequencies in accordance with Article 7'.[136] Many NRAs limit the number of radio licences granted, both to limit the risks of interference and also to encourage operators to invest in areas where they may not otherwise invest.

First, a Member State must 'give due weight to the need to maximise benefits for users and to facilitate the development of competition'.[137] Secondly, if a Member State wants to limit the number of grants, it must consult interested parties, including users and consumers, in accordance with Article 6 of the Framework Directive. Thirdly, Member States must publish and state their reasons for any decision to limit the number of radio licences. Fourthly, once the procedure for allocating licences is established, Member States must invite applications for rights of use.[138] Fifthly, the procedures for selecting candidates must be objective,

135 Authorisation Directive, Art 5(2).
136 Authorisation Directive, Art 5(5).
137 Authorisation Directive, Art 7(1)(a).
138 Ibid, Art 7(1)(d).

transparent, non-discriminatory and proportionate. Sixthly, the section criteria must give due weight to the achievement of the key principles of the Article 8 'mission statement' of the Framework Directive.

The Authorisation Directive does not detail what selection criteria an NRA must use leaving considerable latitude to each NRA to determine its own selection and grant procedures. The Authorisation Directive does, however, allow NRAs to verify whether an applicant will be able to comply with the conditions attached to the licence, and the applicant can be asked to submit any necessary information to prove such compliance (with, for example, minimum coverage obligations and network-built commitments).

7. Beauty contest/auction
Where the number of licences is limited, Member States may organise a competitive or comparative selection procedure. A pure auction where the only selection criteria is the price that candidates are willing to pay for the frequency would not appear to give due weight to the achievement of the Article 8 Framework Directive objectives (which include promoting competition and encouraging infrastructure investment). Member States that wish to hold an auction procedure may have to implement a hybrid beauty contest/auction procedure where candidates are first shortened by qualitative selection criteria and then invited to bid for frequency.

8. Time periods
If the frequency use is foreseen in the national frequency plan, the time period for allocating rights of use for frequency is six weeks. If a Member State uses competitive or comparative selection procedures, the Member State can extend the six-week period for up to a further eight months.

9. Conditions attached to rights to use radio frequencies
Part B of the Authorisation Directive's Annex contains a list of eight conditions that can be imposed on entities benefiting from an individual right to use frequencies (in addition to conditions associated with the general authorisations):

Condition 1: *Designation of service or type of network or technology for which the rights of use for the frequency has been granted, including, where applicable, the exclusive use of a frequency for the transmission of specific content or specified audiovisual services.*

This condition grants NRAs a broad discretion as to how to control how an operator runs its business. A Member State may simply require an operator to operate a mobile network or, alternatively, mandate the form of technology used; the type of service provided (voice, data or both); whether an operator can provide audiovisual content; whether an operator must provide audiovisual services from particular content providers.

Condition 2: *Effective and efficient use of frequencies in conformity with the Framework Directive, including, where appropriate, coverage requirements.*

This condition will, in most cases, include network roll-out and coverage obligations, allowing NRAs, where necessary, to take spectrum away from an operator which fails to deploy its network within the time stipulated in the grant.

Condition 3: *Technical and operational conditions necessary for the avoidance of harmful interference and for the limitation of exposure of the general public to electromagnetic fields, where such conditions are different from those included in the general authorisation.*

This condition will include frequency coordination obligations vis-à-vis other users of the frequency band, obligations relating to regions situated on national borders, as well as health-related obligations. Due to public concern at the proliferation of radio transmitters, Member States have begun to enact laws that implement a 1999 European Council Recommendation on the maximum permitted exposure levels to radio emissions.[139]

Condition 4: *Maximum duration in conformity with Article 5 of the Authorisation Directive, subject to any changes in the national frequency plan.*

The duration of radio usage rights was discussed above.

Condition 5: *Transfer of rights at the initiative of the rights holder and conditions for such transfer in conformity with the Framework Directive.*

The transfer of rights to use frequency is discussed below.

Condition 6: *Usage fees in accordance with Article 13 of the Authorisation Directive.*

Usage fees are discussed below.

Condition 7: *Any commitments which the undertakings obtaining the right have made in the course of a competitive or comparative selection procedure.*

This condition permits NRAs to impose numerous public interest obligations under the guise of 'voluntary commitments' made by candidates in a beauty contest. In the course of a beauty contest, NRAs may suggest to candidates that undertakings committing to roll out their networks to cover both rural and urban areas to avoid a 'digital divide' would maximise their chances of success. Such

---

139 Recommendation 1999/519/EC of the Council of July 1999 ([1999] OJ L199/59) on the limitation of exposure of the general public to electromagnetic fields (OH2 to 300GHZ).

commitments would become part of the conditions attached to the usage rights for frequency.

Condition 8: *Obligations under relevant international agreements relating to the use of frequencies.*

This clause will cover any rules defined by the ITU Convention, and any other international rules and agreements.

10. Usage fees for frequencies

The Authorisation Directive permits Member States to impose frequency usage fees in addition to administrative charges. Member States do not have to match the costs incurred by the NRA and they can freely set the level for usage fees for frequencies, subject to compliance with the following principles:

(a) the fees must reflect the need to ensure optimal use of the frequency resources;

(b) the fees must be 'objectively justified, transparent, non-discriminatory and proportionate in relation to their intention and purpose';[140]

(c) in setting the level of fees, Member States must take into account the objectives of Article 8 of the Framework Directive.

The Authorisation Directive requires that usage fees for frequency be used as an instrument to ensure the optimal use of such resources, and that the level of fees 'not hinder the development of innovative services and competition in that market'.[141] Member States must also ensure that the payment arrangements (for example, a lump-sum payment) ensure that the fees 'do not in practice lead to selection on the basis of criteria unrelated to the objective of ensuring optimal use of radio frequencies'.[142]

11. Transferability of usage rights

The Framework Directive suggests that 'the transfer of radio frequencies can be an effective means of increasing efficient use of spectrum'.[143] The Framework Directive does not require Member States to make frequency usage rights transferable but states that Member States 'may' foresee that possibility. Whether a Member State can make frequency transferable depends on each Member State's administrative law.

For countries that decide to allow the transfer of frequency usage rights, the Framework Directive requires that the transfer:

---

140 Authorisation Directive 2002/20/EC ([2002] OJ L108/21), Art 13.
141 Authorisation Directive 2002/20/EC ([2002] OJ L108/21), recital 32.
142 Ibid.
143 Authorisation Directive 2002/20/EC, recital 19.

(a) be notified in advance to the relevant NRA;

(b) take place in accordance with the transfer procedures established by the NRA; and

(c) be made public.[144]

The Framework Directive instructs NRAs to ensure that 'competition is not distorted' as a result of any such transfer.[145]

12. Harmonised frequencies

The Authorisation Directive provides that, in the event that frequency usage rights are allocated pursuant to a pan-European selection procedure, Member States shall grant national usage rights strictly in accordance with the pan-European selection procedure. Member States cannot impose any further conditions, additional criteria or procedures which would restrict, alter or delay the correct implementation of the common assignment of such radio frequencies.

13. Rights to use numbering frequencies

Many of the above comments relating to the right to use frequencies also apply to the right of use of numbering resources. Usage rights for numbering resources can be granted to any entity 'providing' or 'using' electronic communications networks or services under a general authorisation. The recitals confirm that 'Member States are neither obliged to grant nor prevented from granting rights to use numbers ... to undertakings other than providers of electronic communications networks or services',[146] leaving considerable freedom to Member States in deciding what kinds of entities can benefit from the right to numbering resources.

14. Procedure

The procedures for allocating number rights must be 'open, transparent and non-discriminatory'.[147] Member States must ensure that enough numbers and numbering resources are available for all electronic communications services[148] and that 'numbering plans and procedures are applied in a manner that gives equal treatment to all providers of publicly available electronic communications services'.[149] The decisions granting rights to use numbers are made by the NRA within three weeks after receipt of a completed application. Member States can organise competitive or comparative selection procedures for numbers of 'exceptional economic

---

144 Framework Directive, Art 8.
145 Ibid, Art 9(4).
146 Authorisation Directive, recital 14.
147 Authorisation Directive, Art 5(2).
148 Framework Directive, Art 10(1).
149 Ibid, Art 10(2).

value'[150] but only after the public consultation procedure required under Article 6 of the Framework Directive.

15. Conditions attached to usage rights for numbers

The Annex to the Authorisation Directive contains a list of conditions that can be imposed on those granted numbering usage rights. These conditions are similar to those associated with frequency rights.

Condition 1: *The ability of a Member State to link a given numbering resource to a given source.*

This condition is necessary in order to ensure that end-users understand which classes of number are associated with a given service or tariff scheme (freephone v premium services, for example).

Condition 2: *Effective and efficient use of numbering resources in accordance with the Framework Directive.*

This condition allows Member States to impose a 'use it or lose it' rule to ensure that operators do not sit on numbering resources without exploiting them.

Condition 3: *Number portability requirements in conformity with the Universal Service Directive.*

Number portability obligations are discussed below in Chapter 6, 'Universal Service and Users' Rights'.

Condition 4: *Obligations to provide public directory subscriber information for the purposes of Articles 5 and 25 of the Universal Service Directive.*

These obligations are also discussed in Chapter 6.

Condition 5: *Maximum direction in conformity with Article 5 of the Authorisation Directive, subject to any changes in the national numbering scheme.*

Here, the same rules apply as those applicable to rights to use frequency. The direction number should be appropriate for the service concerned.

Condition 6: *Transfer of rights at the initiative of the rights holder and conditions for such transfer in conformity with the Framework Directive.*

As with frequencies, the transferability of numbering resources depends on how the use of numbering resources is characterised in individual Member States.

Condition 7: *Usage fees in accordance with Article 13 of the Authorisation Directive.*

---

150 Authorision Directive, Art 5(4).

Usage fees are discussed below.

Condition 8: *Any commitments that the undertaking obtaining the usage right has made in the course of a competitive or comparative selection procedure.*

Promises made by operations during the selection process may be deemed important enough by the NVLA to incorporate as a condition to obtaining the number.

Condition 9: *Obligations under relevant international agreements relating to the use of numbers.*

This condition refers to existing ITU recommendations on numbers as well as to European agreements on, for example, the single European emergency number 112 and the European single country code 3883.

16. Usage fees for numbers

As with frequencies, Member States may charge usage fees for number resources. Member States are free to set the level of fees as long as they comply with the following principles:

(a) The fees reflect the need to ensure the optimal use of the numbering resources.

(b) The fees are:

– objectively justified;

– transparent;

– non-discriminatory;

– proportionate in relation to their intended purpose.

(c) They take into account the objectives of Article 8 of the Framework Directive and do not hinder the development of innovative services and competition in the market.[151]

However, the raising of revenue for the provision of a national directory service is not one of the permitted purposes of usage fees.

I. RIGHTS TO INSTALL FACILITIES AND RIGHTS OF INTERCONNECTION

The ability to lay cables and/or install antennaes is an essential requirement for operators. Article 4(1) of the Authorisation Directive states that a general authorisation gives the holder the right to have its application for the necessary rights to install facilities considered in accordance with

151 Authorision Directive, recital 32, Art 13.

Article 11 of the Framework Directive. Article 11 of the Framework Directive provides that when a competent authority considers an application for granting rights of way:

> (a) it must act on the basis of transparent and publicly available procedures, applied without discrimination and without delay;
>
> (b) it must follow the principles of transparency and non-discrimination in attaching conditions to any rights.

A 'competent authority' can be a national, regional or local authority, a highway or railtrack company or a canal or port authority. The Framework Directive's provisions fall short of an absolute obligation to grant rights of way. The Authorisation Directive states that a provider holding a general authorisation shall have the right to have its application for rights of way 'considered'. The Framework Directive then continues by stating that when a competent authority 'considers' an application, it must act 'without delay' and apply publicly-available and transparent procedures. But the Directives never state that the competent authorities 'shall grant' rights of way.

Article 9 provides the right to obtain a declaration from the NRA either upon request or, alternatively, as an automatic response to a notification under the general authorisation, on the right to obtain rights of way and/or rights to negotiate interconnection. However, a declaration from the NRA is not required for exercise of the rights contained in the general authorisation.

If providers find that their applications for rights to install facilities are not dealt with in accordance with the principles set out in the Framework Directive, or where decisions are 'unduly' delayed, they maintain the right to appeal against such decisions and delays.

J. COMPLIANCE WITH CONDITIONS OF GENERAL AUTHORISATION OR RIGHTS OF USE

The Directive does not require service providers to be subjected to regular reporting or information obligations given their time-consuming and cumbersome nature. Any such measures would need to be proportionate, objectively justified and limited to what is strictly necessary. However, despite the absence of a requirement on service providers to provide systematic and regular proof of compliance with all the conditions under the general authorisation or those attached to the rights of use, NRAs can require undertakings to verify their compliance.

Where an NRA uncovers a breach of one or more conditions, it must notify the service provider. The service provider will then have usually one month (or a shorter period, eg, in the case of repeated breaches if ordered by the NRA) to respond or remedy any breaches. NRAs are permitted to take 'appropriate and proportionate measures' to ensure compliance and enforce undertakings to remedy their breaches. This includes the imposition of substantial fines.[152] Any proposed regulatory action must be notified to the affected company within one month and state a further reasonable period of time in which to comply with the regulator's decision.

In cases of serious and repeated breaches, NRAs can stop service providers from continuing to operate and provide their network services and suspend or withdraw their rights of use.

Where any breach represents 'an immediate and serious threat to public safety, public security or create[s] serious economic or operational problems' for other providers or users of such networks and services, NRAs can take urgent interim measures to temporarily resolve the situation before reaching any final decision.

Companies have the right to appeal against any measure taken under this Article in accordance with the procedure referred to in Article 4 of Directive 2002/21/EC (the Framework Directive).

K. INFORMATION REQUIRED UNDER THE GENERAL AUTHORISATION AND FOR RIGHTS OF USE

The Authorisation Directive curtails the purposes for which information provided by service providers to NRAs can be used.[153] Any information request must be proportionate and objectively justified and can only be requested with respect to the following:

(a) systematic or case-by-case verification of compliance with conditions 1 and 2 of Part A, condition 6 of Part B and condition 7 of Part C of the Annex and of compliance with obligations as referred to in Article 6(2);

(b) case-by-case verification of compliance with conditions as set out in the Annex (namely, the conditions attached to a General Authorisation) where a complaint has been received or where the NRA has other reasons to believe that a condition is not complied with or in case of an investigation by the NRA on its own initiative;

(c) procedures for and assessment of requests for granting rights of use;

---

152 Member States can also empower NRAs to impose financial penalties on those undertakings that fail to provide information in accordance with obligations imposed under this Directive, Art 11(1)(a) or (b), or Directive 2002/19/EC (Access Directive), Art 9 within a reasonable period stipulated by the NRA.

153 The Authorisation Directive is without prejudice to Member States' obligations to provide information within the context of international agreements and any national legislative reporting obligations which are not specific to the electronic communications sector, eg, competition law.

(d) publication of comparative overviews of quality and price of services for the benefit of consumers;

(e) clearly defined statistical purposes; and

(f) market analysis for the purposes of Directive 2002/19/EC (Access Directive) or Directive 2002/22/EC (Universal Service Directive).

The provision of the above information cannot be made a prerequisite to market access.

L. ADMINISTRATIVE CHARGES

The previous Authorisation Directive required that administrative charges[154] and fees imposed on operators cover only the administrative costs incurred in the issue, management, control and enforcement of the applicable authorisation and licensing schemes. Nevertheless, previous practices in some of the Member States had been criticised in the public consultation for lack of transparency and high fees. The widely diverging range of fees within the Community could be fully accounted for by diverging regulatory workloads.

The present Authorisation Directive permits the imposition of administrative charges on providers of electronic communications services but only to the extent needed to finance the activities of the NRA in the management, control and enforcement of the general authorisation scheme and of rights of use and of specific obligations as referred to in Article 6(2), which may include costs for international cooperation, harmonisation and standardisation, market analysis, monitoring compliance and other market control, as well as regulatory work involving preparation and enforcement of secondary legislation and administrative decisions, such as decisions on access and interconnection.

The Authorisation Directive also provides that the costs incurred by NRAs and the total fees collected should be published yearly.

154 Systems for administrative charges cannot distort competition or create barriers for entry into the market. With a general authorisation system, it will no longer be possible to attribute administrative costs and charges to individual undertakings except for the granting of rights to use numbers, radio frequencies and for rights to install facilities. Any applicable administrative charges must be in line with the principles of a general authorisation system. An example of a fair, simple and transparent alternative for these charge attribution criteria could be a turnover-related distribution key. Where administrative charges are very low, flat rate charges, or charges combining a flat rate basis with a turnover-related element may be appropriate.

M. FEES FOR RIGHTS OF USE AND RIGHTS OF WAY

In addition to administrative charges, the Authorisation Directive provides for the imposition of usage fees on the use of radio frequencies and numbers as a means to ensure their optimal use.

The fees must not hinder the development of innovative services and may be used to finance activities of NRAs that cannot be covered by administrative charges.[155]

N. MODIFICATION OF RIGHTS AND OBLIGATIONS

The Authorisation Directive recognises that Member States may need to amend rights, conditions, procedures, charges and fees relating to general authorisations and the rights of use but can only do so if it can be objectively justified. Any changes must be notified to all interested parties and allow them adequate opportunity to express their views on the proposed amendments.[156]

The Commission may publish, on a regular basis, benchmark studies with regard to best practices for the assignment of radio frequencies, the assignment of numbers or the granting of rights of way.[157]

O. PUBLICATION OF INFORMATION

The Authorisation Directive requires Member States to publish, keep up-to-date and allow easy access to all relevant information on rights, conditions, procedures, charges, fees and decisions concerning general authorisations and rights of use.

If the information is held at different levels of government, NRAs are obliged to make a reasonable effort to create a user-friendly overview of all such information and at least assist applicants by identifying the relevant information-holding government institution.

---

155 For example, in the case of competitive or comparative selection procedures where fees for rights of use for radio frequencies usually consist entirely of a one-off amount, payment arrangements should ensure that such fees do not in practice lead to selection on the basis of criteria unrelated to the objective of ensuring optimal use of radio frequencies.
156 The consultation includes all interested parties and includes users and consumers. The period for consultation must be at least four weeks except in exceptional circumstances.
157 Authorisation Directive 2002/20/EC ([2002] OJ L108/21), recital 32.

P. REVIEW PROCEDURES

The Authorisation Directive requires the Commission to periodically review the functioning of the national authorisation systems and the development of cross-border service provision within the Community. It must make its first report to the European Parliament and to the Council by 24 July 2006.

Q. EXISTING AUTHORISATIONS

The process of the national transpositions of the Authorisation Directive is taking place in parallel with alignment of the existing licences with the new rules in order to implement elements of the new regulatory framework for the electronic communications sector by 24 July 2003.

Where there are specific cases that may lead to either an increase of existing authorised individual service provider's obligations or to a reduction of their rights, Member States may by application to the Commission extend the time period for the alignment of such licences by a further nine months.[158] However, such extension must not have a negative impact on the rights and obligations of other undertakings.

The Commission must take a decision within six months on whether to grant or reject the request.[159] If it decides to grant the request, it may limit the scope and duration of the prolongation granted.

R. TRANSPOSITION

Article 18 confirms 24 July 2003 as the ultimate date for transposition of the Authorisation Directive into national law and its immediate application on 25 July 2003. As at the date of writing, many Member States do not appear to be in a position to implement the Authorisation Directive's provisions. However, the Authorisation Directive appears to be sufficiently precise and unconditional and it can be relied upon by affected electronic communications companies and even enforced in individual Member States' national courts.

---

158 For example, where the Member State concerned can prove that the abolition of an authorisation condition regarding access to electronic communications networks, which was in force before the date of entry into force of this Directive, creates excessive difficulties for undertakings that have benefited from mandated access to another network, and where it is not possible for these undertakings to negotiate new agreements on reasonable commercial terms before the date of application.
159 The Commission must take into account the particular situation in that Member State and of the undertaking(s) concerned, and the need to ensure a coherent regulatory environment at a Community level.

5
ACCESS AND INTERCONNECTION

A. WHAT IS THE ACCESS DIRECTIVE?

The new Directive on Access to and Interconnection of Electronic Communications Networks, Directive 2002/19/EC[160] (the 'Access Directive') harmonises the way in which Member States regulate the market between suppliers of electronic communications networks and services in the Community.

The Framework Directive (Directive 2002/21/EC) lays down the objectives of the new EU regulatory framework covering electronic communications networks and services in the EU. This includes fixed and mobile telecommunications networks, cable telecom networks, networks used for terrestrial broadcasting, satellite and Internet networks. While the Authorisation Directive (discussed in Chapter 4) sets out the conditions for the authorisation of these networks, the Access Directive lays down certain rules relating to the access and interconnection between service providers using publicly available electronic communications services. Non-public networks do not have obligations under the Access Directive.

The Access Directive applies to all forms of communications networks carrying publicly available communications services whether used for voice, fax, data or images in the areas covered under the Framework Directive.

The legislation is designed to provide a framework which will stimulate competing network infrastructures and the provision of services over those networks. Of particular importance here is to ensure that limits of capacity on particularly popular networks do not give rise to bottlenecks which constrain the emergence and growth of innovative services.

For the electronic communications sector to operate effectively for the benefit of users and consumers, networks need to be interconnected with each other in order to allow customers on one network to communicate with customers on another. But the Access Directive is not just about mandating interconnection between networks. It goes far beyond that. The owner or operator of network infrastructure is in a powerful position either as a provider of services to end-users itself or as a provider of transmission services to others or both. Those companies wanting to provide communications services or broadcast services need to have access to that infrastructure to deliver their services to the end-user. The Access Directive therefore seeks to harmonise the way in which Member States regulate

---

160 Access Directive ([2002] OJ L108/7).

access to these networks for service providers. To do this, it sets out rules for access to and interconnection of networks. The old-style, simple relationships in which there were a limited number of suppliers on the narrow band market centred on voice services have changed. The present-day marketplace is considerably more vibrant and flexible. The next generation of communications services, whether they are fixed or mobile, will rely increasingly on broadband networks or transport networks using the Internet Protocol (IP) for the delivery of a whole range of multi-media services. Providing these services will be a large number of operators, service providers, content providers, advertisers and broadcasters, often grouped together in highly complex commercial relationships.

It should be noted, however, that whilst the Access Directive deals with interconnection and access to electronic communications systems, it does not extend to regulating the content of the services actually provided over those networks. This is particularly true of sound or television broadcasting content.

B. NEW REGULATORY FRAMEWORK FOR ACCESS AND INTERCONNECTION

It is essential that there is a harmonised system of access and interconnection across the EU to ensure that competition is not distorted. To do otherwise would lead to different patterns of regulation in the Member States, market variations, increased costs to end-users and a fragmentation of the single market. The benefits of such a harmonised system are that it will encourage sustainable competition at both a network and services level. In an open and competitive market, there should be no restrictions that prevent undertakings from negotiating access and interconnection arrangements between themselves subject to the requirements of competition law. The Access Directive notes in its preamble that these agreements should be perfectly capable of being concluded on a commercial basis and negotiated in good faith by relevant undertakings.

Regrettably, however, the reality does not match the theory. A number of factors detract from this position. In some markets, there continue to be large differences in negotiating power between undertakings. This is usually the case where a former encumbent monopolist still provides the majority of connections giving it a degree of bargaining power significantly above any of its competitors. Another restriction primarily affects those who provide services over other networks controlled by one or a few operators. Examples of this can be found in access to the local loop in the telecommunications environment or conditional access systems for digital television. There are also barriers which arise due to the need to ration the availability of radio spectrum in the mobile market. Limiting the number of operators has had the effect of keeping pricing at supra-competitive levels especially in areas such as termination charges.

In view of these market distortions, the Access Directive establishes a framework to ensure that the market functions effectively. The rules put in place to address these issues are referred to as 'ex-ante' rules. Under their terms, National Regulatory Authorities (NRAs) are given the power to secure adequate access and interconnection between networks and the ability to mandate the use of networks for the provision of services where there is a significant disparity in bargaining power and the commercial process has failed. These ex-ante rules will continue alongside the application of the EU competition rules to regulate access and interconnection until such time as full and effective competition exists on the relevant market.

The Access Directive sets out in clear terms the criteria for mandating access and interconnection. The regime is designed to be flexible based on certain key principles allowing NRAs to address issues as they occur. The Access Directive does not provide a set of ready make solutions to pre-defined problems. Instead, it lays down the criteria for regulatory intervention, a maximum list of obligations that NRAs can impose and identifies those undertakings upon which obligations can be placed. For example, an NRA may ensure end-to-end connectivity by imposing reasonable obligations on undertakings that control access to end-users through ownership or control of the physical link to the end-user and/or the ability to change or withdraw the national number or numbers needed to access an end-user's network termination point. This could be the case if network operators were to unreasonably restrict end-user choice for Internet access.

The Access Directive also sweeps away previous national, legal or administrative measures that link the terms and conditions for access or interconnection to the activities of the party seeking interconnection and specifically to the degree of its investment in network infrastructure and not to the interconnection or access services provided. These conditions are likely to cause market distortion and may not comply with the competition rules. An example of these can be seen in UK Interconnection Regulations Schedule I Operators, ie, those operators who had their own network infrastructure. These rules have now been repealed.

The agreed criteria for interconnection and access maintains a balance between providing legal certainty for market players and providing sufficient flexibility to allow regulatory authorities to adapt the rules to changing market circumstances.

C. WHO IS SUBJECT TO EX-ANTE OBLIGATIONS?

Only those undertakings subject to ex-ante obligations will be required to offer access and interconnection to their network infrastructure. Previously, ex-ante obligations were imposed on undertakings defined by reference to an arbitrary market share level. Under the old Interconnection Directive, undertakings that had 25 per cent share of the relevant market as defined by the NRAs were covered.

This approach drew a lot of criticism from the industry, economists and regulators as not adequately reflecting the true dynamics of the marketplace. Therefore, a new test for Significant Market Power (SMP) was introduced based on the competition law concept of dominance and the leverage of a dominant position on one market into an adjacent upstream or downstream market. The issues associated with the new SMP test are discussed in the context of the Framework Directive in Chapter 3. Under the new test, the definition of the relevant market is an essential part of the analysis. To ensure a consistent approach to market definition, the Commission has published a Decision on the Product and Service Markets susceptible to ex-ante regulation. The markets covered are fixed public telephone networks at both a retail and wholesale level, leased lines and mobile public switched telecommunications networks (see below at para [326] for a more detailed list).

NRAs have the responsibility to determine which undertakings have SMP on those markets and to impose ex-ante obligations on those undertakings. If an NRA wishes to designate that an undertaking outside these markets has SMP, it has to refer to the EU Commission for agreement.

Therefore, after having undertaken an appropriate market analysis, NRAs will be able to notify relevant companies that they have SMP and impose ex-ante obligations. This is likely to occur in situations where there are legacy problems associated with being the previous incumbent monopolist or where problems of vertical integration exist. Clearly, in such cases, the competition law powers are not adequate to address these market issues. However, in many cases, the new SMP test will result in a significant reduction of regulatory burdens for operators. For example, in the UK, the longest established mobile network operators, Vodafone and O2, were designated as having SMP under the old Interconnection Directive. OFTEL, the UK NRA, has now proposed under the new EU telecommunications framework that none of these operators should henceforth be designated as having SMP. T-Mobile and Orange are not SMP operators.

D. TRANSITIONAL PROVISIONS

The new EU telecommunications package has reduced the obligations contained in approximately 20 Directives down to five Directives and one Regulation. In doing so, it was necessary to ensure continuity between the old and new systems of regulation and to avoid a legal vacuum. Therefore, the Access Directive provides for the initial carrying over of certain obligations from the old Directives into the new regime.

These access and interconnection obligations are those set out in the old Interconnection Directive 97/33/EC (see Articles 4, 6, 7, 8, 11, 12 and 14). Obligations on special access in Article 16 of Directive 98/10/EC, and obligations for the provision of leased transmission capacity under Directive 92/44/EC are also included. The provision of Regulation 2887/2000 on unbundled access to the local loop will also be carried over to the new regime.

The approach adopted under the Access Directive is that the provisions of these old Directives will be subject to an immediate review 'in light of prevailing market circumstances'.

This review will be carried out using an economic market analysis based on the competition law methodology of SMP. The aim of this review is to reduce ex-ante sector specific rules as much as possible as competition in the market develops.

However, the Access Directive does provide that if and when new market situations arise which could justify new ex-ante obligations (eg, international roaming and new bottlenecks linked to new technologies), the same market analysis procedure would allow new ex-ante obligations to be introduced provided they are fully justified and focused on remedying the market problem identified.

The Access Directive carries over the main provisions of Directive 95/47/EC on TV standards (the TV Standards Directive), in particular, the obligation to provide conditional access for digital television services on fair, reasonable and non-discriminatory terms, and will allow the extension of these obligations, eg in relation to new gateways, to be imposed by NRAs. The TV Standards Directive was designed to provide an initial regulatory framework for the nascent digital television industry. Its main focus was on behavioural rules for conditional access providers in order to ensure market entry for other broadcasters. The intention was to provide some certainty for investors in the sector while assuming market entry to the digital TV market and safeguarding very public interests such as the interoperability of consumer equipment.

The digital TV market has made reasonable progress, driven in its first phase by substantial pay TV investments and there remains broad support for the approach taken in the Directive. There is, however, some urgency that there should be extension to new gateways that have appeared since 1995, notably electronic programme guides (EPGs) and application program interfaces (APIs). The new Directive, therefore, preserves the current structure under the TV Standards Directive but allows it to be extended to other new gateways where justified.

E. THE DETAILED PROVISIONS

Within the framework set out in Directive 2002/21/EC (the Framework Directive), the Directive harmonises the way in which Member States regulate access to and interconnection of electronic communications networks and associated facilities.

The detailed provisions of the Directive provide how this new regulatory order is to be implemented. In this section, we look in detail at how the new system is to work.

By reason of the complex nature of the provisions, it is helpful to set out an explanation of some of the common terms found in the Directive's provisions:

'*Access*': the making available of facilities and/or services to another undertaking, under defined conditions, on either an exclusive or non-exclusive basis, for the purpose of providing electronic communications services. It covers, inter alia, access to network elements and associated facilities which may involve the connection of equipment by fixed or non-fixed means (in particular, this includes access to the local loop and to facilities and services necessary to provide services over the local loop); access to physical infrastructure including buildings, ducts and masts; access to relevant software systems including operational support systems; access to number translation or systems offering equivalent functionality; access to fixed and mobile networks, in particular, for roaming access to conditional access systems for digital television services; and access to virtual network services.

'*Interconnection*': the physical and logical linking of public communications networks used by the same or a different undertaking in order to allow the users of one undertaking to communicate with users of the same or another undertaking or to access services provided by another undertaking. Services may be provided by the parties involved or other parties who have access to the network. Interconnection is a specific type of access implemented between public network operators.

'*Operator*': an undertaking providing or authorised to provide a public communications network or an associated facility.

'Wide-screen television service': a television service that consists wholly of partially of programmes produced and edited to be displayed in a full height, wide-screen format. The 16:9 format is the reference format for wide-screen television services.

'Local loop': the physical circuit connecting the network termination point at the subscriber's premises to the main distribution frame or equivalent facility in the fixed public telephone network.

F. GENERAL FRAMEWORK AND PRINCIPLES FOR ACCESS

The central focus of the Directive is set out in Article 3 which stipulates that Member States shall ensure that there are no restrictions imposed which prevent undertakings in the same or in different Member States from freely negotiating access and interconnection agreements between them. The undertaking requesting access or interconnection does not need to be authorised to operate in the Member State where access or interconnection is requested if it is not providing services and does not operate a network in that Member State.

This carries over the provisions from the old Directives establishing the freedom for parties to interconnect within and between Member States. It also requires Member States to remove measures that link the interconnection charges paid by a new entrant to their level of restriction in infrastructure. Operators' charges for interconnection must be only related to the access and interconnection services provided and subject to any additional requirements or obligations provided for in the Authorisation Directive.

Article 4 sets out the primary interconnection duty. This is recognition that for networks to work and the Community market to function there must be interconnection between networks. Operators of public communications networks have a right and an obligation when requested by other licensed undertakings to negotiate interconnection with each other for the purpose of providing publicly available electronic communications services.

Operators shall offer access and interconnection to other undertakings on terms and conditions laid down by NRAs on accordance with the general rules set out in the Directive.

The Directive also brings other obligations in relation to the distribution of digital television services from the TV Standards Directive 95/47/EC concerning network operators' responsibilities with regard to the distribution of wide-screen television services.

In negotiating interconnection and access agreements, undertakings may acquire confidential information. The Directive's provisions in Article 4(3) ensure that Member States have a duty to impose upon those undertakings an obligation to respect the confidentiality of the information it was given. In particular, it should not be passed on to other parties of the undertaking which have no reason to see it. This is to ensure such information is not misused for competitive advantage.

The Directive confers upon NRAs a general role with respect to access interconnection and interoperability and gives it powers to intervene and impose obligations on operators and to resolve disputes. NRAs shall be empowered to intervene at their own initiative or in the absence of an agreement or where there is a dispute between the parties at the request of either party.

Any obligations imposed must be objective, transparent, proportionate and non-discriminatory and must be implemented in accordance with the procedures referred to in Articles 6 and 7 of Directive 2002/21/EC (the Framework Directive).

Notwithstanding any measures which may be imposed on operators with SMP under the Authorisation Directive, NRAs shall have the power to impose the following obligations on:

(a) undertakings that control access to end-users when such an obligation to interconnect is not already imposed in situations necessary to ensure end-to-end connectivity;

(b) operators to provide access to application program interfaces and electronic programme guides on fair, reasonable and non-discriminatory terms to ensure accessibility for end-users to digital radio and television broadcasting services specified by the Member State.

Article 5 of the Access Directive also imposes duties on NRAs to ensure that when an operator is required to provide access or interconnection in accordance with the provision of the Directive and in particular Article 12, the NRA may lay down technical or operational conditions to be met by the provider and/or the persons connecting where necessary to ensure the normal operation of the network.

Any conditions referring to the implementation of specific technical standards or specifications must respect the provisions of Article 17 of the Framework Directive (Directive 2002/21/EC). This provides for the Commission to draw up and publish in the Official Journal a list of standards and/or specifications to serve as a basis for encouraging the harmonised provision of electronic communications networks, electronic commmunications services and associated facilities and services. Where such standards and/or specifications have not been drawn up, Member

States must encourage the implementation of standards and specifications adopted by the European Standard Organisations. In the absence of any of the above standards, Member States must encourage the use of international standards adopted by the International Telecommunications Union (ITU), the International Organisation for Standardisation (ISO) or the International Electrotechnical Commission (IEC).

G. CONTINUITY OF OBLIGATIONS

In Articles 6–13 of the Directive, the legislation provides that obligations as to access and interconnection contained in previous Directives, namely TV Stations Directive 95/47, ONP Directives 97/33/EC and 92/44/EC, will continue to be imposed under the new regime. There is, however, a procedure to review all these obligations in light of current market conditions.

Article 6 of the Directive maintains the obligations from the TV Standards Directive 95/47/EC for all operators of conditional digital TV and radio access systems to provide access to broadcasters on fair, reasonable and non-discriminatory terms irrespective of the means of transmission.

The list of obligations are set out in Annex I, Part I of the Directive. Conditional access systems operated on the market in the Community are to have the necessary technical capability for cost-effective transcontrol allowing the possibility for full control by network operators at local or regional level of the services using such conditional access systems:

(a) All operators of conditional access services, irrespective of the means of transmission, who provide access services to digital television and radio services and whose access services broadcasters depend on to reach any group of potential viewers or listeners are to:

– offer to all broadcasters, on a fair, reasonable and non-discriminatory basis compatible with Community competition law, technical services enabling the broadcasters' digitally-transmitted services to be received by viewers or listeners authorised by means of decoders administered by the service operators, and comply with Community competition law,

– keep separate financial accounts regarding their activity as conditional access providers.

(b) When granting licences to manufacturers of consumer equipment, holders of industrial property rights to conditional access products and systems are to ensure that this is done on fair, reasonable and non-discriminatory terms. Taking into account technical and commercial factors, holders of rights are not to subject the granting of licences to conditions prohibiting, deterring or discouraging the inclusion in the same product of:

– a common interface allowing connection with several other access systems, or

– means specific to another access system, provided that the licensee complies with the relevant and reasonable conditions ensuring, as far as it is concerned, the security of transactions of conditional access system operators.

However, there is a recognition that in light of market and technological developments since the original Directive was passed in 1995 there may be a need to vary these obligations. The Framework Directive set up a Communications Committee whose function it is to assist the Commission in reviewing the obligations pursuant to the proceedings set down in Decision 1999/468/EC.

Nevertheless, notwithstanding the above procedure, NRAs are empowered as soon as possible after the entry into force of the Access Directive and thereafter at regular intervals to undertake a market review of the obligations imposed and to determine whether to maintain, vary or withdraw the conditions applied.

If, as a result of that market analysis, an NRA finds that one or more operators do not have SMP in the relevant market, it may amend or withdraw the conditions with respect to those operators to the extent that:

(a) accessibility for end-users to radio and television broadcasters and broadcasting channels and services specified in the Universal Services Directive (see Article 31 of Directive 2002/22/EC) would not be adversely affected by such amendment or withdrawal; and

(b) the prospects for effective competition in the markets for:

– retail digital TV and radio broadcasting services; and

– conditional access systems and other associated facilities;

would not be adversely affected by the removal or variations.

The power should be exercised reasonably and an appropriate period of notice given to parties affected by the amendments or withdrawal of conditions.

The legislation, however, makes it clear that any conditions applied through variation of Annex I rights or amendments to SMP status do not fetter the ability of Member States to impose obligations in relation to the presentational aspect of electronic programme guides and other listing and navigation facilities of a similar nature.

While Article 6 regulates conditional access systems and other associated facilities, Article 7 of the Directive contains the main focus of the legislation. Essentially it carries over the obligations imposed on public communications network operators as to access and interconnection under the old ONP Directives 97/33/EC, 98/10/EC and 92/44/EC. This term is crucial to provide continuity in the transition between the old and new regulatory framework.

However, the new regulatory framework requires NRAs to review all these obligations in light of the new definition of SMP and to decide in light of their conclusions whether to maintain, modify or withdraw these obligations. NRAs will in addition be required to carry out such market review procedures at regular intervals in the future.

To assist the NRAs in this task, the Commission has published a Commission Recommendation on the relevant product and service markets within the electronic communications sector susceptible to ex-ante regulation in accordance with Directive 2002/21/EC and Guidelines for market analysis and assessment of market power referred to in Article 15(2) of the Framework Directive. NRAs are required to take detailed account of these documents in defining relevant markets appropriate to national circumstances in accordance with the principles of competition law. On the basis of this market analysis, NRAs will determine whether these markets are subject to effective competition or not and whether to impose, amend or withdraw ex-ante regulatory obligations.

The new regulatory framework is designed to ensure a harmonised approach to market definition across the Community. The Recommendation plays an important role in achieving this objective.

NRAs will be able to regulate markets which differ from those identified in the Recommendation but only where this is justified by national circumstances and where the Commission does not raise any objections in accordance with the procedures referred to in Articles 7(4) and 15(3) of the Framework Directive. As competition and convergence develops, it is expected that the range of markets identified in this Recommendation will in the future be reduced.

The Recommendation sets out at Table 2 a table of market definitions that NRAs will need to use to conduct their market review procedures, cross-referred to the market areas listed in Annex 1 of the Framework Directive.

Table 2: Treatment of Annex 1 market areas

Market areas listed in Annex I of the Framework Directive	Corresponding competition law market set out in Annex I of the Recommendation
RETAIL	
The provision of connection to and use of the public telephone network at fixed locations	Access to the public telephone network at a fixed location – residential
	Access to the public telephone network at a fixed location – business
	Publicly available local/and or national telephone services provided at a fixed location – residential
	Publicly available local/and or national telephone services provided at a fixed location – business
	Publicly available international telephone services provided at a fixed location – business
	Publicly available international telephone services provided at a fixed location – residential
The provision of leased lines to end-users	The minimum set of leased lines

WHOLESALE	
Call origination in the fixed public telephone network	Call origination on the public telephone network provided at a fixed location
Call termination in the fixed public telephone network	Call termination on individual public telephone network provided at fixed locations
Transit services in the fixed public telephone network	Call termination on individual public telephone network provided at fixed locations
Call origination on public mobile telephone networks	Access and call origination on public mobile telephone networks
Call termination on public mobile telephone networks	Voice Call termination on individual mobile networks

Leased line interconnection (interconnection of part circuits)	Wholesale terminating segments of leased lines Wholesale trunk segments of leased lines
Access to the fixed public telephone network, including unbundled access to the local loop	Wholesale unbundled access (including shared access) to metallic loops and sub-loops, for the purpose of providing broadband and voice services; wholesale broadband access
Access to public mobile telephone networks, including carrier selection	Access and call origination on public mobile telephone networks
Wholesale provision of leased line capacity to other suppliers of electronic communications networks or services	Wholesale or terminating segments of leased lines Wholesale trunk segments of leased lines
Services provided over unbundled (twisted metallic pair) loops	Wholesale unbundled access (including shared access) to metallic loops and sub-loops, for the purpose of providing broadband and voice services
The national market for international roaming services on public mobile telephone networks	The wholesale national market for international roaming on public mobile networks

Where an operator is designated as having SMP (and not otherwise) on a specific market after a market review carried out as above, NRAs are under a duty to impose the following obligations.

H. OBLIGATION OF TRANSPARENCY

SMP operators must publish certain specific information including prices, terms and conditions for access or interconnection, technical specifications, network characteristics and accounting information to ensure their dealings are sufficiently transparent. NRAs can specify the precise information to be made available, the level of detail and how it is to be published. In particular, where an operator has obligations of non-discrimination, NRAs may require the operator to publish a reference offer which shall be sufficiently unbundled to ensure undertakings are not required to pay for facilities which are not necessary for the service requested. It should also give a description of the relevant offerings broken down into components according to market needs and associated terms and conditions including prices.

Notwithstanding the NRAs' discretion in dictating the type of information to be made available and the manner of its dissemination, where an operator has obligations to provide unbundled access to the local loop, all NRAs must ensure publication of a reference offer which contains at least the elements set out in Annex II of the Directive.

Annex II of the Directive lists the following disclosure requirements:

1. 'Local sub-loop' means a partial local loop connecting the network termination point at the subscriber's premises to a concentration point or a specified intermediate access point in the fixed public telephone network.

2. 'Unbundled access to the local loop' means full unbundled access to the local loop and shared access to the local loop; it does not entail a change in ownership of the local loop.

3. 'Full unbundled access to the local loop' means the provision to a beneficiary of access to the local loop or local sub-loop of the notified operator authorising the use of the full frequency spectrum of the twisted metallic pair.

4. 'Shared access to the local loop' means the provision to a beneficiary of access to the local loop or local sub-loop of the notified operator, authorising the use of the notified operator to provide the telephone service to the public.

A. Conditions for unbundled access to the local loop

1. Network elements to which access is offered covering in particular the following elements:

(a) access to local loops;

(b) access to non-voice band frequency spectrum of a local loop, in the case of shared access to the local loop.

2. Information concerning the locations of physical access sites,[161] availability of local loops in specific parts of the access network.

3. Technical conditions related to access and use of local loops, including the technical characteristics of the twisted metallic pair in the local loop.

4. Ordering and provisioning procedures, usage restrictions.

B. Co-location services

1. Information on the notified operator's relevant sites.

---

161 Availability of this information may be restricted to interested parties only, in order to avoid public security concerns.61

2. Co-location options at the sites indicated under point 1 (including physical co-location and, as appropriate, distant co-location and virtual co-location).

3. Equipment characteristics: restrictions, if any, on equipment that can be co-located.

4. Security issues: measures put in place by notified operators to ensure the security of their locations.

5. Access conditions for staff of competitive operators.

6. Safety standards,

7. Rules for the allocation of space where co-location space is limited.

8. Conditions for beneficiaries to inspect the locations at which physical co-location is available, or sites where co-location has been refused on grounds of lack of capacity.

C. Information systems

Conditions for access to notified operators' operational support systems, information systems or databases for pre-ordering, provisioning, ordering, maintenance and repair requests and billing.

D. Supply conditions

1. Lead time for responding to requests for supply of services and facilities, service level agreements, fault resolution, procedures to return to a normal level of service and quality of service parameters.

2. Standard contract terms, including, where appropriate, compensation provided for failure to meet lead times.

3. Prices or pricing formulae for each feature, function and facility listed above.

There is also a similar procedure to the one under the TV Standards Directive and Article 6 of the Directive to update from time to time the requirements under Annex II. Such a review is to be carried out in accordance with Article 14(3) of the Directive, including the Commission and the Communications Committee.

I. OBLIGATION OF NON-DISCRIMINATION

Article 10 allows NRAs to impose obligations for non-discrimination in situations where a market analysis indicates that discriminatory behaviour by an operator could lead to distortion of competition thereby disadvantaging end-users. Obligations of non-discrimination shall ensure, in particular, that the operator applies equivalent conditions in equivalent circumstances to other undertakings providing equivalent services and provides services and information to others under the same conditions and of the same quality as it provides for its own services or those of its subsidiaries or partners.

J. OBLIGATION OF ACCOUNTING SEPARATION

NRAs may impose upon SMP operators obligations for accounting separation in order to make transparent wholesale prices and internal cost transfers within the operators' vertically integrated companies in situations where the operator concerned provides input facilities that are essential to other service providers while competing with them on the same downstream market itself. This ensures compliance with the requirement of non-discrimination but also prevents unfair cross-subsidy. NRAs may specify the format and accounting methodology to be used.

To assist in enforcing these obligations and verifying the statistics given, NRAs can require that accounting records including data on revenues from third parties are provided on request. Whilst respecting commercial confidentiality, NRAs are allowed to publish as much of this information as would assist in creating an open and competitive market.

K. OBLIGATION OF ACCESS AND USE

Article 12 allows NRAs to impose on SMP operators obligations to grant access to and use of specific network elements and/or associated services or facilities in situations where denial of access by the SMP operator would hinder the development of a sustainable competitive retail market and would be contrary to end-users' interests.

Among the obligations operators can be forced to accept and provide in a reasonable and timely manner are the following:

(a) to give third parties access to specified network elements and/or facilities, including unbundled access to the local loop;

(b) to negotiate in good faith with undertakings requesting access;

(c) not to withdraw access to facilities already granted;

(d) to provide specified services on a wholesale basis for resale by third parties;

(e) to grant open access to technical interfaces, protocols or other key technologies that are indispensable for the interoperability of services or virtual network services;

(f) to provide co-location or other forms of facility sharing, including duct, building or mast sharing;

(g) to provide specified services needed to ensure interoperability of end-to-end services to users, including facilities for intelligent network services or roaming on mobile networks;

(h) to provide access to operational support systems or similar software systems necessary to ensure fair competition in the provision of services;

(i) to interconnect networks or network facilities.

When assessing whether to impose any of the above obligations, NRAs have to be mindful of the objections set out in Article 8 of the Framework Directive and how the obligations would reasonably facilitate the achievement of those objectives. Among the criteria they need to take into account in examining their discretion are the following:

(a) the technical and economic viability of using or installing competing facilities in the light of the rate of market development taking into account the nature and type of interconnection and access involved;

(b) the feasibility of providing the proposed owner, including the risks associated with the investment;

(c) the initial investment by the facility owner, including the risks associated with the investment;

(d) the need to safeguard competition in the long term;

(e) any relevant intellectual property rights;

(f) the provision of pan-European services.

L. PRICE CONTROL AND COST ACCOUNTING

Where an operator has SMP, situations will arise where it is necessary to impose certain restrictions on pricing to prevent supra-competitive pricing or pricing practices which could lead to a price squeeze. To avoid this mischief, NRAs may impose on SMP operators obligations relating to cost recovery and price controls. This may involve obligations for cost orientation of prices and obligations concerning cost accounting systems for provision of certain types of interconnection and/or access. In doing so, NRAs will have to have regard to any investment made by the operator and to allow it to make a reasonable rate of return on the capital employed. Any cost recovery mechanism used must promote efficiency and sustainable competition and maximise consumer benefits. To benchmark the appropriate mechanisms, account may be taken of prices available in comparable competitive markets.

NRAs have wide powers and discretions when enforcing obligations with regard to cost orientation of an operators' prices. It is for the operator to prove that the changes are derived from costs including a reasonable rate of return on the investment. NRAs are not constrained in doing so with the accounting methods used by the operator and are at liberty to use other cost accounting methods. If the operator fails to justify its prices, NRAs are entitled to require price adjustment. Transparency is an important issue when justifying to the industry and consumers that price controls have been adhered to. Therefore, NRAs can ensure that a description of the cost accounting system used is made publicly available showing the main categories under which costs have been grouped and the rules used for allocation of costs. Compliance with the cost accounting system shall be verified by a qualified independent body and a statement verifying compliance shall be published annually.

M. REVIEW AND IMPLEMENTATION

The final procedural provisions of the Directive impose obligations on NRAs to ensure up-to-date information is published on the obligation imposed on undertakings and that the specific product/service markets upon which they operate are identified. Member States must send a copy of this information to the Commission.

There are also notification requirements. NRAs are required to notify the Commission of the names of operators deemed to have SMP and the obligations imposed upon them.

By Article 17, the Commission is tasked with reviewing the functioning of this Directive and reporting back to the Council and the European Parliament not later than three years after the date of implementation of this measure.

Member States are required to implement the obligations contained in the Directive into their own laws by 25 July 2003 at the latest and to inform the Commission that this has been done.

N. CONCLUSION

The Access Directive is designed to achieve a harmonised framework for access and interconnection in the Community and to stipulate the role of NRAs in that process to ensure that necessary decisions are taken at the most appropriate level (eg, national).

The new regulatory framework on the Directive therefore:

    (a) places emphasis on commercial negotiation between parties on the terms and conditions of access and interconnection agreements;

(b) defines a framework in which NRAs need to work to address issues of access and interconnection;

(c) ensures continuity with the old regulatory framework but with a requirement on NRAs to review and possibly roll back certain obligations on certain operators following an assessment under the new definition of SMP;

(d) enables NRAs to impose upon SMP operators obligations of transparency, non-discrimination and accounting separation as well as price controls.

The above measures are designed to ensure that the EU electronic communications market can develop in a sustainable, harmonised way on a Community-wide basis which will reward investment risks but also benefit end-users with a growth of innovative and cost-effective services of high quality.

6
UNIVERSAL SERVICE AND USERS' RIGHTS

A. INTRODUCTION

This chapter describes the provisions of the new Universal Service Directive[162] which sets out the minimum level of services that Member States must make available to all end-users at an affordable price. It also describes the steps Member States can take to meet the cost of providing such services. The Directive also deals with the retail controls National Regulatory Authorities (NRAs) can impose on operators with Significant Market Power (SMP). Lastly, in this chapter, we review the rights of telephone users and the protection afforded to them in the provision of the basic telephony service.

The Universal Service Directive brings together the law relating to the provisions of Universal Service contained in several other Directives (the Interconnection Directive, the ONP Voice Telephony Directive, and the ONP Leased Lines Directive).[163]

B. PRE-EXISTING OBLIGATIONS

The old law was based principally on the Interconnection Directive and the ONP Voice Telephony and Leased Lines Directives. The ONP Voice Telephony and Leased Lines Directives set out the conditions to ensure open and efficient access and use of fixed telephone networks and services. The Directives also established the list of services to which all users, including consumers, should have access at an affordable price, regardless of their geographical situation.

The Interconnection Directive was introduced to ensure fair competition throughout the EU by establishing the conditions for access to fixed telecommunications networks. It also established a structure for the financing and funding of Universal Service and set out the principle that funding Universal Service is only justified when the cost imposed by the mandatory provision of Universal Service outweighs the benefits of being a Universal Service provider.

If it was felt that the overall cost of the Universal Service obligation subjected the operator, which was under the obligation to provide such a

---

162 Directive 2002/22/EC ([2002] OJ L108/51).
163 Interconnection Directive 97/33/EC ([1997] OJ L199/32); ONP Voice Telephony Directive 98/10/EC ([1998] OJ L101/51); ONP Leased Lines Directive 97/51/EC ([1997] OJ L295/23).

service, to an unfair financial burden, two mechanisms could be used if it was decided that the costs should be shared among the various market players. The first of these mechanisms involved supplementary charges. In this system, operators, who had the responsibility of providing the service directly, collected payments from competitors through additional charges to interconnection charges. The second mechanism, known as the Universal Service fund, required that operators and service providers made contributions which were collected at the national level with the overall fund being managed by an independent body. Money was then transferred to any operators who were entitled to receive Universal Service payments.

The Interconnection Directive stated that the calculation of the net cost, along with the mechanism chosen, must be based on objective, transparent, non-discriminatory and proportionate criteria and that the costs of Universal Service should be calculated on a long-run incremental cost methodology. Member States also had the power to set extra Universal Service obligations on top of those defined in the EU Directives. However, these obligations could not be funded through a Universal Service funding mechanism and any costs resulting from these additional obligations had to be met either by the relevant operator or directly by the State.

These Directives were repealed on 25 July 2003 and replaced by the new Universal Service Directive.

C. THE NEW UNIVERSAL SERVICE DIRECTIVE

So how does the Universal Service Directive compare with the old system. The new Directive defines the scope of Universal Service, the rights of users and provides the possible measures Member States can take for financing Universal Service without distorting competition. The scope of the Universal Service Directive compared to the old legislation remains largely unaltered in the new regulatory framework. The Directive does, however, clarify that the scope includes access to data communications, such as the Internet, via the public telephone network from a fixed location. Nevertheless, the legislation does provide a mechanism for the review of the scope of Universal Service from time to time.[164] The EU Commission was keen to avoid the emergence of a digital divide as technology develops which could result in a lack of access by low income groups to high speed services. The rapid evolution of technology and the increased availability of broadband access could result in a substantial rethink about the extent of Universal Service in the years ahead. This review mechanism lets that happen.

164 Article 15.

D. OVERVIEW OF THE DIRECTIVE

1. Basic Aim
The aim of the Universal Service Directive is 'to ensure the availability throughout the Community of good quality publicly available services through effective competition and choice and to deal with circumstances in which the needs of the end-users are not satisfactorily met by the market'.[165]

2. Universal Service
As mentioned above, the Universal Service Directive does not change the basic definition of Universal Service contained in the old legislation.[166] Universal Service is still limited to a telephone connection to the public switched telephone network at speeds capable of handling fax and narrowband Internet access.[167] ISDN provision is excluded from the scope of Universal Service (recital 8).

However, the following services are included in the basic definition:

(a) the publication of a universal telephone directory (at least one a year) (Article 5(1)(a));

(b) the provision of directory enquiries (Article 5(1)(b));

(c) the provision of public telephone boxes (Article 6(1));

(d) access to basic services for the disabled (Article 7(1)).

The Universal Service Directive talks about Universal Service covering technologies used by the 'majority of subscribers'. This leaves open the possibility of broadening the scope of Universal Service to include new services (such as broadband) when such technologies become a basic part of the life of the majority of users. According to the Commission, the difference between Universal Service and Information Society policy is that, while Information Society policy is about rolling out new services, Universal Service is about the requirement to make services that are available to the majority also available to the minority even if the majority has to cross-subsidise this through higher charges.

Disabled services: Disabled services are included within the scope of the Universal Service even though they go beyond what might be termed 'basic'. They include services such as the provision of public text telephone for the deaf or speech impaired, free directory assistance for blind or partially sighted people, and special access to emergency services.

Affordability: Universal Service must be made available to all end-users in a Member State's territory, regardless of geographic location

---

165 Directive 2002/21/EC, Art 1(1).
166 Interconnection Directive, ONP Leased Lines Directive and ONP Voice Telephony Directive.
167 Article 4.

and in the light of specific national conditions, at an 'affordable price'. So a basic telephone service at a standard price of connection and usage must be as equally available to end-users in London as to to those in northern Scotland.

'Affordable price' is not defined in the Universal Service Directive as the pricing levels for the basic service fall to national governments and regulators to decide, but the Directive does give certain indicators as to what constitutes affordable.

By Article 9 of the Directive, NRAs are mandated to ensure that the tariffs imposed for the delivery of Universal Service are affordable so as not to exclude people on low incomes or those with special social needs. Member States can ensure that price levels are enforced by the introduction of price caps, geographical averaging, or the provision of direct subsidies to end users.

Guidance as to what constitutes affordability is also provided in recital 10 of the Universal Service Directive. This links affordability with a consumer's ability to monitor and control expenditure. Methods of controlling expenditure include itemised billing, the ability to selectively block certain calls (such as high priced calls to premium services), the ability to pre-pay and the possibility for consumers to offset up-front connection fees (recital 15).

Universal Service providers have to supply these services as part of the basic menu of services and facilities. We examine in more detail the characteristics of each of these services below:

(a) *Itemised billing:* As part of Universal Service, operators must provide itemised billing free of charge if requested. The Universal Service Directive leaves it to the discretion of the Member States to define the extent of a carrier's liability in providing itemised bills but the Directive requires a level of detail sufficient to allow verification and control of the charges incurred in using the public switch telephone network (PSTN) from a fixed location and to be able to adequately monitor their usage and expenditure (Annex I, Part A, point (a)(ii)). The legislation does, however, allow operators to charge for billing information which exceeds the legal minimum. Annex I, Part A also makes it clear that an operator shall not provide details regarding calls made to free telephone numbers such as helplines.

(b) *Call blocking:* Another facility designed to help consumers control their expenditure is the ability to block calls to certain numbers. Under Annex I(b) of the Universal Service Directive, users must be able to block calls of defined types or to defined types of numbers free of charge. This is a useful feature designed to allow customers to block calls to premium numbers or to long-distance or international numbers.

(c) *Pre-payment schemes:* This is another means of allowing customers to control and monitor expenditure. Member States are under a duty to ensure that regulators are given the discretion to impose on designated undertakings a requirement to provide customers with a means of paying for access to PSTN on pre-paid terms. This discretion should also extend to terms allowing payments for connection to the PSTN to be phased over time.

(d) *Non-payment of bills:* Member States are to authorise specific measures relating to the non-payment of telephone bills for use of the public telephone network at fixed locations. Any measures imposed relating to the disconnection or the suspension of services needs to be proportionate, non-discriminatory and transparent. These measures must warn the subscriber of the imminent disconnection or service interruption. Any disconnection must also be limited to the service in question. Member States may allow a period of limited service prior to complete disconnection during which only calls that do not incur a charge to the subscriber are permitted (eg, emergency calls or incoming calls).

Who is the Universal Service provider?: In accordance with the principle of subsidiarity, it is at the discretion of Member States to decide on the basis of objective criteria which undertakings have Universal Service obligations under the Universal Service Directive. In doing so, they may take into account the ability and willingness of undertakings to accept all or at least some of the Universal Service obligations. Whoever is appointed must fulfil the function of providing a basic service for an affordable cost efficiently. Many Member States have appointed the incumbent operator to fulfil this requirement (eg, BT in the UK), but the Directive does exhort Member States to consider other undertakings in helping to provide all or part of the Universal Service obligations and choice. They may designate different undertakings or sets of undertakings to provide different elements of Universal Service and/or to cover different parts of the national territory.

To allow Member States to allocate these duties in the most cost effective way, the Directive provides that Member States can consider using competitive or comparative selection procedures to make their appointment. This refers to a possible competitive tender situation where operators may vie with each other to provide Universal Service at a lower subsidy than that presently received.

Recital 9 makes clear that Member States, if they so wish, can designate different undertakings to provide the network and service elements of Universal Service. There is therefore the flexibility to apportion responsibility to provide Universal Service. Those undertakings providing the network elements may be required to ensure such construction and maintenance as may be required to meet all reasonable requests for connection at a fixed location to the PSTN while the service provider satisfies the requirements for the other service-driven Universal Service obligations.

Universal Service costs: One of the most controversial issues associated with the operation of Universal Service obligations is its costing and funding. Universal Service operators are required to be reimbursed where it is demonstrated that the obligations can only be provided at a loss or a net cost outside normal commercial standards. It is important to ensure that the net cost is properly calculated. This needs the undertaking to take into account not only direct costs and revenues but also intangible goodwill derived from being seen everywhere in that territory as the Universal Service provider. In calculating the net costs of its provision, NRAs should follow the mechanism set out in Article 12 of the Universal Service Directive.

NRAs shall calculate the net cost of the Universal Service obligation taking into account any market benefit which accrues to an undertaking designated to provide Universal Service in accordance with Annex IV, Part A.

Annex IV, Part A provides that the calculation is to be based upon the costs attributable to:

(a) Elements of the identified services which can only be provided at a loss or provided under cost conditions falling outside normal commercial standards.

This category may include service elements such as access to emergency telephone services, provision of certain public pay telephones, provision of certain services or equipment for disabled people, etc;

(b) Specific end-users or groups of end-users who, taking into account the cost of providing the specified network and service, the revenue generated and any geographical averaging of prices imposed by the Member State, can only be served at a loss or under cost conditions falling outside normal commercial standards. This category also includes those end-users or groups of end-users who would not be served by a commercial operator which did not have an obligation to provide Universal Service.

The calculation of the net cost of specific aspects of the Universal Service obligation is to be made separately and so as to avoid the double counting of any direct or indirect benefits and costs. The overall net cost of the Universal Service obligation to any undertaking is to be calculated as the sum of the net costs arising from the specific components of the Universal Service obligation, taking account of any intangible benefits. The responsibility for verifying the net cost lies with the NRA.

Alternatively, Article 12(1)(b) allows NRAs the discretion to use the net costs of providing Universal Service identified by the mechanism set out in Article 8(2). This mechanism provides that any undertakings carrying out part or all of the Universal Service obligation must ensure that they do so in an efficient, objective, transparent and non-discriminatory way. In calculating what is efficient and cost effective, Member States are allowed to ask undertakings to bid for carrying out Universal Service for a set subsidy figure. This is a type of competitive tendering approach.

Financing of the Universal Service obligation: If the net cost calculation set out in Article 12 shows that an undertaking is subject to an unfair burden in providing Universal Service, Member States may, upon a request from the Universal Service provider in question, decide to set up a reimbursement mechanism using either or both of the following methods:

(a) to compensate the undertaking from government funds; and/or

(b) to share the net cost of the Universal Service obligation between providers of electronic communications networks and services.

If the net cost is to be shared among other industry members, Member States have to establish a sharing mechanism administered by the NRA or a body independent from beneficiaries under the supervision of the NRA. This would seem to indicate that payments would be distinct and separate. They are not allowed to be recouped, for example, as increased interconnection charges. Such an industry fund can only finance the net costs as determined according to the formula above (see also Article 12 and Annex IV). The industry scheme must adhere to the principles of transparency, non-discrimination and proportionately, and be designed to minimise any market distortion (see Article 13(3) and Annex IV, Part B).

In this connection, the Universal Service Directive recommends that the contributions are spread as widely as possible. However, the criterion does allow for some flexibility. The charge could be imposed on a section of operators or those providing a specific service or new entrants could be exempt from the payment until such time as they had achieved a significant market presence.

In Article 13(4), the Universal Service Directive makes clear that any changes related to the sharing of the cost of the Universal Service obligation shall be unbundled and identified separately for each undertaking. Only undertakings providing services in the Member State that has established the charging mechanism are liable to pay. The Directive requires NRAs to publish details on how any cost sharing method is applied and an annual report must be published giving the calculated cost of the Universal Service obligation, identifying the contributions made by all the undertakings involved and identifying the market benefits, if any, that may have been gained by undertakings designated to provide Universal Service (Article 14).

SMP regulatory controls: The second part of the Directive provides NRAs with the power to impose certain restrictions upon the retail activities of SMP operators in markets where there is inadequate competition.

In such markets, competition does not provide a sufficient disciplinary influence and there is a risk that an undertaking with SMP may act in various ways to inhibit entry or distort competition. Such practices may extend to setting predatory prices, unlawfully bundling together retail services or discriminating in favour of certain customers.

Therefore, NRAs are given the power to impose remedial measures to combat such abusive behaviour. These powers, which should be used as a last resort, include price cap regulation, geographical averaging or similar measures. In addition, regulators are given power to impose a wide range of non-regulatory measures such as mandating the publication of retail tariffs, the maintenance of Universal Service or access to appropriate accounting information and separation (recital 26). This is referred to as 'ex-ante' regulation. It is similar but different to competition law. Ex-ante regulation is designed to open up markets previously dominated by monopoly providers where there is a lack of competition with a view to stimulating the growth of effective competition in the future.

This power to fetter the behaviour of SMP operators is one of the most important powers in the new EU electronic communications package.

Retail controls: In markets which are not subject to effective competition, the Universal Service Directive provides that, until NRAs have undertaken an updated market analysis of relevant retail markets as required by the Framework Directive (see Article 16), they must enforce the existing retail controls which are provided by the old ONP Directives (the ONP Voice Telephony and ONP Leased Lines Directives). The relevant product and service markets for the purposes of Articles 16–18 of the Universal Service Directive are defined on a European level by the Commission in its Recommendation on Relevant Product and Service Markets within the electronic communications sector susceptible to ex-ante regulation in accordance with Directive 2002/21/EC of the European Parliament and of the Council on a common regulatory framework.[168] These are follows:

> (1) Access to the public telephone network at a fixed location for residential customers.

---

168 COM(2003)497, 11 February 2003.

---

(2) Access to the public telephone network at a fixed location for non-residential customers.

(3) Publicly available local and/or national telephone services provided at a fixed location for residential customers.

(4) Publicly available international telephone services provided at a fixed location for residential customers.

(5) Publicly available local and/or national telephone services provided at a fixed location for non-residential customers.

(6) Publicly available international telephone services provided at a fixed location for non-residential customers.

These six markets are identified for the purpose of analysis in respect of Article 17 of the Universal Service Directive.

Together, markets 1 to 6 correspond to 'the provision of connection to and use of the public telephone network at fixed locations', referred to in Annex I(1) of the Framework Directive. This combined market is also referred to in Article 19 of the Universal Service Directive (for possible imposition of carrier call-by-call selection or carrier selection).

(7) The minimum set of leased lines (which comprises the specified types of leased lines up to and including 2Mb/sec as referenced in Article 18 and Annex VII of the Universal Service Directive).

This market is referred to in Annex I (1) of the Framework Directive in respect of Article 16 of the Universal Service Directive ('the provision of leased lines to end users'). A market analysis must be undertaken for the purposes of Article 18 of the Universal Service Directive which covers regulatory controls on the provision of the minimum set of leased lines.

Under the new structure, once the national regulatory authorities have undertaken their review of the relevant markets, and have concluded that those markets are not effectively competitive, then if measures relating to interconnection under the Access Directive (access to SMP networks on cost orientated prices) are not sufficient, the NRA concerned must impose appropriate retail controls on the SMP operator.

There are situations which could arise where an NRA has ordered access to an SMP operator's network at cost orientated prices to promote vigorous competition, but the SMP operator has abused its market power at a retail level. The SMP operator concerned could in response reduce its retail tariff to exclude new competition. Consequently, there may be a need for retail tariff regulation.

This is an important policy issue as the Commission has clearly signalled in the drafting of the terms of Article 17(1) that it regards wholesale access to networks as the primary focus of opening up markets and only when this is insufficient will retail controls be regarded as permissible. So expect detailed but favourable scrutiny by the Commission of the steps taken by NRAs to stimulate competition through wholesale access and a restrictive interpretation of measures seeking retail controls.

The different types of control open to the NRA are retail price caps, prior appeal of tariff obligations, cost orientated prices and a prohibition on predatory prices or bundled services.

Article 17(2) of the Universal Service Directive places the only limit on the NRA discretion in relation to these measures when it dictates that the measures must be based on the nature of the problem identified and be proportionate and justified in light of the objectives laid down in Article 8 of Directive 2002/21 (the 'Framework Directive').

Once measures have been taken, they will have to be notified to the Commission on request (Article 17(3) of the Universal Service Directive). This is a substantial watering down of the obligation first suggested to be imposed on NRAs and is in accordance with the desire of the Commission to promote wholesale competition.

Where the NRA subjects an SMP operator to retail tariff regulation or other retail controls, there is an obligation to implement appropriate cost accounting systems. An NRA may specify the format and accounting methodology used. Adherence to the cost accounting system should be verified by a qualified independent body and an annual compliance statement must be published giving the system added transparency.

The Universal Service Directive is an attempt to approximate the behaviour of NRAs. While the principle behind the Directive is to leave to the NRA the discretion to police its own markets, it does attempt to ensure that the NRA follows standard procedures in reviewing the market, applying necessary retail controls, and then notifying them to the Commission. This is a hallmark of the new framework system.

The new powers of NRAs to impose retail controls may require certain Member States to alter their national regulatory systems where the power is vested in government, rather than in an independent regulator, to impose these measures. This is part of a drive to separate the exercise of regulatory powers from political considerations. The European Commission stated in its Seventh Report on the Implementation of the Telecommunications Regulatory Package:[169]

> It is also vital that political considerations are not allowed to justify intervention in the regulatory and market process, for example, by imposing or supporting retail tariffs that are set at artificially low levels [eg, to promote broadband in schools and hospitals]. The dangers of this to competition are clear: in the market for local

169 COM(2001)706, pp 13–14.

broadband access for example the combination of a high price for local loop, unbundling and collation, a lack of shared access, failure to provide as wholesale DSL service by the incumbent and authorisation by the regulator for the incumbent to provide its own DSL services at low retail prices will conspire to keep entrants out of the market.

Regulation on leased lines: NRAs are under an obligation to review under Article 16(3)(c) whether the market for the provision of part or all of the 'minimum set' of leased lines is effectively competitive. If those markets do not pass this test, NRAs shall identify undertakings with SMP in the provision of those specific parts of the 'minimum set of leased lines service' in all or part of their territory. The NRAs shall impose obligations regarding the provision of the 'minimum set of leased lines' in accordance with Article 17 of and Annex VII to the Framework Directive. These provisions must be based on the following:

(a) *Non-discrimination:* SMP operators identified by NRAs must provide leased lines to all on the same terms (including quality) as they provide for their own services. The SMP operator must apply similar conditions in similar circumstances to companies providing similar services (Annex VII, Part 1).

(b) *Cost orientation:* All SMP operators must provide leased lines on tariffs based on cost orientation, and put in place suitable accounting systems to support it. NRAs must make available information on such operators' cost accounting systems and make that information available to the Commission on request (Annex VII, Part 2).

(c) *Transparency:* NRAs must ensure that SMP operators publish information in respect of their leased line offerings. This must include the technical characteristics, tariffs and supply terms.

This applies only to the 'minimum set'. The minimum set of leased lines is defined under the ONP Leased Lines Directive as 64 kbit/sec and 2mbit/sec circuits. Leased lines within the minimum set are mandatory services and SMP operators are under a duty to provide them (see recital 28). Leased lines falling outside the minimum set are not covered by the non-discrimination, cost orientation or transparency criteria. However, they may still be included under the general Article 17 provisions governing the control of retail tariffs.

Lifting of regulatory controls: Article 18(2) of the Universal Service Directive dictates that NRAs have a duty to lift regulatory controls in markets where the supply of leased lines (2mbit/sec) is effectively competitive. To comply with this duty, NRAs have an ongoing duty to review markets for leased lines to identify areas (even local markets) within their testing where the supply of leased lines is sufficiently competitive.

Carrier selection and pre-selection: The Universal Service Directive imposes upon SMP operators obligations to provide the subscribers of providers of interconnected publicly available telephone services with access to their networks:

(a) on a call-by-call basis by dialling a carrier selection code ('carrier selection'); or

(b) by means of pre-selection with a facility to override that pre-selected choice on a call-by-call basis by dialling a carrier selection code ('carrier pre-selection') (see Article 19(1)).

The Universal Service Directive maintains the current position on carrier selection and pre-selection. However certain technical problems arise from carrier pre-selection. For example, is it possible to pre-select more than one carrier for all calls or just long distance international, fixed local calls and possibly even mobile operators, or a mixture of some or all of the above. The technical choice will need to be resolved by each NRA.

One controversial aspect of the new system is whether the obligations of carrier selection and pre-selection extend to mobile operators. The Universal Service Directive appears to be silent on this point. However, under Article 19(2), it appears that these services may be implemented 'on other networks or in other ways' following market review under the provisions of the Framework and Access Directives. Readers should note that the term 'carrier selection' only relates to public telephone services. Carrier selection and pre-selection do not extend to Internet access services or other value added data services.

In accordance with Article 19(3), NRAs must ensure that pricing for access and interconnection to carrier selection and pre-selection is cost orientated and that direct charges to subscribers do not act as a disincentive for the use of these facilities.

End-user interests and rights: Wherever a consumer enters into an agreement for connection or access to the public telephone network, the undertaking providing that service must provide the consumer with a contract in writing. That contract shall contain the following particulars at least:

(a) the identity and address of the supplier;

(b) services provided, the service quality levels offered, as well as the time for the initial connection;

(c) the types of maintenance service offered;

(d) particulars of prices and tariffs and the means by which up-to-date information on all applicable tariffs and maintenance charges may be obtained;

(e) the duration of the contract, the conditions for renewal and termination of services and of the contract;

(f) any compensation and the refund arrangements which apply if contracted service quality levels are not met; and

(g) the method of initiating procedures for settlement of disputes in accordance with Article 34.

Under Article 20(3) of the Universal Service Directive, the above obligations are also extended to contracts between consumers and electronic communications service providers other than those providing connection and/or access to the public telephone network. These include the likes of voice resellers, telephone card providers and Internet service providers.

It will be noted that the legislation only provides mandatory information provision requirements in relation to consumer contracts. It is up to Member States to extend these requirements to other end-users (eg, small and medium-sized businesses). Should an electronic communications provider wish to alter the terms of its contract with a consumer, it must give adequate prior notice, no shorter than one month, of the change. Subscribers shall have a right to withdraw from their contracts without any penalty if they take objection to proposed modifications (Universal Service Directive, Article 20(4)).

The Universal Service Directive sets out a number of obligations imposed upon service providers when dealing with consumers which are set out in Articles 21–31. These are as follows:

(a) *Transparency and publication of information:* Member States shall ensure that clearly understandable and up-to-date information on service providers' prices and tariffs and on standard terms and conditions for access to aid use of publicly available telephone services is available to end users and consumers in accordance with the provisions of Annex II of the USD.

Annex II makes clear that it is for the NRA to decide which of the information is to be published by the undertakings concerned and which information is to be published by the NRA itself to help consumers make informed choices about the services provided.

The information to be provided is:

(i) Name(s) and address(es) of undertaking(s), ie, names and head office addresses of undertakings providing public telephone networks and/or publicly available telephone services.

(ii) Publicly available telephone services offered.

(iii) Scope of the publicly available telephone service and description of the publicly available telephone services offered, indicating what is included in the subscription charge and the periodic rental charge (eg, operator services, directories, directory enquiry services, selective call barring, itemised billing, maintenance, etc).

(iv) Standard tariffs covering access, all types of usage charges, maintenance, and including details of standard discounts applied and special and targeted tariff schemes.

(v) Compensation/refund policy, including specific details of any compensation/refund schemes offered.

(vi) Types of maintenance service offered.

(vii) Standard contract conditions, including any minimum contractual period, if relevant.

(viii) Dispute settlement mechanisms including those developed by the undertaking.

(ix) Information about rights as regards Universal Service, including the facilities and services mentioned in Annex I.

(b) *Quality of services:* NRAs are to have the power to require electronic communications service providers to publish comparable, adequate and up-to-date information to end-users on the quality of their services. Such details shall be provided in advance to the NRAs. To aid the provision of comparable information for consumers and end users, NRAs may provide how the quality service parameters are to be measured, and the content and form of information to be published.

Article 22 stipulates that, where appropriate, the parameters definition and measurements methods referred to in Annex III can be used. However, the language of the text seems to suggest that this is purely advisory and the chosen method of measurement if left to the NRA in question.

(c) *Emergency services:* NRAs shall take steps to ensure that undertakings providing publicly available telephone services at fixed locations take all reasonable steps to ensure uninterrupted access to emergency services. It is for the Member States to take the necessary steps to keep the public telephone network working in the event of catastrophic network breakdown or in cases of force majeure.

However, the Directive is vague on how this is to be done, leaving this to the discretion of the Member States.

In the interests of harmonisation, Member States are under a duty to make available a single European emergency call number '112' free of charge in addition to any other national emergency call numbers specified by the NRAs.

(d) *Operator assistance and directory enquiries:* Subscribers to publicly available telephone services are entitled to be listed in a publicly available telephone directory. Operators that assign numbers to subscribers must make those numbers available for publicly available directories and directory enquiry services on a non-discriminatory basis and at cost oriented prices.

(e) *European access codes:* To ensure EU harmonisation, all Member States must ensure that the 'O' code is the standard international access code, and that all public network operators handle such calls (provided their costs are covered). Although this is without prejudice to any special arrangements that exist for making calls between adjacent locations across Member State borders, end users of publicly available telephone services shall be fully informed of any such arrangements

End-users from other Member States must also be able to access non-geographic numbers within another Member State where this is technically and economically possible. This obligation on Member States does, however, allow a subscriber to limit access to calling parties located in particular geographic areas if he wishes to do so for commercial reasons.

(f) *Tone dialling and caller line identification:* Under Article 29 of the Universal Service Directive, Member States are required to ensure that NRAs have the discretion to require operators of public telephone networks to provide, 'subject to technical feasibility and economic viability', end-users with the following:

(i) Tone dialling or DTMF (dial tone multi-frequency operation) as defined in ETSI ETR 207: The public telephone network must support end-to-end signalling throughout the network both within a Member State and between Member States.

(ii) Caller line identification: This facility allows the calling party's number to be displayed to the called party prior to the call being answered. To facilitate the provision of this service, operators should provide data and signals to facilitate the offering of caller line identity and tone dialling across Member State boundaries. The provision of caller line identification gives rise to data protection issues, and NRAs and public network operators need to ensure that such facilities are provided in accordance with EU personal data protection legislation and, in particular, Directive 97/66/EC.

While a Member State has a duty to provide NRAs with the power to mandate the provision of these facilities, it is purely discretionary upon the part of the NRAs to do so. Issues associated with the provision of caller line identification arise from the use of GSM[170] Gateways. In many Member States, the use of GSM Gateways is technically illegal but in others it is permitted. Certain Member States, including the UK, are considering their positions in relation to these facilities.

The attraction of GSM Gateways is that they collect fixed calls and send them through a single point to a mobile network thereby transforming a fixed-to-mobile call into a mobile-to-mobile connection. Mobile-to-mobile retail tariffs are far cheaper than interconnecting a fixed call to the mobile network. Use of GSM Gateways prevents the transmission of the calling party's caller line identification but instead substitutes the Gateway number.

If an NRA mandates the provision of caller line identification, the use of GSM Gateways could be a breach of this duty unless technical grounds are accepted as an objectively justified reason for non-compliance.

(h) *Number portability:* A duty imposed upon Member States which is fundamental to competition in the voice telephony sector is number portability. Member States must ensure that all subscribers of publicly available telephony services who so request can retain their numbers.

This duty extends to all fixed and mobile services provided by all public network operators whether or not they have SMP. It does not, however, include email addresses. It also applies to both the transfer of geographic numbers at a specific location and non-geographic numbers. However, this obligation does not apply if a subscriber wants to port his fixed line number to a mobile network and vice versa.

Number portability shall not be discouraged or hindered by discriminatory or unfair pricing. NRAs must ensure that pricing for interconnection relating to the provision of number portability is cost oriented and that direct charges to the subscriber do not act as a disincentive to use these facilities.

170 Global system for mobile communications.

Article 25(3) ensures that all end-users who are connected to the public telephone network have access to operator assistance services and directory enquiry services. In addition, there shall not be any restrictions on consumers in one Member State obtaining access to operator directory enquiry services in another Member State, subject to the requirements of EU legislation on personal data and privacy.

E. MISCELLANEOUS PROVISIONS

1. Additional mandatory services
Mandatory services, in addition to the Universal Service specifications referred to above, can be imposed upon public network operators by NRAs but NRAs are not permitted to impose any compensation mechanism or Universal Service fund to recompense those extra duties provided by the undertakings in question.

2. Public consultation
Member States are under a duty to ensure adequate consultation among end-users and consumers, manufacturers and public network operators if any change in consumer rights are contemplated or issues arise upon which the NRA has to act in connection with such rights. The Directive encourages consumers/end-users to form with consumer/user groups and service providers in cooperation with the NRAs to develop and monitor codes of conduct and operating standards to improve the standard and quality of service provision.

This public consultation obligation reflects the general policy trend from Brussels which can be seen elsewhere in the Framework Directives (see the Framework Directive, Article 6) to seek public comment and views before embarking upon any new major policy initiative. Some NRAs, such as OFTEL in the UK, are accustomed to seeking public views on their proposals. Other NRAs (eg, in France) have been loath to involve the public in policy and formulation and to seek views on proposed regulatory changes. In view of the duties set out in Article 33, this culture will need to change. However, it is hard to see what effective disciplinary mechanism could be brought to bear against any reluctant Member State given the wide nature of the duty and the fact that consultation shall be carried out 'as far as appropriate'. As such, it is really an expression of intent on behalf of the Member States to open up their procedures more in the future.

3. Dispute resolution
One of the most common and irretractable problems that consumers face, given their inequality of bargaining power, is a dispute over the size of their bill or in connection with other services provided by a network provider, including the provision of Universal Service. To resolve these

issues, it is important that end-users should have at their disposal simple and cheap dispute resolution procedures. Such procedures are without prejudice to any existing court procedures and Member States may have to deal with such issues.

Article 34 of the Universal Service Directive mandates Member States to ensure that 'transparent, simple and inexpensive out of court procedures are available for dealing with unresolved disputes involving consumers relating to issues covered by this Directive'.

The principal object of any dispute resolution mechanism is that it shall enable disputes to be settled fairly and promptly. In addition, Member States may at their discretion adopt a system of reimbursement or compensation in appropriate cases.

Although the obligation imposed on Member States under Article 34(1) extends only to 'consumers', Member States are free to extend those duties to other end-users (eg, businesses).

Member States must ensure that none of their legislation hampers or prevents the establishment of a Complaints Office and the provision of online services to facilitate access to dispute resolution by consumers and end users. The wording of Article 34(2) is strange. The Directive does not mandate Member States to set up a Complaints Office or to provide online services to facilitate access to dispute resolution by consumers, but requires them merely not to introduce or maintain legislation that would 'prevent or hinder their establishment or provision'. In short, this gives the Member States unlimited discretion in setting up the dispute resolution mechanisms required by the Directive. The Complaints Office for instance could be part of government or it could be entirely independent.

The only specified duty is for Member States to ensure they coordinate with each other in relation to disputes involving two or more Member States to ensure a speedy resolution of a dispute.

7
THE COMMUNICATIONS DATA PROTECTION DIRECTIVE

A. INTRODUCTION

The deployment of advanced digital technologies and new electronic communications services by all the major European public telecommunications operators has given rise to specific concerns with respect to the protection of users' personal data and privacy. Digital networks possess the capacity to store and process a large amount of personal information and the confidence of users that their privacy will not be at risk will partly dictate whether the development of these cross-border networks will be a success or not. The Communications Data Protection Directive,[171] therefore, places specific legal, regulatory, and technical obligations on public telecommunications networks to protect the fundamental rights of individual users[172] and the legitimate interests of companies.[173]

1. Objectives

The Communications Data Protection Directive aims to harmonise the level of protection with respect to privacy and the processing of personal data within the electronic communications data sector and thereby encourage the free movement of such data and electronic communications equipment and services within the European Union.

The Communications Data Protection Directive replaces the 1997 Telecommunications Data Protection Directive.[174] However, the new Communications Data Protection Directive does not introduce major changes to the substance of the previous Directive; its provisions have been adapted and updated to developments in electronic communications services and technologies. It seeks to 'particularise and complement',[175] ie,

171 Directive 2002/58/EC of the European Parliament and of the Council of 12 July 2002 ([2002] OJ L201/27) concerning the processing of personal data and the protection of privacy in the electronic communications sector (the 'Communications Data Protection Directive').
172 The Directive refers to individual users as 'natural persons'.
173 The Directive refers to companies are 'legal persons'.
174 Directive 97/66/EC of the European Parliament and of the Council of 15 December 1997 ([1998] OJ L24/24) concerning the processing of personal data and the protection of privacy in the telecommunications sector.
175 Communications Data Protection Directive, Art 1(2).

it supplements the provisions of the General Data Protection Directive[176] (which continue to apply) for the electronic communications sector. For those areas not expressly covered by this Directive, for example, transfers of personal data to third countries and rights for data subjects to access their personal information, the General Protection Data Directive applies. Both Directives must therefore be read together as a whole.

B. APPLICATION OF THE COMMUNICATIONS DATA PROTECTION DIRECTIVE

1. Scope

The Communications Data Protection Directive applies 'to the processing of personal data in connection with the provision of publicly available electronic communications services in public communications networks in the Community'.[177]

2. Personal data

The General Data Protection Directive defines personal data as 'any information relating to an identified or identifiable natural person; an identifiable person is one who can be identified, directly or indirectly, in particular by reference to an identification number or to one or more factors specific to his physical, physiological, mental, economic, cultural or social identity'.[178] In short, 'personal data' is data that can be traced to an individual. Information that cannot be linked to an individual is not personal data. In particular, according to the recitals of the General Data Protection Directive, it must not be possible to trace data to an individual using 'means likely reasonably to be used either by the controller [of the data] or by any other person'.[179] Data that can be linked to a company (a 'legal person') is not 'personal data' and is not covered by the Directive.

The position is not clear if the customer of a telecommunications company or Internet service provider (ISP) is a company and its employees can be identified by a particular telephone number or IP address. Although the communications provider would be not be able to link the number with a particular individual, an employer may retain the ability to identify its employees through a telephone number or IP number. Some Member States may therefore interpret the provider's data as 'personal data'.

---

176 Directive 95/46/EC of the European Parliament and of the Council of 24 October 1995 ([1995] OJ L281/31) on the protection of individuals with regard to the processing of personal data and on the free movement of such data.
177 Communications Data Protection Directive, Art 3(1).
178 General Data Protection Directiv, Art 2(a).
179 Ibid, recital 26.

3. Processing

The processing of personal data is defined as 'any operation or set of operations which is performed upon personal data, whether or not by automatic means, such as collection, recording, organization, storage, adaptation or alteration, retrieval, consultation, use, disclosure by transmission, dissemination or otherwise making available, alignment or combination, blocking, erasure or destruction'.[180]

4. Private networks

The processing of personal data in connection with 'non-public communication services' is excluded from the scope of this Directive and is only covered by the General Data Protection Directive. The provisions of the Communications Data Protection Directive will not apply to private network environments. Therefore, companies that manage their own private networks will be able to retain traffic data and copies of email longer than permitted under the new Directive subject only to the provisions of the General Data Protection Directive.

A potential conflict arises in future outsourcing arrangements whereby a public network service provider manages the private network of a company. Do the provisions of the Communications Data Protection Directive or the General Data Protection Directive apply, for example, with respect to the retention of employee traffic data for longer than is permitted under the new Directive? The issue will have to be examined in future outsourcing and private network contracts. It may be that the network provider will have to distinguish between its role as a public communications provider and its role as manager of a customer's private network.

5. Content providers

The wording of Article 3(1) is sufficiently broad as to cover not only providers of electronic communications networks and services, but also entities that make use of such networks and services. This means that the Communications Data Protection Directive's provisions apply also to content providers. However, its application to content providers must be examined on a case-by-case basis. In some areas, for example, the provision concerning the sending of unsolicited emails will apply to entities that are not electronic communications service providers. In others, for example, network security, they will not be covered.

6. Rights of 'legal persons'

The Communications Data Protection Directive does not extend the application of the General Data Protection Directive to companies but it does provide some protection to the 'legitimate interests of subscribers who

180 Communications Data Protection Directive, Art 2(b).

are legal persons'.[181] The actual protections must be determined on a case-by-case basis as some provisions (eg, unsolicited email) apply only to individual subscribers. Other provisions (eg, network security) apply regardless of whether the subscriber is a company or an individual consumer.

C. OBLIGATIONS UNDER THE COMMUNICATIONS DATA PROTECTION DIRECTIVE

1. Obligation to ensure security of services

The Communications Data Protection Directive imposes on providers of publicly available electronic communications services an obligation of security. They must take 'appropriate technical and organisational measures to safeguard security of its services, if necessary, in conjunction with the provider of the public communications network with respect to network security'.[182] 'Security' is defined in the General Data Protection Directive as protection against 'accidental or unlawful destruction or accidental loss, alteration, unauthorised disclosure or access, in particular where the processing involves the transmission of data over a network, and against all other lawful forms of processing'.[183]

The level of security must have regard 'to the state of the art and the cost of implementation' and 'ensure a level of security appropriate to the risk presented'.[184] In short, the more significant the risk, the more security measures should be taken to prevent the risk from occurring. However, the difficulty of applying this test will be that the state of the art in network security evolves very quickly. It will be difficult to judge 'state of the art' as of the time the product is sold as selling electronic services is a continuous activity. The test will presumably be applied as of the time the service is provided and the time that the relevant security breach occurs. This places a particularly high burden on service providers to continuously update their security measures. The concept will also partly depend on Member States' applicable legislation on encryption software. In France, for example, the sale of particular encryption software is restricted and so, although technologically available, particular network security tools cannot be used due to government legislation.

The Communications Data Protection Directive requires providers of publicly availably electronic communications services to take appropriate measures to safeguard the security of their services. In particular, they must inform subscribers of a 'particular risk of a breach of security of the

---

181 Communications Data Protection Directive, recital 24, Art 1(1).
182 Communications Data Protection Directive, Art 4(1).
183 General Data Protection Directive, Art 17(1).
184 Communications Data Protection Directive, Art 4(1).

network' and 'where the risk lies outside the scope of the measures to be taken by the service provider, of any possible remedies, including an indication of the likely costs involved.'[185] Service providers must therefore inform users of particular measures they can take to protect the security of their communications, for example, by their use of specific types of software or technologies. Despite the requirement to inform users and subscribers of particular security risks, service providers are still required to take appropriate and immediate measures to remedy new, unforeseen security risks and restore the normal security level of the service.

2. Obligation of confidentiality

Article 5 of the Communications Data Protection Directive requires that Member States ensure the confidentiality of both communications and related traffic data by enacting appropriate national laws. Confidentiality means, in particular, protection against unauthorised 'listening, taping, storage or other kinds of interception or surveillance of communications and related traffic data, by persons other than users, without the consent of the users concerned.'[186] Although the obligation of confidentiality clearly overlaps with the obligation of security as it can be seen as part of the service provider's duty of implementing 'appropriate' security measures under Article 4, Article 5's objective is to ensure that national laws are enacted to prevent third parties from attempting to intercept communications.

A 'communication' means 'any information exchanged or conveyed between a finite number of parties by means of a publicly available electronic communications service'.[187] In other words, it is the content of a telephone conversation or email, the content of a web page, movie or song called up by a particular user, or audiovisual content ordered through a video on demand function. However, broadcast content that can be received by the general public without it being possible to trace the content to a given user is not considered a 'communication' for purposes of the Communications Data Protection Directive.[188]

'Traffic data' is information that is necessary for conveying the communication (for example, the phone number being called or the recipient's email address) or data necessary for billing purposes (for example, duration of the call, number of the calling party, size of the email sent).[189] It can also include some location data as mobile networks need to know in what cell a person is located in order to convey a call to that person. Traffic data has traditionally been given less privacy protection

185 Communications Data Protection Directive, Art 4(2).
186 Communications Data Protection Directive, Art 5(1).
187 Communications Data Protection Directive, Art 2(d).
188 Ibid.
189 Communications Data Protection Directive, Art 2(b).

than communications data. For example, it has been easier for police forces to obtain access to traffic data than to listen to 'communications'.

3. Exceptions

There are a number of exceptions to the confidentiality obligation and these are discussed below.

Storage: The first exception relates to the storage of a communication or traffic data by a user himself. For example, users can keep copies of their incoming and outgoing emails on their computers. More controversial is the practice of recording a telephone conversation when the other person on the call is not aware that his words are being recorded. This practice is currently prohibited in certain Member States. Under the Communications Data Protection Directive, however, Member States would be free to permit such recordings. However, under the principles of the General Data Protection Directive, the data subject would have to be informed of the recording and the reason for the recording.

Consent: The second exemption relating to confidentiality is an interception 'with the consent of the users concerned'.[190] Confidentiality can be waived if the parties to the communication agree. There is no guidance as to the form of consent. That will be covered by national law and by the General Data Protection Directive, Article 2(h), which provides:

> 'the data subject's consent' shall mean any freely given specific and informed indication of his wishes by which the data subject signifies his agreement to personal data relating to him being processed.

Law enforcement: The third exception relates to interceptions by law enforcement authorities. The Communications Data Protection Directive does not restrict law enforcement interceptions which, with national defence measures, is excluded completely from the scope of the new Directive.[191]

Technical reasons: The fourth exception to the confidentiality obligation is for 'technical storage which is necessary for the conveyance of a communication without prejudice to the principle of confidentiality'.[192] The preamble states:

> The prohibition of storage of communications and the related traffic data by persons other than the users or without their consent is not intended to prohibit any automatic, intermediate and transient storage of this information insofar as this takes place for the sole purpose of carrying out the transaction in the electronic communications network and provided that the information is not

---

190 Communications Data Protection Directive, Art 5(1).
191 Communications Data Protection Directive, recital 11, Art 1(3).
192 Communications Data Protection Directive, Art 5(1).

> stored for any period longer than is necessary for the transmission and for traffic management purposes, and that during the period of storage the confidentiality remains guaranteed.[193]

Such 'automatic, intermediate and transient storage' includes the storage of emails until they are opened by the recipient. The exception also covers the catching of web pages provided that the information relating to the identity of subscribers or users having requested access to the website is erased.[194]

Business practices: The fifth exception to the confidentiality obligation allows third party interception and storage of communications when doing so is part of a lawful business practice for the purpose of providing evidence of a commercial transaction. However, this exception is only available if the laws of the Member State authorise such interception and, secondly, the parties to the communication are informed of the recording, its purpose and the duration of its storage.[195] The Directive states that the recorded communication should be 'erased as soon as possible and in any case at the latest by the end of the period during which the transaction can lawfully be challenged'.[196]

Billing purposes: The final exception relates to the storage of traffic data to the extent required for billing purposes, which is examined below.

4. Cookies

'Cookies' are software that remain on a user's hard disk to record the user's preferences and habits on a particular website. They are therefore related to confidential data in that they can record traffic data and communications without the user's knowledge.

Terminal equipment, such as a personal computer and mobile phone, is considered part of an individual's 'private sphere' protected against unauthorised intrusion.[197] By the unknowing introduction of cookies into a user's hard drive, an obvious privacy risk is created. Other similar devices that trace the activities of the user may also seriously intrude upon the privacy of the user.[198] The Communications Data Protection Directive states that the use of such devices should be allowed only for legitimate purposes, and only with the knowledge of the user concerned.[199] The Communications Data Protection Directive draws a distinction between so-called spy-ware and cookies, noting that the latter can be legitimate and

193 Ibid, recital 22.
194 Ibid.
195 Communications Data Protection Directive, Art 5(2), recital 23.
196 Ibid, recital 23.
197 Communications Data Protection Directive, recital 24.
198 Ibid.
199 Ibid.

useful tools for navigation and interactive services.[200] However, it does not attempt to draw a technical distinction between legitimate 'cookies' and illicit 'spy-ware'. Instead, the Directive adopts an 'opt-out' regime for cookies and requires service providers to provide 'clear and comprehensive information in accordance with Directive 95/46/EC, *inter alia* about the purpose of the processing'[201] and an option to refuse the use of cookies. The notification and right of refusal should be offered in as 'user-friendly' a manner as possible.[202] The notification and possibility to opt out may be given to the user once, and then remains valid for the entire duration of the connection and for any subsequent connections.[203]

The Communications Data Protection Directive does provide two exceptions to the requirement of offering an 'opt-out'. First, the requirement to give users an 'opt-out' 'shall not prevent any technical storage or access for the sole purpose of carrying out or facilitating the transmission of a communication'.[204] This would allow, for example, a software feature that searches the user's address book to obtain the email address of the intended recipient of an email. The second exception states that the requirement to give an 'opt-out' shall not prevent any technical storage or access 'strictly necessary in order to provide an information society service explicitly requested by the subscriber or user'.[205] The term 'information society service' includes any service normally provided for remuneration, at a distance, by means of electronic equipment for the processing and storage of data, and at the individual request of a recipient of a service.[206] The term includes most forms of online services exposing a potentially large gap in the opt-out regime.

Finally, the Communications Data Protection Directive indicates that service providers may make access to their website conditional on 'well-informed acceptance' of a cookie or similar device, provided that the cookie is used for a legitimate purpose.[207]

The Communications Data Protection Directive's provisions appear considerably watered down compared to those advocated by some privacy groups. The principal obligation is to inform users of the use of cookies and give them the possibility to opt out. Alternatively, service providers may make access to their websites conditional on users accepting cookies. The

---

200 Ibid, recital 25.
201 Ibid, Art 5(3).
202 Ibid, recital 25.
203 Ibid.
204 Communications Data Protection Directive, Art 5(3).
205 Ibid.
206 Directive 98/34/EC of the European Parliament and of the Council of 22 June 1998 laying down a procedure for the provision of information in the field of technical standards and regulations and of rules on information society services.
207 Communications Data Protection Directive, recital 25.

Communications Data Protection Directive's provisions only apply to 'publicly available' communications services. Therefore, corporate intranets may use cookies and spy-ware without restriction (subject to those contained in the General Data Protection Directive).

5. Erasing traffic data

The Communications Data Protection Directive requires that service providers erase or make anonymous all traffic data as soon as the data is no longer needed for the purpose of the transmission of the communication.[208] However, this 'immediate erasure' rule does not apply in certain circumstances.

The Communications Data Protection Directive permits service providers to store and process traffic data for the purpose of billing and interconnection payments.[209] Storage and processing for billing and interconnection are only allowed 'up to the end of the period during which the bill may lawfully be challenged or payment pursued'.[210] Each Member State is free to set the applicable limitation period for challenging invoices. When data is retained for billing purposes, users and subscribers must be informed of the types of traffic data processed and the duration of the processing.[211] The kinds of data retained must be limited to the elements necessary for billing. For example, the date, time and size of email may be important for billing purposes but not the subject line of emails, which must be erased or rendered anonymous as soon as the recipient of the email has collected the message. Even after the period available for challenging bills, if there is a dispute regarding billing or interconnection, service providers can provide the relevant information to competent bodies in charge of settling the dispute.[212]

The Communications Data Protection Directive also authorises service providers to store and process traffic data to the extent required by national law for police or national security purposes.[213]

Finally, the Communications Data Protection Directive allows service providers to use traffic data to market electronic communications services or to provide 'value added services' but only if the subscriber or user to whom the data relates has given his consent.[214] A value added service is defined as 'any service which requires the processing of traffic data or location data beyond what is necessary for the transmission of a

---

208 Communications Data Protection Directive, Art 6(1).
209 Communications Data Protection Directive, Art 6(2).
210 Ibid, Art 6(2).
211 Ibid, Art 6(4).
212 Ibid, Art 6(6).
213 Communications Data Protection Directive, Arts 6(1) and 15(1).
214 Communications Data Protection Directive, Art 6(3).

communication or the billing thereof.'[215] Such service may include advice on road traffic directions, directions, and weather forecasts. Consent may be given in the same way as provided under the General Data Protection Directive.[216] Ticking a box while visiting an Internet website is a valid means of consent.[217] The user or subscriber must have the opportunity to withdraw his consent at any time.[218] Before giving his consent, the subscriber or user must be informed of the type of traffic data processed and the duration of the processing. Only persons acting under the authority of the public network or communications service provider may process traffic data, including for value added services.[219] However, many value added services are offered by service providers that are not part of the communications operator. In such cases, third party service providers will not be allowed to process traffic data for the purpose of providing the service, unless they do so 'under the authority of' the operator. If the operator allows a third party service provider to process traffic data under operator's authority, then the operator will also bear the responsibility for any violations of privacy regulations by the third party.[220] Transferring the data to the third party will also require the data subject's specific consent pursuant to Articles 7 and 10 of the General Data Protection Directive.

6. Location data other than traffic data

As discussed above, certain location data also qualifies as 'traffic data' because it is used to complete the call. However, mobile network operators can generate location data that is much more detailed than what is needed to complete the call. Such information, including the exact location of the mobile phone and its direction of travel, is 'locating data other than traffic data'. It includes the following information:

> The latitude, longitude and altitude of the user's terminal equipment ... the direction of travel ... the level of accuracy of the location information ... the identification of the network cell in which the terminal equipment is located at a certain point in time and ... the time the location information was recorded.[221]

Location data of this sort cannot be processed without the prior consent of the data subject, ie, an 'opt-in' regime. Before giving consent, the user or subscriber must receive information regarding 'the type of location data other than traffic data which will be processed ... the purposes and duration

215 Ibid, Art 2(g).
216 Ibid, recital 17; General Data Protection Directive, Art 2(h).
217 Communications Data Protection Directive, recital 17.
218 Ibid, Art 6(3).
219 Ibid, Art 6(5).
220 Ibid, recital 32
221 Communications Data Protection Directive, recital 14.

of the processing and whether the data will be transmitted to a third party for the purpose of providing the value added service'.[222] Once the user or subscriber has given his written consent, he must be able to withdraw the consent at any time, or suspend temporarily the consent, free of charge and using a simple means, for a given connection to the network, or for a given communication.[223] This privacy option for location data can be overridden by emergency services,[224] and will not affect law enforcement authorities' ability, under appropriate national legislation, to obtain such data for the purpose of investigating criminal activity.[225]

As with traffic data, the Communications Data Protection Directive states that only people acting under the authority of the public network or communications service provider may process location data.[226] Unlike the provision of traffic data, however, Article 9 also permits third party value added service providers to process location data, even in situations where they are not acting under the authority of the mobile operator. But the transfer to the third party cannot happen unless the user has given his prior consent. In any case, the processing 'must be restricted to what is necessary for the purposes of providing value added service'.[227] As with traffic data, precise location data should be erased or made anonymous as soon as the processing is no longer needed for the value added service.[228]

7. Unsolicited communications

The use of unsolicited emails for the purpose of direct marketing will only be allowed in respect of subscribers who have given their prior consent (an 'opt-in' regime).[229] This prohibitions covers emails sent for the purposes of direct marketing.

The term 'email' is defined as 'any text, voice, sound, or image sent over a public communications network which can be stored in the network or in the recipient's terminal equipment until it is collected by the recipient'.[230] The term therefore covers traditional emails, SMS messages sent over GSM networks[231] and voicemail messages.

The term 'direct marketing' is not defined in the Communications Data Protection Directive or in the General Data Protection Directive. There is therefore some uncertainty as to whether the term is synonymous with the term 'commercial communications' as used in the Electronic Commerce

---

222 Communications Data Protection Directive, Art 9(1).
223 Ibid, Art 9(1).
224 Ibid, Art 10(b).
225 Ibid, Art 15(1).
226 Communications Data Protection Directive, Art 9(3).
227 Ibid, Art 9(3).
228 Ibid, recital 26.
229 Communications Data Protection Directive, Art 13 (1).
230 Communications Data Protection Directive, Art 2(h).
231 Ibid, recital 40.

Directive and whether it includes marketing by charitable organisations or other associations or foundations of a political nature as under the General Data Protection Directive. If the prohibition were to cover political speech, it might breach freedom of speech principles. Whether emails for the purposes of direct marketing will be interpreted in the same way as 'commercial communications' will depend on the language of implementing legislation in the Member States.

8. Exceptions to the 'opt-in' principle

Unsolicited emails to subscribers that are 'legal persons': The Communications Data Protection Directive in effect excludes from its prohibition unsolicited emails sent to employees of an organisation via their company email addresses. For a company email address, the 'subscriber' is the company, not the individual employee. The individual employee is the 'user'. This exception would therefore cover emails sent to the employee in the context of his job, such as unsolicited emails sent to the IT manager of a company to advertise computer equipment, or unsolicited emails to a lawyer promoting law books. But the exception also covers emails sent to the employee in his personal capacity, such as advertisements for ski holidays. The determining factor is whether the email address belongs to the company rather than the employee. Such emails fall under the 'opt-out' rule established by the Electronic Commerce Directive. Article 7 of the Electronic Commerce Directive requires Member States that permit the sending of unsolicited commercial communications to establish at a minimum 'opt-out' registers, in which 'natural persons not wishing to receive such commercial communications can register themselves'.[232] The Electronic Commerce provisions on 'opt-out' are a legal minimum. For example, Member States are permitted to do more. Five Member States (Germany, Austria, Italy, Finland and Denmark) impose an 'opt-in' regime for all unsolicited emails.

Advertising 'similar' products or services: The Communications Data Protection Directive permits companies that have already made one sale to a customer to later send an unsolicited email to the same customer. A number of rules limit this provision. First, in accordance with General Data Protection Directive, the supplier must inform the consumer the first time the supplier obtains the customer's email address that it might later be used for direct marketing by the supplier.[233] Secondly, the consumer must be given the opportunity, both when he first gives his email address to the supplier, and all subsequent times, to object to the use of his email for direct marketing purposes (an 'opt-out'). Thirdly, the subsequent use of the

232 Electronic Commerce Directive, Art 7(2).
233 General Data Protection Directive, Art 10.

email for direct marketing must follow an initial sale to the consumer.[234] Fourthly, the subsequent email must be sent for the purpose of 'direct marketing of [the supplier's] own similar products or services.'[235] The definition of 'similar products or services' will depend on national laws and their interpretation by local data protection authorities.

9. Rules applicable to all unsolicited emails

In all cases where emails are sent for direct marketing purposes, the email must have a valid return address that the recipient can use in order to send a request to 'opt-out'.[236] The Directive also prohibits any attempt to hide the sender's address or the use of other anonymity tools. If the email is an 'unsolicited commercial communication', it must be clearly and unambiguously identified as such.[237]

10. Extraterritorial application

The Communications Data Protection Directive is silent on the question of its extraterritorial application. Article 4 of the General Data Protection Directive provides some guidance which the Article 29 Data Protection Working Party analysed in the context of non-EU websites.[238] The general rule established under EU data protection law for conferring jurisdiction is the place of establishment of the controller[239] or, if the controller is established outside the EU, then the country in the EU (if any) in which processing equipment is located.[240] For non-EU based direct marketers, the issue is whether the sender of the email 'makes use of equipment for the purposes of processing personal data which is situated on the territory of a Member State.'[241] The question is complex and fact specific. However, the threat of potential enforcement action means that undertakings with significant European marketing activities will have more incentive to comply with the Directive's provisions compared to non-EU-based entities that do not specifically target European consumers.

11. Other forms of unsolicited communication

Automatic calling machines and faxes are treated like emails except that the 'prior sale' exception does not apply to them. The use of automatic calling machines and faxes for direct marketing purposes is therefore

---

234 Communications Data Protection Directive, Art 13(2).
235 Ibid.
236 Communications Data Protection Directive, Art 13(4).
237 Electronic Commerce Directive, Art 7(1).
238 Article 29 Data Protection Working Party, 'Working document on determining the international application of EU data protection law to personal data processing on the Internet by non-EU based websites', 5035/01/EN, 30 May 2002.
239 General Data Protection Directive, Art 4(1)(a).
240 Ibid, recital 47.
241 Article 29 Data Protection Working Party, 'Working document', see note 1 above, p 8.

prohibited unless the subscriber has given his prior consent. The provisions on automatic calling machines and faxes only apply to 'individual' subscribers. Their use when a subscriber is a company is not regulated and Member States are adopting an 'opt-in' or 'opt-out' approach.

12. Itemised billing

Subscribers have the right to receive itemised bills. The Communications Data Protection Directive also encourages Member States to apply national measures in order to 'reconcile the rights of subscribers receiving itemised bills with the right to privacy of calling users and called subscribers'.[242] The Communications Data Protection Directive suggests the use of service options and payment mechanisms, such as calling cards, which permit callers to make anonymous calls.[243] It also suggests that Member States could require operators to offer their subscribers a different type of detailed bill in which a certain number of digits of the called number have been deleted.

13. Caller line identification

Caller line identification is a service that displays the number of the calling party on a screen before the person being called picks it up. Connected line identification permits the person calling to see on a screen the number of the person being called. The Communications Data Protection Directive requires that users have the ability to block both caller line identification and connected line identification.

Blocking by the user or subscriber: The Communications Data Protection Directive requires that users be given the ability, free of charge on a call-by-call basis, to block the service so that the person being called does not see the number of the caller.[244] The subscriber must also have the ability to block caller line identification on a per-line basis. A subscriber (such a company) can elect to block caller line identification on a per line basis[245] or on a systematic basis for all outgoing calls, so that people called cannot see who is calling. If the company does not block caller line identification for all its lines, each employee ('user') could block caller line identification on a call-by-call basis. The same holds true for a family. The family as 'subscriber' could ask that the caller line identification be blocked for all outgoing calls but an individual member of the family could block the transmission of caller line identification on a call-by-call basis for certain confidential calls.

Blocking by the called subscriber: In some cases, an organisation may want caller line identification to be blocked on all incoming calls so that

---

242 Communications Data Protection Directive, Art 7(2).
243 Ibid, recital 33.
244 Communications Data Protection Directive, Art 8(1).
245 Ibid.

employees do not see the identity of the person calling. The Directive indicates that this might be the case for organisations providing telephone counselling or anonymous help lines.[246] The Directive therefore provides that the called subscriber may ask that the caller line identification be blocked for all incoming calls.[247]

Override of caller line identification blocking: The Communications Data Protection Directive recognises that there is justification to override caller line identification blocking in specific cases. For example, it is important for the emergency services to be able to see the identity of the calling party and, if possible, his location. Article 10 provides that fire stations, police, ambulance services and other organisations identified by Member States shall always have access to caller line identification even it has been blocked by the calling party. These organisations will also have access to location data when the call is made from a mobile phone. Article 10 also proves that, notwithstanding any blocking, network operators should provide the caller line identification to the called party if necessary to trace nuisance calls.[248]

Rejecting incoming calls: The Communications Data Protection Directive requires that subscribers have the right to reject incoming calls for which caller line identification has been blocked by the calling party.[249]

Blocking the connected line identification: Called subscribers have the right to block the presentation of the connected line identification (ie, the telephone number of the called party).[250] This could be useful, for instance, when the called party has a direct dial number that he does not want the calling party to see (for example, in cases where the calling party may have dialled the switchboard number and then transferred to the employee's direct line).

Informing the public: Service providers are encouraged to inform their subscribers of the privacy options available with respect to caller line and connected line identification which will allow them to make an informed choice as to their usage. The privacy facilities offered by the service provider do not necessarily have to be available as an automatic network service but should be available following a simple request from the subscriber.

14. Subscriber directories

The Communications Data Protection Directive describes the rights of subscribers in connection with directories. Entities collecting personal data for directories must inform subscribers of the purposes of the directories,

246 Communications Data Protection Directive, recital 34.
247 Ibid, Art 8(2).
248 Communications Data Protection Directive, Art 10(a).
249 Communications Data Protection Directive, Art 8(3).
250 Communications Data Protection Directive, Art 8(4).

and of any further usage possibilities based on search functions embedded in electronic versions of the directory.[251] These search functions might include reverse search functions enabling users to find the name or address of a subscriber based only on the subscriber's telephone number.[252] Subscribers must be told in advance that not only their name, numbers, email, address, street address, etc will be included in a directory, but also that users of the directory may be able to perform reverse search functions.[253] Subscribers may elect not to have their number, name and address included in the directory at all. Subscribers must have free of charge access to the information contained in the database in order to modify it or withdraw it.[254] Any processing of data that goes beyond basic search functions can only be done if the subscriber gives his additional consent.[255] The right to be informed of the purposes and functions of the directory, the right to modify and withdraw information, or not be listed at all, belong only to subscribers who are individuals. As regards companies, Member States are free to grant similar rights, but the Directive does not require it.[256]

15. Automatic call forwarding

Call forwarding allows individuals to instruct their network provider to forward particular calls to another person's number. To prevent the abuse of this facility, Article 11 of the Communications Data Protection Directive requires that the subscriber to whom the calls are directed be able to stop the call forwarding through a 'simple means and free of charge'.[257] This provision does not extend to emails even though some of the same forwarding abuses could occur. This is perhaps because emails are less invasive than telephone calls and email forwarding can be eliminated through filtering options in the email software.

16. Technical standards and terminal equipment

Member States must not impose equipment standards linked to data protection and privacy if those standards might impede the equipment being placed on the market, or their free circulation between Member States.[258] The rule has two exceptions. First, if privacy provisions can only be implemented by imposing specific standards, Member States must inform the Commission in advance, as required by the Transparency

---

251 Communications Data Protection Directive, Art 12(1).
252 Ibid, recital 38.
253 Ibid, Art 12(1).
254 Ibid, Art 12(2).
255 Ibid, Art 12(3).
256 Ibid, Art 12(4).
257 Communications Data Protection Directive, Art 11.
258 Communications Data Protection Directive, Art 14(1).

Directive.[259] Secondly, a Member State may implement a standard if it has been adopted by the Commission as a means of enhancing the privacy of terminal equipment.[260] The Directive confers power on the Commission to adopt measures necessary to ensure that terminal equipment is designed to give individuals the right to ensure their privacy as required under the Directive:

> It may therefore be necessary to adopt measures requiring manufacturers of certain types of equipment used for electronic communications services to construct their product in such a way as to incorporate safeguards to ensure that the personal data and privacy of the user and subscriber are protected.[261]

Terminal features might include a privacy button that allows a mobile phone user to indicate that he does not want his location data processed at a given time.

D. LAW ENFORCEMENT EXCEPTION

Law enforcement measures are completely outside the scope of the Communications Data Protection Directive.[262] Member States can adopt national laws requiring service providers to retain traffic data for law enforcement purposes.[263] However, such measures cannot contravene Article 8 of the European Convention for the Protection of Human Rights and Fundamental Freedoms (the 'European Convention').

National law enforcement measures allowing interception or requiring retention of traffic data must be 'appropriate, strictly proportionate to the intended purpose and necessary within a democratic society'.[264] The law enforcement measure should define the purpose for which the data may be used, the duration of retention and the kind of data retained.[265] Measures that amount to 'exploratory or general surveillance' are prohibited under case law applying the European Convention.[266] Public authorities therefore

---

259 Directive 98/34/EC of the European Parliament and of the Council of 22 June 1998 laying down a procedure for the provision of information in the field of technical standards and regulations and of rules of information society services.
260 Communications Data Protection Directive, Art 14(3).
261 Ibid, recital 46.
262 Communications Data Protection Directive, Art 1(3).
263 Ibid, Art 15(1).
264 Communications Data Protection Directive, recital 11.
265 Article 29 Data Protection Working Party, Recommendation 3/99 on the preservation of traffic data by Internet Service Providers for law enforcement purposes, 5085/99, adopted on 7 September 1999.
266 Klass v Germany, Series A No 28, 6 September 1978, European Court of Human Rights.

should only have access to traffic data on a case-by-case basis and 'never proactively and as a general rule'.[267]

Under the Communications Data Protection Directive, individual Member States are responsible for ensuring that there are appropriate remedies provided in national legislation for violations of the Communications Data Protection Directive's provisions.

---

267 Article 29 Data Protection Working Party, Recommendation 3/99, see note 2 above.

8

THE COMPETITION DIRECTIVE

A. HISTORY

Historically, the provision and operation of telecommunication networks and the provision of related services in all Member States has generally been vested in one telecommunications organisation holding exclusive or special rights. These rights were granted by Member States in connection with their power to regulate access to the national telecommunications market. Such organisations were predominantly public undertakings entrusted with the provision and operation of the public telecommunications network. They therefore fell within the definition of undertakings under Article 86 (ex Article 90(1)). As all Member States had to some degree imposed restrictions on the free provision of telecommunications services, the European Commission sought through Commission Directive 90/2888/EEC on competition in the markets for telecommunications services to progressively create an open Community market for telecommunications services.[268]

Directive 90/388/EEC established that the granting of special or exclusive rights to telecommunications services was in breach of Articles 49 (ex Article 59) and 86 (ex Article 90) of the EC Treaty because it limited the provision of cross-border services.

1. Freedom to provide services

Article 49 (ex Article 59) of the EC Treaty requires the abolition of any other restrictions on the freedom of Member State nationals who are established in a Member State country to provide services to persons in other Member States. The maintenance or introduction of any exclusive or special right which hinders this objective is a breach of Article 49 and Article 86.

The restrictions imposed on the provision of telecommunication services to and from other Member States, within the meaning of Article 49, included the prohibition of connecting leased lines through concentrators, multiplexers and other equipment to the switched telephone network; imposing access charges for connection that were out of

---

268 In 1988, the Commission set out in a Green Paper its proposals for the development of a common market for telecommunications services and equipment and for progressively introducing competition into the telecommunications market. In Directive 90/388/EEC ([1990] OJ L192/10), the Commission adopted the programme as set out in the Green Paper. The programme did not include mobile telephony, paging services or radio or television. Satellite communications were included in the scope of the Directive through Directive 94/46/EC, and mobile and personal communications were included in the scope of Directive 90/388/EEC through Directive 96/2/EC.

proportion to the service provided; prohibiting the routing of signals to or from third parties through leased lines; applying volume sensitive tariffs without any economic justification; and refusing to give service providers access to the public network. Articles 45, 46 and 56 of the EC Treaty (ex Articles 55, 56 and 66) allow exceptions on non-economic grounds to the freedom to provide services. These restrictions, however, are narrowly interpreted and, according to the Commission, had no application in the provision of telecommunications services.[269]

The only essential justifications for derogating from Article 49 (ex Article 59) and imposing restrictions on the use of a public telecommunications network were those relating to the maintenance of the integrity of the network, security of network operations and also cases involving interoperability and data protection. The Commission found that such essential requirements could be included as part of individual Member State telecommunications licensing regimes which could specify objective, non-discriminatory and transparent licensing conditions with respect to public service requirements.[270]

2. Exclusive rights

Directive 90/388/EEC also found infringements of Articles 86 (ex Article 90) and 82 (ex Article 86) where exclusive rights were granted for the provision of telecommunications services to telecommunications companies which also enjoyed exclusive or special rights for the establishment and the provision of telecommunications networks. This amounted to the reinforcement or the extension of a dominant position or led to other abuses contrary to Article 82 (ex Article 86). It is interesting to compare the similarity of this approach in attacking monopolist incumbent telecommunications companies to the recent approach taken by the European Commission in condemning Microsoft's unlawful tying practices for extending its near monopoly by leveraging its dominant position in the operating systems market to acquire dominance over related neighbouring markets (see Commission Decision, 24 March 2004).

---

269 See Directive 90/388/EEC, recital 7.

270 However, in 1990, the Commission granted a temporary exception under Art 90(2) in connection with exclusive and special rights for the provision of voice telephony. It was felt that the opening up of this service would reduce the revenue and could threaten the financial stability of some national telecommunications companies and obstruct performance of their particular national mandates, for example, the provision of a Universal Service. At that time, concerns were also expressed against the immediate introduction of competition in voice telephony because the price structures of national telecommunications companies were substantially out of line with costs. Competing operators could therefore potentially target highly profitable services, such as international voice calls, and gain market share only on the basis of substantially distorted tariffs. This exception was ended by Directive 96/19/EC and Member States had to discontinue special and exclusive rights after 1 January 1998. Member States with less developed or very small networks were eligible for an additional temporary transitional period.

The Commission thus relied on Article 82 (ex Article 86) to prohibit Member State telecommunications companies from engaging in any conduct that involved an abuse of a dominant position. The Commission highlighted how the provision of a telecommunications network constituted a separate services market which was not interchangeable with any other services, and that the competitive market in which the national telecommunications network and associated telecommunications services were provided in each national market was sufficiently homogenous to evaluate the market power held by national telecommunications companies. The Commission found that, in each Member State, the national telecommunications company held a dominant position for the creation and exploitation of the public network, because they were the only telecommunications companies with networks covering the whole country and, furthermore, their respective governments had granted them the exclusive right to provide this network.

Where a Member State granted special or exclusive rights to provide telecommunications services to those companies which already held a dominant position in the creation and operation of the public telecoms network, the effect of such a grant was to strengthen this dominant position by extending it to cover those services. It also allowed national telecoms operators to prevent or restrict access to the market for these telecommunications services by their competitors, thus reducing consumer choice. The Commission recognised that this type of conduct represented a specific abuse of a dominant position which would be likely to have an appreciable effect on trade between Member States, as all the services in question could in principle be supplied by providers from other Member States. Special or exclusive rights for particular services gave rise to a situation which ran contrary to the objective in Article 3(g) of the EC Treaty which provides for the institution of a system ensuring that competition in the common market is not distorted. Member States are required under Article 3(g) to refrain from any measure that could frustrate the achievement of any Treaty objectives.

3. Removal of dual regulatory and commercial functions

Under some Member States' national legislation, national telecommunications companies were also given responsibility for regulating telecommunications services, for example, with respect to licensing, equipment approval and frequency allocation. This dual regulatory and commercial function had a direct impact on competitor firms who were subject to the national operators' substantial influence on their own supply of services. The Commission recognised that the delegation of regulatory responsibility to a national operator, which already held a dominant position for the provision and utilisation of the public network, constituted a strengthening of a dominant position. The regulatory and commercial roles represented a conflict of interest and an abuse of a dominant position under Article 82 (ex Article 86) and were incompatible with Article 86(1) (ex Article 90(1)).

4. Liberalisation of alternative infrastructure

National telecommunications companies retained the benefit of the exclusive or special right to establish and provide the underlying infrastructure, including the acquisition of indefeasible rights of use in international circuits. This allowed them a degree of flexibility and provided them with the economies of scale which allowed them to prevent their dominant position being challenged in the normal course of competition. This made it possible for the national telecommunications companies to shore up their dominant position on their home markets if new entrants were not entitled to the same rights and obligations. If new entrants were not granted free choice with respect to the underlying infrastructure to provide their services in competition with the dominant operator, the restriction would de facto prevent them from entering the market for the provision of cross-border services. The maintenance of special rights limiting the number of undertakings authorised to establish and provide infrastructure therefore limited the freedom to provide services contrary to Article 49 (ex Article 59) of the EC Treaty.

In effect, new entrants would be obliged to use the public telecommunications network of the incumbent telecommunications organisations with whom they competed in the wider market. Reserving the task of supplying the indispensable raw material to all its competitors, ie, the transmission capacity, was tantamount to conferring upon the national operator the power to determine at will where and when services could be offered by its competitors, and at what cost, and the ability to monitor their clients and the traffic generated by its competitors. It would place the national telecommunications company in a position where it would be induced to abuse its dominant position. Directive 90/388/EEC did not explicitly address the establishment and provision of telecommunications networks, as it granted a temporary exception under Article 86(2) (ex Article 90(2)) of the EC Treaty in respect of exclusive and special rights for voice telephony. However, the Directive provided for an overall review by the Commission of the situation in the whole telecommunications sector in 1992.

Council Directive 92/44/EEC of 5 June 1992 on the application of open network provision to leased lines, amended by Commission Decision 94/439/EC, harmonised the basic principles regarding the provision of leased lines, but it only harmonised the conditions of access and use of leased lines. The aim of that Directive was to remedy the conflict of interest of the telecommunications organisations as infrastructure and service providers. However, it did not impose a structural separation between the national telecommunications companies as providers of leased lines and as service providers. The number and variety of complaints illustrated that, even among those Member States which had implemented the Directive, their national telecommunications companies still used their control of the access conditions to the network at the expense of their competitors in the services market. In addition, national telecommunications companies applied excessive tariffs and used information acquired as infrastructure providers, regarding the services planned by their competitors, to target clients in the services market.

What Directive 92/44/EEC did was to provide for the basic principles of cost orientation and transparency to ensure that the tariffs for leased lines were directly related to the costs of providing the service according to the formula laid down in the legislation. However, this did not prevent national telecommunications companies from using the information acquired as capacity provider as regards subscribers' usage patterns, necessary to target specific groups of users, and on price elasticities of demand in each service market segment and region of the country. The regulatory framework did not resolve this conflict of interest. The most appropriate remedy to this conflict of interest was therefore to allow service providers to use own or third party telecommunications infrastructure to provide their services to the final customers, instead of the infrastructure of their main competitor. In its Resolution of 22 December 1994, the Council approved the principle that infrastructure provision should be liberalised. Member States therefore had to abolish exclusive rights on the provision and use of infrastructure which infringed Article 86(1) (ex Article 90(1)) of the EC Treaty, in combination with Articles 49 and 82 (ex Articles 59 and 86), and allow providers to use own and/or any alternative infrastructure of their choice.

5. Notification of Member State licensing requirements

Certain Member States began to impose disproportionate obligations on new entrants under the authorisation requirements under Directive 90/388/EEC. These measures were being used to prevent the dominant position of the incumbent operators being challenged by competition, making it possible for them to maintain their dominant position in the voice telephony and public telecommunications networks markets. The Commission therefore required Member States to notify any licensing or declaration requirements to it before they were introduced, to enable the Commission to assess their compatibility with the EC Treaty and in particular the proportionality of the obligations imposed.[271]

---

271 Under Directive 96/13/EC, amending Directive 90/388/EC.

6. Financial transparency requirements

It was hoped that the abolition of special and exclusive rights in the telecommunications markets would encourage undertakings enjoying special and exclusive rights in sectors other than telecommunications to enter the telecommunications markets. But this raised the possibility of anti-competitive cross-subsidies between, on the one hand, areas for which providers of telecommunications services or telecommunications infrastructures enjoy special or exclusive rights and, on the other, their business as telecommunications providers. Member States therefore had to adopt appropriate measures to achieve financial transparency and were required to ensure that telecommunications companies with a turnover of more than ECU 50 million should keep separate financial accounts which distinguished between, among other things, the costs and revenues associated with the provision of services under their special and exclusive rights and those provided under competitive conditions.

B. THE COMPETITION DIRECTIVE

Commission Directive 2002/77/EC (the 'Competition Directive') has its roots in the enactment of Directive 90/388/EC.[272] The aim of the Competition Directive was twofold: first, to codify the amendments made to Commission Directive 90/388 and produce a single simplified text. Secondly, the amendments would have the effect of extending its scope to cover broadcasting infrastructure and services for the first time. The Competition Directive does not utilise any new substantive provisions which affect the telecommunications sector, save that it opens up competition in broadcasting networks and services.

The Competition Directive, although part of the new electronic communications framework package, is separate and distinct from the other liberalisation directives.[273] The Competition Directive has a completely separate basis; the Commission and not the National Regulatory Authority has the role in determining whether a relevant market has become effectively competitive, and the Competition Directive contains its own definitions instead of incorporating by reference the definitions in the Framework Directive.

The Competition Directive prohibits Member States from granting or maintaining in force exclusive or special rights for the establishment and/or provision of publicly available electronic communications

272 [2002] OJ L249/21.
273 See Directive 2002/21/EC (the Framework Directive), Directive 2002/20/EC (the Authorisation Directive), Directive 2002/19 (the Access Directive), Directive 2002/22 (the Universal Service Directive), Directive 2002/58 (the Directive on Privacy and Electronics Communications) (together the 'liberalisation directives').

services.[274] It follows in the footsteps of Directive 90/388/EC and is a Commission Directive made under Article 86(3) of the EC Treaty to break up national monopolies which contravene the rules of the EC Treaty and in particular the EC competition rules.[275] This legislative power was recognised by the European Court of Justice with respect to the first telecommunications liberalisation Directive.[276] In contrast, the Framework Directive, the Authorisation Directive, the Access Directive, the Universal Directive and the Communications Data Protection Directive were initially proposed by the Commission, then adopted by the European Council and European Parliament pursuant to Articles 95 and 251 of the EC Treaty.

1. Abolition of special and exclusive rights

Article 2 of the Competition Directive mandates Member States to remove (if they have not already done so under the previous legislative enactments) and not grant any exclusive or special rights for the establishment and/or the provision of electronic communications networks or for the provision of publicly available electronic communications services. As discussed above, 'electronic communications services' includes traditional telecommunications, Internet and broadcasting services. 'Exclusive rights' are defined as rights granted by a Member State to an undertaking by any legislative, administrative or regulatory measure reserving to it the right to provide an electronic communications service or to undertake an electronic communications activity within a given geographic area. 'Special rights' are those rights granted by a Member State to a number of different undertakings by any legislative, administrative or regulatory measure, which either (a) reserves to two or more of them the right to provide an electronic communications service or to undertake an electronic communications activity on grounds that are not otherwise objective, proportional and based on non-discriminatory criteria, or (b) confers on undertakings legal or regulatory advantages which substantially affect the ability of other undertakings to offer the same electronic communications services in the same geographical area under substantially equivalent conditions.

A mobile network spectrum allocation tender procedure based on objective, proportional and non-discriminatory criteria would not be considered as conferring 'special rights'. This in contrast to an

---

274 Competition Directive, Art 2(1).

275 Article 86(3) of the EC Treaty authorises the Commission to act alone to adopt directives to mandate Member States to ensure that public undertakings or undertakings enjoying 'special or exclusive rights' comply with the EC Treaty's competition rules, unless doing so would interfere with them complying with their general economic interest duties.

276 Commission Directive 88/301/EEC of 16 May 1988 on competition in the markets in telecommunications terminal equipment ([1988] OJ L131/73); Case C-202/88 France v Commission, 19 March 1991, ECJ.

administrative law provision that for historic reasons permitted only one entity to provide broadcasting services to a national television channel. Such a restriction would be illegal.

Also, Member States are required to take all measures necessary to ensure that any undertaking is able to provide electronic communications services or to establish electronic communications networks.[277] This means that any undertaking has the right to provide electronic communications services or establish or provide electronic communications networks so long as the undertaking complies with the relevant licensing rules. In addition, Member States cannot impose restrictions on the kinds of network that may be used to carry electronic communication services, or the kinds of electronic services that may be offered over a given network.[278] This general rule that any type of network can provide any type of service is subject to the rules contained in the other directives. For example, Member States can limit the services that can be offered using a particular radio frequency under the Authorisation Directive.

Finally, the Competition Directive obliges Member States to ensure that general authorisations granted to undertakings to provide electronic communications services or establish electronic communications networks are granted on objective, non-discriminatory, proportionate and transparent criteria.[279] Any refusal on grounds set out in the Authorisation Directive must be justified, and an aggrieved party must be able to challenge the decision before an independent court or tribunal.[280]

2. Vertically integrated public undertakings

The desire to stop anti-competitive behaviour by dominant public undertakings which own and operate both networks and supply services over that network gave rise to the provisions of Article 3 of the Competition Directive. Where these vertically integrated public network operators operate networks which have been established under special or exclusive rights, they must ensure that they do not discriminate in favour of their own downstream operations to the extent that they enjoy a dominant position in a relevant market. Member States are placed under a positive duty to prevent any discrimination between such vertically integrated operators and their competitors.

3. Rights of use of frequencies

In Article 4, the Competition Directive repeats various conditions on the licensing of radio frequencies contained in the Authorisation Directive.

---

277 Any violation would therefore breach the harmonisation measures of the Universal Service Directive and the EC Treaty competition rules.
278 Competition Directive, Art 2(3).
279 Competition Directive, Art 2(4).
280 Competition Directive, Art 2(5).

Member States are prohibited from granting exclusive or special rights of use of radio frequencies for the provision of electronic communications services, and shall not grant usage rights for frequencies other than through objective, proportionate, transparent and non-discriminatory criteria. However, as in the Authorisation Directive, the Competition Directive contains a cultural exception to normal licensing rules which covers 'procedures adopted by Member States to grant rights of use of radio frequencies to providers of radio or television broadcast content services with a view to pursuing general interest objectives in conformity with Community law'.

4. Directory services

Readers will be familiar with the recent liberalisation of directory services in the UK and the plethora of suppliers it produced. As directory services have historically been provided by former monopoly telecommunication operators, the principle of liberalisation was to provide the consumer with a choice of service provider and more effective competition. The rules stated in Article 5 of the Directive repeat the various provisions contained in the Universal Service Directive. Any violation would therefore breach the harmonisation measures of the Universal Service Directive and the EC competition rules. This Article stipulates that Member States shall abolish all exclusive and special rights with respect to the establishment and provision of directory services. The abolition extends to cover not only the provision of directory enquiry services but also the publication of telephony directories themselves.

5. Universal Service obligations

The Competition Directive states that any national Universal Service scheme adopted under the Universal Service Directive must be based on objective, transparent and non-discriminatory criteria which are consistent with the principle of proportionality and cause the least market distortion. These rules also repeat various provisions contained in the Universal Service Directive. As above, any violation would therefore breach the harmonisation measures of the Universal Service Directive and the EC competition rules as applied to the Member States and to public undertakings.

6. Satellites

Member States must ensure that all providers of space segment capacity can sell their capacity to authorised operators of earth station networks.[281] Historically, national operators have enjoyed territorial exclusivity and were protected under international satellite agreements. Further, the Competition Directive obliges those Member States who have signed

---

281 Competition Directive, Art 7(1).

international conventions establishing international satellite organisations to take all steps to eliminate any provisions which are contrary to the competition rules of the EC Treaty.[282]

7. Cable television networks

The Competition Directive maintains obligations imposed on Member States by Directive 1999/64/EC, which ensures that dominant providers of electronic communications networks and publicly available telephone services operate their respective public electronic communications and cable television networks as separate legal entities. In essence, this provision is targeted at incumbent telecommunication operators who retain high market shares and a powerful market position in their respective countries. They will likely satisfy the qualifying criteria set out at Article 8(1), as such undertakings must:

(a) be controlled by a Member State or benefit from special rights;

(b) be dominant in a substantial part of the common market in the provision of public electronic communications networks and publicly available telephone services; and

(c) operate a cable television network which has been established under special or exclusive rights in the same geographic area.

If an undertaking satisfies the above criteria, it must impose structural separation between its cable and telecommunications networks. There is no mandatory divestiture requirement,[283] and the cable network company can remain under the control of the incumbent operator.

Consistent with the principle of removing regulation as soon as a market becomes competitive, the Competition Directive allows for the Commission to make a determination that the above structural separation requirement will no longer be imposed when there is 'sufficient competition in the provision of local loop infrastructure and services' in the relevant country.[284] The Commission, and not National Regulatory Authorities, assumes the role of deciding whether sufficient competition in the provision of local loop infrastructure exists, as the Competition Directive is a competition law enforcement instrument enacted under Article 86(3), unlike the other directives in the electronic communications package as described above.

---

282 Competition Directive, Art 7(2). Previously, under the Services Directive, Member States were only required to inform the Commission of provisions of those conventions that violated the competition rules.

283 However, under European merger rules, the Commission can require divestiture as a condition to agreeing a merger, eg, Case No COMP/M.2803 – Telia/Sonera, p 35, in which Telia agreed to divest its cable network subsidiary in Finland.

284 Competition Directive, Art 8(3).

8. Conclusion

The Competition Directive brings into one single text all the relevant provisions of all previous liberalisation directives in the telecommunications sector. Its objective is to bring more competition into local communications markets and to introduce greater flexibility in the face of new technology and market changes. It restates the obligations imposed on Member States to abolish exclusive and special rights in the field of telecommunications, which is an obligation deriving directly from the EC Treaty itself. In this sense, the Competition Directive merely interprets and clarifies the scope of the EC Treaty's fundamental provisions relating to freedom to provide services and competition (including any enactments made under them) as they relate to the provision of telecommunication services.

C. LOCAL LOOP UNBUNDLING

1. Introduction

In order for Europe to seize the growth and job potential of the digital, knowledge based economy, businesses and citizens needed to have access to an inexpensive, world-class communications infrastructure and a wide range of services. Various earlier EU liberalisation directives from the late 1980s, prior to the present legislative package, opened this sector progressively up to competition. However, there was one significant impediment to greater competition and the widespread provision of low cost services (including Internet access), and that was access to the local network. The lack of competition in this part of the market, or, as it is sometimes called, the local loop, was considered a significant obstacle to the widespread provision of low cost Internet access.

The 'local loop' refers to the physical circuit connecting the network termination point at the subscriber's premises to the telecommunications operator's local switch or equivalent facility in the local access network.

2. What is local loop unbundling?

Local loop unbundling (LLU) is the process where the incumbent operator makes its local network (the copper cables that run from the customer's premises to the telephone exchange) available to other companies. This means that small businesses and other consumers have a greater choice over the provision of their telecommunications services, and operators are able to upgrade individual lines using DSL technology to offer services such as always-on, high-speed Internet access, direct to the customer.

LLU became necessary due to the high cost of duplicating the local access infrastructure, which was driving competitors out of the market. New entrants did not have widespread alternative network infrastructures and were unable, with traditional technologies, to match the economies of scale and the coverage of operators designated as having significant market power in the fixed public telephone market. This resulted from the fact that these operators rolled out their metallic local access infrastructures over significant periods of time, protected by exclusive rights, and were able to fund investment costs through monopoly rents. It was therefore not economically viable for new entrants to duplicate the incumbent's local access infrastructure in its entirety within a reasonable time.

3. The EC Regulation on Local Loop Unbundling

The European Council of Ministers decided that it was urgent to implement unbundling in order to inject greater competition into the EU telecoms market, to stimulate technical innovation on the local access market and to foster competitive provision of a wide range of electronic communication services, including greater Internet usage. Consequently, the Council gave its unanimous agreement to the Commission proposal for a regulation on unbundled access to the local loop, which aimed to introduce fair competition in local access networks. The EC Regulation on Local Loop Unbundling (EC/2887/2000) was passed on 18 December 2000 as an internal market measure pursuant to Article 95 of the EC Treaty and required Member States to implement rules on local loop unbundling by 31 December 2000.

This Regulation was passed and implemented ahead of the directives which formed part of the 2002 legislative package on telecommunications liberalisation, discussed above, but it is still an essential part of the EU liberalisation programme.

4. Main provisions

The Regulation requires incumbent operators throughout Europe to offer unbundled access to their local loops on reasonable request and thereby allow new entrants to compete with notified operators in offering high bitrate data transmission services for continuous Internet access and for multimedia applications based on DSL technology, as well as voice telephony services. A reasonable request for unbundled access implies that the access is necessary for the provision of the services of the beneficiary and that a refusal of the request would prevent, restrict or distort competition in this sector. However, the obligation to provide unbundled access to the local loop does not imply that notified operators have to install entirely new local network infrastructures specifically to meet beneficiaries' requests.

The Regulation mandates unbundled access to the local loop only of notified operators that have been designated by their National Regulatory Authorities as having significant market power in the fixed public telephone network supply market.

Notified operators must offer local loop unbundling on terms that are no less favourable than those on which it provides equivalent services to its own operations and should offer terms that have been agreed between willing parties in an equal bargaining position.

5. Pricing of reference offers

Costing and pricing rules for the unbundling of the local loop and related facilities are also covered by the Regulation. All costs and pricing should be transparent, non-discriminatory and objective to ensure fairness, and pricing rules should ensure that the local loop provider is able to cover its appropriate costs in this regard, plus a reasonable return, in order to ensure the long term development and upgrade of local access infrastructure. Pricing rules for the unbundling of the local loop should foster fair and sustainable competition, bearing in mind the need for investment in alternative infrastructures, and ensure there is no distortion of competition.

The publication by notified operators of an adequate reference offer for unbundled access to the local loop, within a short time frame and ideally on the Internet, and under the supervisory control of the National Regulatory Authority, also contributes towards the creation of transparent and non-discriminatory market conditions. In the UK, both BT and Kingston have published reference offers, as required under the Regulation.

6. Sub-loop unbundling

The Regulation also requires that other operators can interconnect with the local access network at a point between the incumbent's site and the end user. This arrangement is referred to as sub-loop unbundling. In sub-loop unbundling, the connection point refers to the primary connection points (PCPs), which are the green street-side cabinets. Sub-loop unbundling can be used for emerging technologies, such as VDSL, where the equipment needs to be much closer to the home to deliver very high bandwidth services. An optical fibre delivers the high-speed services to the local green street-side cabinet, and VDSL technology is used to send those services along the copper pair to the consumer's premises.

On the whole, the Regulation has been kept short and simple, focusing on what is strictly necessary to achieve the objective of greater competition. It sets out basic obligations for Member States to meet, but does not go beyond what is necessary.

7. UK example

An example of local loop unbundling can be seen in the UK where, in November 1999, Oftel issued a statement, 'Access to Bandwidth: Delivering Competition for the Information Age', which set out its decision to require BT to make its local loop available to other operators. This followed a

12-month consultation. UK thinking was marginally ahead of the EU proposals.

The statement set out Oftel's conclusion that the opening up of the local loop was necessary to introduce competition into the provision of higher bandwidth services, such as high-speed, always-on Internet access and video on demand. The introduction of competition into this area should mean a wider range of services to consumers and better value for money. The statement also concluded that local loops should be available at cost based prices (which Oftel would determine). The requirement for BT to provide loops would be through a licence condition to be inserted into BT's licence. Oftel would conduct a policy review of the position on LLU after four years and then at two yearly intervals. The statement also set out Oftel's approach to BT's wholesale ADSL service. As a result, a new condition (Condition 83) was inserted into BT's licence in April 2000. Condition 83 came into effect on 8 August 2000. Condition 83 sets out the co-location products BT must offer, the conditions which apply to the supply of these products and unbundled loops, how the prices will be set and how disputes can be resolved.

8. Conclusion

In promoting competition in EU telecommunications markets, a balance has to be struck between the twin goals of promoting competition in the local access network and encouraging innovation and investment by all participants in the telecommunications market. It is hoped that the LLU Regulation, in opening the final mile to customers' homes, will encourage market entry by new players, whilst encouraging those same entrants to deploy new technologies such as VDSL on the local loop and to invest in alternative telecommunications infrastructure to help sustain long term competition in this market.

9

INTERNATIONAL TELECOMMUNICATIONS REGULATORY REGIME

The international telecommunications regime had traditionally comprised the principles, norms, rules and decision making procedures that governments have agreed to govern the organisation of international telecommunications networks and services.

This chapter broadly examines three substantive areas of international telecommunications law:

(a) the establishment and operation of satellite and submarine cable infrastructure;

(b) the structure and procedures of the International Telecommunications Union (ITU) and European standard-making bodies; and

(c) the World Trade Organisation's (WTO) trade agreements relating to telecommunications.

A. SATELLITE REGULATION

1. Introduction

The idea of using satellites for telecommunications can be dated back to 1945, when the popular science fiction writer Arthur C Clarke speculated on the possibility of using space technology to deliver low cost international communications. That idea effectively spawned a brand-new industry, with scientists in the US and Europe beginning work on designing and launching prototype systems just a few years later. During the early 1960s, large numbers of governments and enterprises trialled satellite technology. In July 1962, AT&T's Telstar satellite was the first to complete a transatlantic telecast, with the first commercial system, known as Intelsat-1 or Early Bird, being successfully deployed three years later, in April 1965.

Satellites were first put to use to deliver long-distance telecommunications to areas which – for reasons of geography or economics – lacked the infrastructure to support landline connection. Their cost-effectiveness over long distances meant they quickly grew to become the preferred means of delivering long-haul international traffic to countries which did not have access to long-distance cable systems. In addition, their 'point-to-multipoint' capabilities helped them quickly become an important element of regional and international broadcasting systems, a role which they continue to fulfil, *par excellence*, today.

Satellite systems are effectively orbiting radio repeating stations, taking information 'uplinked' via radio waves from a terrestrial Earth station and retransmitting it – or 'downlinking' it – through transponders which beam the information back to receiving stations on the ground. Most commercial satellites contain a series of transponders, and the ground area covered by the combined transponder beams is known as the system's 'footprint'.

2. Geostationary/non-geostationary

Almost all commercial communications satellites in use today are *geostationary systems*. This means they are positioned in a linear cluster some 36,000km above the equator, orbiting in synchronisation with the planet's own rotation. Geostationary systems have several important advantages. First, because they maintain the same spatial relationship to the surface of the Earth, they can provide continuous service to the area covered by their footprint. In addition, their considerable distance from the Earth means their footprints can be extremely large, covering close to one-third of the globe, which makes them a very cost effective solution. Finally, their stable position deep in space ensures a relatively long lifespan – an important consideration with systems that cost several billion dollars to build and launch.

But while geostationary systems remain by far the most common species, the last few years have seen the development of new types of system which make use of *non-geostationary* orbits to deliver services such as data messaging and person-to-person voice communications.

These systems are collectively known as GMPCS – Global Mobile Personal Communications by Satellite – but are perhaps more commonly (although sometimes erroneously) called Big and Little LEO systems, with LEO standing for Low Earth Orbit. Low in this sense is purely relative – at between 700km and 1,500km from the Earth's surface these systems certainly occupy a lower orbit than their geostationary cousins, but are still far higher up than the space station Mir, for example, which is stationed some 400km from the surface of the Earth.

Non-geostationary systems are generally made up of several satellites, the position of which changes in relation to the surface of the planet. In operation, they form a moving constellation, circling the globe and relaying messages back and forth between each other, Earth stations, and users on the ground.

3. The changing face of the satellite industry

Because satellite systems need to occupy a unique portion of space and rely on exclusive use of particular radio frequencies to perform their uplinks and downlinks, they need to be managed at an international level. The ITU has fulfilled the function of international registrar of all satellite systems since they began to be launched back in the mid-1960s. The ITU performs the essential coordination functions that ensure satellites are positioned in such a way as to ensure smooth operation without harmful interference to other systems. Such coordination, performed early in a satellite's design phase, determines system characteristics which are eventually incorporated into the manufacture of the satellite itself. Coordination is performed by engineers and mathematicians working in the Space Services Department of the ITU's Radiocommunication Bureau, and generally takes around six months to complete.

Coordination of geostationary systems requires each satellite to be positioned at least two degrees away from any other system. Because they are in constant motion, coordination of non-geostationary systems can be more complex, especially for large constellations such as Iridium, Globalstar and new broadband systems like Skybridge and Teledesic. The coordination process also determines the frequencies on which the satellite system may broadcast.

ITU figures show there were a total of 998 geostationary satellites and 178 non-geostationary satellites registered in operation by September 1997, with those figures forecast to grow to 1,768 geostationary and 245 non-geostationary satellites in operation by September 2003. While satellites continue to play an important role in long-haul telecommunications, the plethora of high-capacity undersea fibre optic cables now in place or being laid is fast eating into this market. But while the satellite industry might be losing on the swings of long-distance telecommunications, it's winning on the roundabouts of new applications like VSAT, Satellite Broadcasting and GMPCS.

4. The United Nations space treaties

Since the early 1960s, the United Nations has been active in the creation and implementation of a special system of space law within the framework of existing international law. Since the establishment of the United Nations Committee on the Peaceful Uses of Outer Space (COPUOS) in 1958, five major international treaties and conventions have been negotiated and ratified by many countries. A large number of bilateral and multilateral treaties also set out international agreements and obligations in relation to space.

The five main space treaties are:[285]

(a) the 1967 Treaty on Principles Governing the Activities of States in the Exploration and Use of Outer Space, including the Moon and other Celestial Bodies (commonly known as the Outer Space Treaty);

(b) the 1968 Agreement on the Rescue of Astronauts, the Return of Astronauts and the Return of Objects Launched into Outer Space (commonly known as the Rescue Agreement);

(c) the 1972 Convention on International Liability for Damage Caused by Space Objects (commonly known as the Liability Convention);

(d) the 1975 Convention on Registration of Objects Launched into Outer Space (commonly known as the Registration Convention); and

(e) the 1979 Agreement Governing the Activities of States on the Moon and other Celestial Bodies (commonly known as the Moon Agreement).

These five treaties, together with several United Nations General Assembly declarations and resolutions,[286] form the cornerstone of international space

---

285 Treaty on Principles Governing the Activities of States in the Exploration and Use of Outer Space, including the Moon and Other Celestial Bodies (the 'Outer Space Treaty'), adopted by the General Assembly in its resolution 2222 (XXI), opened for signature on 27 January 1967, entered into force on 10 October 1967, 98 ratifications and 27 signatures (as of 1 January 2003); Agreement on the Rescue of Astronauts, the Return of Astronauts and the Return of Objects Launched into Outer Space (the 'Rescue Agreement'), adopted by the General Assembly in its resolution 2345 (XXII), opened for signature on 22 April 1968, entered into force on 3 December 1968, 88 ratifications, 25 signatures, and 1 acceptance of rights and obligations (as of 1 January 2003); Convention on International Liability for Damage Caused by Space Objects (the 'Liability Convention'), adopted by the General Assembly in its resolution 2777 (XXVI), opened for signature on 29 March 1972, entered into force on 1 September 1972, 82 ratifications, 25 signatures, and 2 acceptances of rights and obligations (as of 1 January 2003); Convention on Registration of Objects Launched into Outer Space (the 'Registration Convention'), adopted by the General Assembly in its resolution 3235 (XXIX), opened for signature on 14 January 1975, entered into force on 15 September 1976, 44 ratifications, 4 signatures, and 2 acceptances of rights and obligations (as of 1 January 2003); Agreement Governing the Activities of States on the Moon and Other Celestial Bodies (the 'Moon Agreement'), adopted by the General Assembly in its resolution 34/68, opened for signature on 18 December 1979, entered into force on 11 July 1984, 10 ratifications and 5 signatures (as of 1 January 2003).

286 Declaration of Legal Principles Governing the Activities of States in the Exploration and Uses of Outer Space (General Assembly resolution 1962 (XVIII) of 13 December 1963); Principles Governing the Use by States of Artificial Earth Satellites for International Direct Television Broadcasting (resolution 37/92 of 10 December 1982); Principles Relating to Remote Sensing of the Earth from Outer Space (resolution 41/65 of 3 December 1986); Principles Relevant to the Use of Nuclear Power Sources in Outer Space (resolution 47/68 of 14 December 1992); Declaration on International Cooperation in the Exploration and Use of Outer Space for the Benefit and in the Interest of All States, Taking into Particular Account the Needs of Developing Countries (resolution 51/122 of 13 December 1996).

law. The following sections provide a brief outline of the main treaties and their impact on governmental and commercial activities in outer space.

The Outer Space Treaty: Under the Outer Space Treaty, a country is internationally responsible for its 'national activities' in outer space regardless of whether they are conducted by governmental agencies or by non-governmental entities (Outer Space Treaty, Article VI). The Treaty further provides that, as the 'appropriate State', that country's government is required to undertake authorisation and continuing supervision of the activities of non-governmental entities, which is generally understood to include private and commercial entities (Outer Space Treaty, Article VI).

Should a space object be registered in the registry of a country, that country retains jurisdiction and control over that space object (Outer Space Treaty, Article VIII). For example, if a country launches or procures the launching of a space object into outer space which causes 'damage to another State Party to the Treaty or to its natural or juridical persons by such object or its component parts on the Earth, in air or in outer space', that country is liable for the damage caused (Outer Space Treaty, Article VII). While the issue of third party liability is more particularly addressed by the Liability Convention, this is a general principle of space law that binds States that are party to the Outer Space Treaty but not to the Liability Convention.

Other provisions of the Outer Space Treaty include:

(a) the prohibition of launching nuclear weapons and other weapons of mass destruction in outer space (Outer Space Treaty, Article IV), and

(b) the duty not to interfere detrimentally with the interests of other States in the exploration and use of outer space (Outer Space Treaty, Article IX).

The Liability Convention: The Liability Convention entered into force in September 1972. The European Space Agency and European Telecommunications Satellite Organisation have declared their acceptance of the rights and obligations provided for in this Agreement.

There are two distinct regimes of liability that are established by the Liability Convention. If the damage is caused by the space object on the surface of the Earth or to an aircraft in flight, the liability to compensation shall be absolute. However, if the damage caused by a space object is incurred on another space object not on the surface of the Earth, then the launching State will be liable only if it can be established that the damage caused is due to fault on the part of the launching State or its nationals.

In the complicated event where the space object of one launching State causes damage to a space object of another launching State that is not on the surface of the Earth and subsequently causes damage to a third State, then the launching States of the two space objects shall be jointly and severally liable to the third State. Similarly, when two or more States jointly launch a space object, the launching States will also be jointly and severally liable for any damage caused. In cases of two or more launching States with joint and several liability, the burden of compensation will be apportioned between them in accordance with the extent of fault or, otherwise, it will be apportioned equally between them unless there is an agreement purporting to the contrary.

How the mechanisms for settling such international claims will work under the Convention has been heatedly debated among academic circles but has never really been put to the test in practice. The only notable international compensation claim for damage to date, the case of Cosmos-954 where the Soviet satellite unexpectedly returned and landed in Canada, was resolved without explicit reference to any particular provision of the Liability Convention. If it did, the process is likely to have been drawn out for many years, thus placing a heavy financial burden on any commercial undertaking outside the government sector.

Summary of Liability under the Liability Convention:

Article II	Damage on Earth or to aircraft in flight	Absolute liability
Article III	Damage to another space object not on the surface of the Earth	Fault liability
Article IV	Damage to another space object in outer space which subsequently causes damage on Earth or to aircraft in flight	Joint and several absolute liability
Article IV	Damage to another space object in outer space which subsequently causes damage to another space object not on the surface of the Earth	Joint and several fault liability
Article V	More than one launching State	Joint and several liability

In terms of determining what damages are payable under the Liability Convention, Article XII provides that:

> The compensation which the launching State shall be liable to pay for damage under this Convention shall be determined in accordance with international law and the principles of justice and equity, in order to provide such reparation with respect to the damage as will restore the person, natural or juridical, State or international organisation on whose behalf the claim is presented to the condition which would have existed if the damage had not occurred.

Within the context of the Convention, 'a claimant would be required to show that the harm flowed directly or immediately from, and as the probable or natural result of, the malfunctioning of the space object'. Once this required causation is established, compensation will presumably be payable to the claimant State for the following:

(a) lost time and earnings;

(b) impaired earning capacity;

(c) destruction or deprivation of use of property;

(d) rendering the property unfit for the use for which it was intended;

(e) loss of profits resulting from an interruption in business activities;

(f) loss of rents;

(g) reasonable medical, hospital and nursing costs occasioned by the harm to the person;

(h) physical impairment, including impairment of mental faculties;

(i) pain and suffering;

(j) humiliation;

(k) reasonable costs of the repair of property that has been wrongfully harmed;

(l) costs incurred in mitigating existing wrongful harm; and

(m) loss of services of a third party to which the injured party was entitled.

With respect to personal injuries, recovery can be made when the harm results from both physical impact with the debris of a space object as well as by contamination emanating from such an object. Furthermore, most academic scholars argue that the Convention covers indirect damage as the Convention 'allow[s] for the additional consequences produced as a result of the initial hit'. The liability of the launching States under the Convention is unlimited but there is no provision for the award of punitive damages as liability under the Convention is purely compensatory in nature.

If malfunction of a space object occurs and consequently injury and damage is sustained by a third State, all launching States will be liable under the present Liability Convention regime. For example, where a German telecommunications company contracts with a British aerospace company to produce a satellite which is to be launched using a Russian launch vehicle from an Australian launch site operated by a South African company, all five countries would be regarded as launching States and, therefore, liable for any damage caused by the space object.

The Registration Convention: Countries that are parties to the Registration Convention are obliged to register all space objects for which they are the launching State and provide the Secretary-General of the United Nations with information about every space object in the registry as soon as is practicable (Registration Convention, Article II). This information should include the name of the launching State or States, a designator or registration number, the date and location of launch, the general function and the basic orbital parameters (including the nodal period, inclination, apogee and the perigee) of a space object (Registration Convention, Article IV).

5. International satellite organisations

The operation of satellite systems has historically been the preserve of national, State-owned, monopoly operators, subject to international treaty. However, the rapid commercialisation of the industry has led to the privatisation of commercial operations of international satellite organisations and a proliferation of new bodies.

Intelsat: The International Telecommunications Satellite Organization (Intelsat) was created on an interim basis by its initial member states in 1964.[287] Intelsat was formally established in 1973 upon entry into force of an intergovernmental agreement.[288] On 18 July 2001, Intelsat was privatised by the transfer of substantially all of its assets and liabilities to Intelsat Ltd and its subsidiaries.

This privatisation resulted in the elimination of various restrictions on its operations to which the company was subject as an intergovernmental organisation (IGO). At the same time, however, this privatisation resulted in the loss of several privileges, exemptions and immunities enjoyed by the intergovernmental organisation. However, through the elimination of these restrictions on the IGO's operations, the old organisation has transformed itself, in the face of the rapid commercialisation of the market, to be in a better competitive position to respond to the requirements of its customers in the industry and take advantage of market opportunities. For example, Intelsat can now enter new markets from which the IGO was restricted, acquire and operate ground facilities, provide new services complementary to wholesale satellite capacity and establish a more flexible management structure.

Inmarsat: The International Mobile Satellite Organisation (Inmarsat) was established in 1979 as an intergovernmental organisation providing satellite services for the maritime and aeronautical sectors, particularly

---

287 Under the Interim Arrangements for a Global Commercial Communications Satellite System.
288 Agreement relating to International Telecommunications Satellite Organisation (Intelsat) (with operating Agreement).

communications in situations of distress and safety.[289] INMARSAT was the world's first global mobile satellite communications operator and is still the only one to offer a mature range of modern communications services to maritime, land-mobile, aeronautical and other users.

Formed as a maritime-focused intergovernmental organisation over 20 years ago, Inmarsat has been a limited company since 1999, serving a broad range of markets. Starting with a user base of 900 ships in the early 1980s, it now supports links for phone, fax and data communications at up to 64kbit/s to more than 250,000 ship, vehicle, aircraft and portable terminals. That number is growing by several thousand a month.

Inmarsat Ltd is a subsidiary of the Inmarsat Ventures plc holding company. It operates a constellation of geostationary satellites designed to extend phone, fax and data communications all over the world. The constellation comprises five third-generation satellites backed up by four earlier spacecraft. The satellites are controlled from Inmarsat's headquarters in London, which is also home to Inmarsat Ventures as well as the small IGO created to supervise the company's public-service duties for the maritime community (Global Maritime Distress and Safety System) and aviation (air traffic control communications).

Today's Inmarsat system is used by independent service providers to offer a range of voice and multimedia communications. Its business strategy is to pursue a range of new opportunities at the convergence of information technology, telecoms and mobility while continuing to serve traditional maritime, aeronautical, land-mobile and remote-area markets.

Eutelsat: A third organisation, the European Telecommunications Satellite Organisation (Eutelsat), was established as an intergovernmental organisation in 1977,[290] initially on a provisional basis, before achieving permanent status in 1985. Its aim was 'the provision of the space segment required for international public telecommunication services in Europe'[291] in line with Europe's objective to develop autonomy in the space sector. As with Intelsat and Inmarsat, Eutelsat was restructured as a private company under French law on 2 July 2001.

6. Barriers to access

The European Union policy regarding satellite communication has had three main objectives: the liberalisation of the earth segment, the liberalisation of access to the space segment, and the commercial freedom of space segment providers. Satellite Directive 94/46/EC eliminated special

289 See Convention on the International Maritime Satellite Organisation (Inmarsat) (with operating Agreement), 3 September 1976, London.
290 See Convention establishing the European Telecommunications Organisation (Eutelsat), 15 July 1982, Paris; TS 15 (1990); Cmnd 956 as amended by a Protocol of 15 December 1983, Cmnd 9154.
291 Ibid, Art III(a).

rights or monopoly barriers to access, and required Member States to create regulatory structures for satellite services and licensing.

The regulatory working group of the Satellite Action Plan ('SAP') issued a paper on regulatory barriers in early 1998 that described in detail the barriers to access facing the satellite industry.[292] The SAP working group summarised these access barriers within the Community in the following terms:

> In the EU, difficulties in market access can be summarised as being due to the following reasons:
>
> (a) lack of implementation of EC directives and lack of the necessary regulatory mechanisms at the national level;
>
> (b) lack of harmonization between existing legislation further to the implementation of the EC directives;
>
> (c) slow appraisal of licence requests (causing delays in the provision of the service or the near impossibility in providing it);
>
> (d) significant differences in the amount of licence fees;
>
> (e) privileges to the incumbent PTO;
>
> (f) difficulty to access space segment; and
>
> (g) complexity of type approval processes.

One barrier specifically mentioned in the SAP working group report that the Satellite Directive did not eliminate, however, is created by international satellite organisations (ISOs) and the rules arising from their signatory structure. The ISOs traditionally permitted national signatories to hold the exclusive right to sell capacity within their national territory. This right has been a barrier to competition as national signatories were able to block use of capacity bought from other signatories and at the same time were able to apply large mark-ups for the ISO capacity. Such exclusivity has eroded due to trends towards 'direct access' designed to permit customers to obtain satellite capacity from any signatory or directly from the ISO itself.

However, these historical and future potential concerns revolving around, for example, the opening up of shareholding to non-participant entities (through a public offering) and the restriction of access to space-segment capacity and satellite service by former State incumbent telecommunication companies, are now increasingly resolved through the decisions of competition regulators in the same way as other multinational

---

292 'Market Access: Problems and Solutions, Report of the Satellite Action Plan Regulatory Working Group', www.ispo.cec.be/infosoc/telecompolicy/en/study-en.htm.

satellite ventures.[293] The full privatisation and commercialisation of treaty-based satellite organisations has contributed towards the achievement of the EU's main objectives mentioned above. As a result, these organisations are becoming less relevant as a feature of international telecommunications law.

B. SUBMARINE CABLES

Europe witnessed the beginnings of international submarine cable telegraphy in 1850 when the first cable crossing the English Channel to France was laid. It was over 100 years later, however, before the first coaxial trans-Atlantic telephone cable was laid in 1956 carrying 36 simultaneous analog telephone channels. Ever since that time, and especially in the last few years, the increase in capacity and growth requirements for submarine cables has been amazingly swift.

Thanks to new technologies such as WDM, or Wavelength Division Multiplexing, the capacity of submarine systems has expanded tremendously in recent years. The new capacity is being laid in response to huge increases in demand for digital data flows, which the new capacity in turn permits to grow even faster in a synergy of demand and supply. The balance between the demand for the systems to carry information and the capacity to cope with such demand is an outstanding feature of the history of submarine cables and is a key factor in the current competitive market situation.

1. Infrastructure

The physical infrastructure that is relevant from a regulatory perspective can be divided into the 'wet' portion of submarine cables, the landing stations or 'headends,' and backhaul facilities.

'Wet' portion: The 'wet' portion of submarine cables comprises the submarine cable itself. From a regulatory or market perspective, it is important to focus on three elements: the construction, provisioning and support of cable facilities. With respect to construction, it is sometimes argued that there are barriers to entry into submarine cable markets due to lead times, limited number of undersea cable supply and construction companies, or limited number of qualified personnel.[294] However, these

---

293 For example, see Commission competition decisions in International Private Satellite Partners (Case IV/34.768) [1994] OJ L354/75, and Iridium (Case IV/35.518) [1997] OJ L16/87.
294 See, eg, Global Crossing Ltd Form 8-K Current Report, 1 February 1999, at p 51. Similarly, the UK's OFTEL noted that there can be 'difficulties in laying new cable,' which may take up to two years to install. OFTEL, 'Mercury as a Well Established Operator,' June 1997, para 2.10 ('OFTEL 1997 Mercury Determination'), www.oftel.gov.uk/licensing/merweo.htm (accessed 8 March 1999).

would not seem to be major barriers, or at least no more significant than in any other large management project.

The process of planning and installing submarine cables is very complicated. The regulations that apply mainly fall into the realm of land use planning, environmental, maritime and (sometimes) defence, rather than telecommunications. Before selecting marine routes, very comprehensive desktop and shipboard surveys are undertaken of the routing options. These determine the nature of the sea-bed, its suitability for ploughing, the topology of the submarine mountain ranges, the location of deep sea currents, and the trends of fishing and off-shore exploration activity.[295] The planning process also must include assessment of landing rights or best available landing points.

A second element to the cable is the provisioning of cable transmission capacity. Competitors have argued that cable owners do not sell transmission capacity in a timely or sufficient manner, or at prices that match either the cost of the facilities or the price that the cable owners charge themselves. This second element is critical in assessing whether there are barriers to access.

The third element is the support of cable facilities, including repair and restoration. The cable owners have a maximum interest in restoring capacity and it is not obvious that they could impede competition using non-competitive restoration policies.

Cable landing stations: The argument is frequently raised that submarine cable landing stations are essential facilities. Even with multiple cable landing stations in a country, there still will usually be only one or two operators that control access to these stations. Normally the cable operator or owner will manage landing stations – for club cables, the club member in each country where the cables land typically manages the landing station. It is conceivable, nevertheless, that 'dark' fibre can be sold that permits customers to manage their own landing stations.

Backhaul: This facility is the high capacity inland circuit which is required by operators to link the cable landing station to an operator's existing domestic infrastructure. In most respects, this capacity is indistinguishable from domestic capacity, and arguably should be subject to the same rules as any other domestic infrastructure.

2. Elements of submarine cable transactions

As described below, submarine cables were traditionally sponsored by consortia of owners, almost always the dominant or monopoly operators from a large number of countries. The defining legal document for these

---

295 Most cable faults are caused by anchors of vessels and fishing gear. The cable and fishing industries make substantial efforts to avoid such problems. See, eg, International Cable Protection Committee, 'Fishing and Submarine Cables, Working Together,' 15 April 1996, www.iscpc.org/home.htm.

consortia has been the 'Construction and Maintenance Agreement' (C&MA) which the owners negotiate. These are not generally public documents, but the carriers are required to file them as part of FCC authorisations in the United States.

Capacity in submarine cables owned by consortia traditionally has been divided into Minimum Investment Units (MIUs). This concept does not necessarily apply to private cables, which are owned outright by the operator. Both consortia and private cable operators sell capacity on the cables in terms of Indefeasible Rights of Use (IRU). These IRUs are sold through Capacity Purchase Agreements (CPAs), often committing a buyer to obtain a unit of capacity for the remaining design life of a particular cable.

Traditional cable transactions were based on operating agreements that established correspondent relations between carriers. The traditional cable transaction involved two or more carriers, each dominant in its own national territory, exchanging traffic (ie, corresponding) and relying on the international system of accounting rates and settlements for remuneration. As part of this correspondent arrangement, carriers would own half circuits on submarine cable, and 'hand off' traffic to each other at a mythical midpoint on the cable. (This model was somewhat more realistic for satellite traffic, since each carrier owned a half circuit linked to the satellite, which is a physical midpoint to the service.) Operating agreements defined the terms and conditions for this activity – without an operating agreement in a country, a carrier could not correspond with its foreign counterpart or terminate service to or from that country.

This correspondence model is no longer the sole or even preferred approach for most international telecommunications traffic. Carriers are increasingly seeking to rely on full circuit arrangements and interconnection agreements, especially for data and private line traffic. As described in the next section, there is increasing customer demand for end-to-end solutions that include submarine and terrestrial cable combined into networks without correspondent relations. This development in turn decreases some of the original justification for consortium cables, by eliminating the need for operators to correspond with another operator at the midpoint of the cable.

3. Evolutionary change in ownership
The submarine cable industry is currently undergoing a change in ownership patterns at a pace that is speeding up, not as fast as capacity is expanding, but extremely fast compared to the past. Ownership of submarine cables is moving relatively rapidly from the 'club' model, in which consortia of dominant Telecommunications Operators (TOs) jointly owned the cables, to a private ownership model where private companies

or new operators finance the construction of the cable and then sell capacity to whomever requires it.

The historic model for cables is based on cooperation between monopoly and incumbent providers. International telecommunications services were provided for well over 100 years by monopoly operators, providing half-circuit facilities to connect with other monopoly TOs. International submarine cables classically were owned by consortia of national carriers. This ownership pattern produced a small number of cables, owned by a small group of carriers in the monopoly environment, almost entirely to provide capacity for their needs. The consortia members had joint control of these 'club cables', offered service mainly in correspondent relations, and sold wholesale capacity mainly for shore-to-shore or shore-to-midpoint connectivity.

This pattern is changing. The new model appears to be based on private companies or consortia building cable capacity without heavy representation of the traditional TOs, or TOs building their own cables without forming a large club of other TO investors. Project Oxygen, although reportedly still working to obtain its goal of $10 billion in financing, seeks to build cables around the world outside the 'club' model, with plans to complete a network connecting 96 landing points in 75 countries by 2003.

Global Crossing Ltd (GCL) financed its initial $750 million AC-1 trans-Atlantic cable and argued that 'the cost of constructing a submarine cable system is well within the means of a single company'.[296] Meanwhile, GCL purchased a US facilities-based operator for $11.2 billion, announced plans for yet another trans-Atlantic cable,[297] and at almost the same time sought a merger with Regional Bell Operating Company US West.

European TOs are building their own cables. For example, Telefónica announced a $900 million joint development agreement with Tyco International for a South American cable project,[298] and Esat Telecoms has sought its own Ireland-UK cable.[299]

These examples are mainly trans-Atlantic, where the most enormous traffic flow is concentrated. The same pattern, however, appears to be true

---

296 Reply of Global Crossing Ltd in the matter of AT&T Corp et al, FCC File No SCLLIC-19981117-00025, filed 26 January 1999, at p iv.

297 On 24 March 1999, GCL announced that it will construct a 2.5 terabits capacity AC-2 cable, scheduled to commence in the first quarter of 2001. GCL press release at www.globalcrossing.bm/pressreleases/pr_032499.asp (accessed 31 March 1999).

298 Telecommunications Reports, TR Daily, 14 May 1999. See the Tyco news release at http://investors.tycoint.com/news/19990511-8331.htm (accessed 18 May 1999).

299 C Daly, Esat, 'Why Esat Telecoms invested in a subsea cable system in Ireland and the UK', Proceedings, Submarine Fiber-Optic Cables Summit, 23 February 1999 (London, SMi Ltd). Esat specifically mentioned its desire to be 'independent' of the incumbent national carrier as a reason to build its own cable.

of intra-Community traffic. For example, on the high-capacity UK to continental Europe path, BT estimated that its net capacity for submarine links was only 3.5 per cent of total capacity as of October 1998. MCI WorldCom owns substantial non-consortium facilities that include two submarine crossings of the English Channel. Hermes owns at least two cable links between the UK and Belgium and the Netherlands. Esprit has built links through the Channel Tunnel and other companies have announced further independent submarine cable projects.

Thus, while club cables are still planned, observers argue that there is decreasing credibility to the argument that this model is required by financial requirements. Given rapid development of new cable projects, at a minimum the market model is changing from one dominated by large club cables, to one with a mix of large and small club cables together with private cables.

4. Regulation of international submarine transmission facilities

WTO rules: On 5 February 1998, the results of the WTO negotiations on market access for basic telecommunications services entered into force.[300] The ensuing agreement is formally referred to as the Fourth Protocol to the General Agreement on Trade in Services (GATS) and is only a page or so long. However, the specific commitments from the countries that participated add another 400 pages of text.[301] These commitments generally open telecommunications markets, to varying degrees, to competition under general GATS principles.

As part of their GATS commitment, EU Member States also committed to comply with a Reference Paper on regulatory principles attached to the Fourth Protocol. The Reference Paper derives from and elaborates on principles already set forth in the GATS, including transparency (Article III), regulatory procedures (Article VI) and competition principles (Article XIX). At least the three following elements of the Reference Paper are relevant to regulation of submarine cable facilities:

(a) Interconnection with a 'major supplier' (a defined term) will be ensured at 'any technically feasible point in the network', provided under non-discriminatory terms, conditions, rates and quality; in a timely fashion; and at requested points subject to construction charges.

(b) Public availability of licensing criteria: this requirement includes making publicly available information on criteria, the normal time

---

300 The WTO Agreement, and the GATS are set out at (1994) 33 International Legal Materials 11, 44. See also E McGovern, International Trade Regulation (Exeter: Globalfield Press, 1996).
301 The commitments of EU Member States are set out officially in Council Decision of 28 November 1997 ([1997] OJ L347/45) concerning ... the results of the WTO negotiations on basic telecommunications services.

period required for decisions, and the terms and conditions of individual licences.

(c) Allocation and use of scarce resources: any procedures for allocation and use of such resources, 'including frequencies, numbers and rights of way', will be carried out in an 'objective, timely, transparent and non-discriminatory manner'.

This last factor could be especially important. To the extent that this WTO commitment focuses on access to rights of way, Member States have an obligation to ensure that national procedures meet the conditions for allocating and using those scarce resources.

Law of the sea: The traditional law of the sea entitles countries to lay submarine cables on their continental shelf. This principle has been enshrined in Article 79 of the Law of the Sea Convention, which is now part of EU law.[302] Further, Article 112 provides that all States are entitled to lay submarine cable on the high seas as well. Articles 113–115 require States to adopt laws and regulations concerning the breaking or injury of submarine cables, including liability rules and indemnity for losses by ships who sacrifice anchors, nets or other gear in order to avoid damaging cables. There also exist a body of international conventions on cable, dating back as far as the 1884 Convention on protecting submarine cables, which have been implemented in national legislation.[303] For example, Ireland's Submarine Telegraph Act of 1885 transposed this Convention into national law.

The Access and Interconnection Directive: Articles 6-13 of the new Access and Interconnection Directive provide that obligations as to access and interconnection contained in previous Directives, namely the Interconnection Directive 97/33/EC and ONP Leased Lines Directive 92/44/EC, will continue to be imposed under the new regime. There is, however, a procedure to review all these obligations in light of current market conditions. In any event, many of the primary duties under the Interconnection and Leased Lines Directives are carried over into the new Access and Interconnection Directive.

The new Access and Interconnection Directive, at the most basic level, lays down the principle that interconnection and special access should normally be left to commercial negotiations between parties, while

302 The Convention is reprinted in Council Decision of 23 March 1998 ([1999] OJ L179/1) concerning the conclusion by the European Community of the United Nations Convention of 10 December 1982 on the Law of the Sea and the Agreement of 28 July 1994 relating to the implementation of Part XI thereof.

303 A compendium of international law on submarine cable is available at the International Cable Protection Committee website under 'information, government and law', at www.iscpc.org/home.htm.

imposing a certain number of detailed obligations on operators notified by Member States as having Significant Market Power (SMP) (now to be defined by reference to dominance under competition law principles) on a relevant market. It includes obligations to meet all reasonable requests for interconnection and special access and to respect the principle of non-discrimination, in particular between subsidiaries and other parties. National Regulatory Authorities (NRAs) are under a duty to ensure that, when an operator is required to provide access or interconnection in accordance with the provision of the Directive, and in particular Article 12, the NRA may lay down technical or operational conditions to be met by the provider and/or the persons connecting where necessary to ensure the normal operation of the network. Notwithstanding any measures which may be imposed on operators with SMP under the Authorisation Directive, NRAs also have the power to impose the following obligations on undertakings that control access to end-users when such an obligation to interconnect is not already imposed in situations necessary to ensure end-to-end connectivity.

In the context of submarine cable capacity, two questions arise: (a) is access to cable headends covered by the Access and Interconnection Directive; and (b) should conditions for access to cable headends be included as part of the reference interconnection offer of the incumbent operator? These questions are crucial since any traffic on an international cable has to pass through the cable landing facilities at each end in order to be terminated in the country concerned.

Submarine cable headends are part of the 'public communications network,' in that they are part of 'a network used for the provision of publicly available communication services', ie, international calls. Thus, in answer to the first question, we take the view that access to cable headends is covered by the Directive. As to the second question, it is for NRAs to agree on the precise interconnection offerings to be included in the interconnection offer.

There is no clear statement of the application of the Access and Interconnection Directive to submarine cable facilities in official EU documents.

C. THE INTERNATIONAL TELECOMMUNICATIONS UNION

The International Telecommunications Union (ITU) began as the International Telegraph Union, which was founded at a conference of 20 European countries in 1865. The stated purpose of the organisation was to universalise telegraph services among nations. While its membership at first included only European States, countries from other continents were represented within a short time after the organisation's founding. In 1947, the ITU voted to become a specialised agency of the United Nations and moved its headquarters from Berne to Geneva. In 1992, the ITU approved a fundamental reorganisation designed to make it more responsive to the rapid pace of technological change in international communications. The reorganised ITU was officially reborn on 1 July 1994.

1. Structure and proceedings of the ITU

The ITU's highest authority is its Constitution, supplemented by a document called the Convention. These two documents together set out the mission, structure, and working methods of the ITU and define the rights and obligations of the organisation's members. The provisions of both documents are binding on the ITU's members.

As the Constitution provides, the supreme authority of the ITU is the Plenipotentiary Conference, or 'Plenipotentiary', which meets every four years. All member countries are represented at the Plenipotentiary, which sets long-term policy, elects officers, sets the budget, amends the Convention, and elects the 41 members of the Council. The Council acts as the chief policy-making body between meetings of the Plenipotentiary. It meets once a year.

Day-to-day administration of the ITU is the job of the General-Secretariat, headed by a Secretary-General who is elected by the Plenipotentiary for a four-year term. The detailed work of the ITU is done at periodic conferences, each devoted to a particular area of the ITU's responsibility, and by permanent groups known as 'sectors', each of which is headed by a director elected by the Plenipotentiary.

ITU oversight of radio matters is delegated to a permanent Radiocommunications Sector – called ITU-R. It is supervised by a World Radiocommunications Conference (WRC) that meets every two years to adopt revisions to the ITU's Radio Regulations. Regional conferences convene as needed to consider issues associated with particular geographic areas. The WRC also organises and oversees the work of the study groups that deal with ongoing technical questions posed by radio frequency spectrum use (for both terrestrial and satellite communications), radio systems performance, and radio-related emergency and safety questions. Administration of the Radiocommunications Sector is entrusted to the Radiocommunication Bureau, which is headed by a director.

ITU oversight of telecommunications standards (including the interconnection of radio systems used for telecommunications) is delegated to the Telecommunication Standardisation Sector, the ITU-T, which is supervised by a World Telecommunication Standardisation Conference that meets every four years. Similar to the Radiocommunications Sector, the Telecommunication Standardisation Sector includes a number of study groups that work on technical problems associated with the performance and compatibility of telecommunications systems and equipment. This sector also includes a permanent Telecommunication Standardisation Bureau, which is headed by a director elected by the Plenipotentiary.

The ITU's mandate to assist in international development is the province of the Telecommunication Development Sector (ITU-D), which is supervised by a World Development Conference that meets every four years. Like other sectors, the Telecommunication Development Sector works through a number of study groups. It also includes a bureau, which is headed by a director, and an advisory board.

Aside from the provisions of the Constitution and the Convention, the ITU enacts rules known as Administrative Regulations. Some of these regulations, for example, Radio Regulations, are treaty undertakings that bind all member governments. Others, notably the telecommunications standards and development regulations, are non-binding regulations.

As the ITU is a treaty organisation, the delegations that work with its sectors and advisory bodies have traditionally been accredited by the governments of the member countries. Where member countries' telecommunications networks are operated by the State, the delegations are made up of civil servants. Where private companies provide these services, delegations could include employees of those private companies who were accredited by their governments to participate. In 1998, the Convention was amended to enable such 'Sector Members' to apply directly to join the ITU. With the liberalisation of the telecommunications industry and the proliferation of commercial operators, tension has recently been mounting over the position of industry members within the ITU structure.

D. EUROPEAN STANDARD-MAKING BODIES

In addition to the international organisations above, there are European bodies which prescribe standards of regional scope.

1. ETSI

ETSI (the European Telecommunications Standards Institute) based in Antipolis, south of France, was founded in 1988 and is officially recognised by the European Commission and the EFTA secretariat. The principal role of the Institute is the technical pre-standardisation and standardisation at the European level in telecommunications, information technology and broadcasting. It has a broad membership comprising administrative bodies, national standards organisations, network operators, manufacturers, users, service providers, research bodies, and consultancy companies.

Like the ITU, ETSI works through a large number of technical committees and subcommittees. Standards produced by ETSI are known as

European Telecommunications Standards (ETS). To ensure coordination with the work of the ITU, ETSI is also a member of ITU-T.

2. CEPT

The European Conference of Postal and Telecommunications Administrations (CEPT) was established in 1959 by 19 countries. Original members were the incumbent monopoly-holding postal and telecommunications administrations. CEPT's activities included cooperation on commercial, operational, regulatory and technical standardisation issues.

In 1988, CEPT decided to create ETSI, the European Telecommunications Standards Institute, into which all its telecommunication standardisation activities were transferred.

In 1992, the postal and telecommunications operators created their own organisations, Post Europe and ETNO respectively. In conjunction with the European policy of separating postal and telecommunications operations from policy-making and regulatory functions, CEPT thus became a body of policy-makers and regulators. At the same time, Central and Eastern European Countries became eligible for membership of CEPT. With its 45 members, CEPT now covers almost the entire geographical area of Europe.

The role and purpose of CEPT was redefined at its plenary assembly on 5–6 September 1995 in Weimar as follows. CEPT offers its members the chance of:

(a) establishing a European forum for discussions on sovereign and regulatory issues in the field of post and telecommunications issues;

(b) providing mutual assistance among members with regard to the settlement of sovereign/regulatory issues;

(c) exerting an influence on the goals and priorities in the field of European post and telecommunications through common positions;

(d) shaping, in the field of European post and telecommunications, those areas coming under its responsibilities;

(e) carrying out its activities at a pan-European level;

(f) strengthening and fostering more intensively cooperation with Eastern and Central European Countries;

(g) promoting and facilitating relations between European regulators (eg, through personal contacts);

(h) influencing, through common positions, developments within ITU and the Universal Postal Union in accordance with European goals;

(i) responding to new circumstances in a non-bureaucratic and cost-effective way and carrying out its activities in the time allocated;

(j) settling common problems at committee level, through close collaboration between its committees;

(k) giving its activities more binding force, if required, than in the past; creating a single Europe in the post and telecommunications sectors.

CEPT after this agreement deals exclusively with sovereignty/regulatory matters, and has established three committees, one on postal matters, CERP (Comité Européen de Réglementation Postale) and two on telecommunications issues, ERC (European Radiocommunications Committee) and ECTRA (European Committee for Regulatory Telecommunications Affairs). The field of responsibility for each committee is decided by CEPT's Plenary Assembly, while each committee establishes its own rules of procedure and elects its chairman.

The committees handle harmonisation activities within their respective fields of responsibility, and adopt recommendations and decisions. These recommendations and decisions are normally prepared by their working groups and project teams.

On 6 May 1991, the European Radiocommunications Committee established a permanent office in Copenhagen, the European Radiocommunications Office (ERO), with the purpose of supporting the activities of the Committee and conducting studies for it and for the European Commission. On 1 September 1994, ECTRA also established a permanent office in Copenhagen, the European Telecommunications Office (ETO), for the same purpose.

At its Plenary Assembly meeting in Bergen on 20–21 September 2001, CEPT made a number of important steps to strengthen the organisation. As such, the basic instruments, the CEPT Arrangement and Rules of Procedure, have been amended. A Presidency has been created, and a policy agenda has been adopted, to give CEPT a more active role as a forum for strategic planning, decision-making, and preparing for conferences of the International Telecommunications Union.

E. THE WORLD TRADE ORGANISATION

The World Trade Organisation (WTO) was established in 1994 as part of the final act for embodying the results of the Uruguay Round of multilateral trade negotiations. The function of the WTO is to facilitate the implementation, administration and operation of certain multilateral trade agreements. It also established a dispute settlement duty to enforce the obligations accepted by Member States within the context of the agreements.

The most directly relevant of the WTO-administered trade agreements for telecommunications are the General Agreement on Tariffs and Trade (GATT) in respect of telecommunications equipment, and the General Agreement on Trade in Services (GATS). The following sections focus on the GATS as a framework for international telecommunications law.

1. Annex on telecommunications

The GATS contains the Principles for trade in all services. Included in the GATS is the Annex on telecommunications which deals with specific points pertaining to trade in telecom services, such as access to public networks.

The Annex is composed of seven sections, but its core obligations are contained in a section on access to and use of 'public telecommunications transport networks and services' (meaning essentially basic public telecommunications). The Annex requires each Member to ensure that all service suppliers seeking to take advantage of scheduled commitments are accorded access to and use of public basic telecommunications, both networks and services, on a reasonable and non-discriminatory basis.

Members incur these obligations whether or not they have liberalised or scheduled commitments in the basic telecommunications sector. This is because the Annex addresses access to these services by users rather than the ability to enter markets to sell such services; the latter is addressed in schedules of commitments. As such, the beneficiaries of the disciplines in the Annex will be firms that supply any of the services included in a Member's schedule of commitments; not only value added and competing basic telecommunications suppliers, but banking or computer services firms, for example, that wish to take advantage of market access commitments made by a WTO Member. The Annex obligations strike a fragile balance between the needs of users for fair terms of access and the needs of the regulators and public telecommunications operators to maintain a system that works and that meets public service objectives.

The Post-Uruguay round negotiators, for basic telecommunications, attached to the GATS the Fourth Protocol to the General Agreement on Trade in Services, commonly referred to as the 'Basic Agreement on Telecommunications'. This WTO agreement on basic telecommunications services came into effect on 5 February 1998. At the conclusion of the main negotiations, 69 countries made binding commitments on market access for basic telecom services (voice, fax and data). Further offers have been made subsequently by other countries.

At the outset of the negotiations, governments agreed to set aside national differences on how basic telecommunications might be defined domestically and to negotiate on all telecommunications services both public and private that involve end-to-end transmission of customer supplied information (eg, simply the relay of voice or data from sender to receiver). They also agreed that basic telecommunications services provided over network infrastructure, as well as those provided through resale (over private leased circuits), would both fall within the scope of commitments. As a result, market access commitments will cover not only cross-border supply of telecommunications but also services provided through the establishment of foreign firms, or commercial presence, including the ability to own and operate independent telecom network infrastructure. Examples of the services covered by this agreement include voice telephony, data transmission, telex, telegraph, facsimile, private leased circuit services (ie, the sale or lease of transmission capacity), fixed and mobile satellite systems and services, cellular telephony, mobile data services, paging, and personal communications systems.

Value added services (or telecommunications for which suppliers 'add value' to the customer's information by enhancing its form or content or by providing for its storage and retrieval) were not formally part of these negotiations. Examples include online data processing, online database storage and retrieval, electronic data interchange, email or voice mail. Value-added services were already included in 44 schedules (representing 55 governments) that are in force as a result of the previous Uruguay Round.

The result is that the two central GATS disciplines of 'most favoured nation' (MFN) and 'national treatment' now apply to the telecoms sector. Under the MFN discipline, concessions offered to a supplier from one WTO country must be offered to suppliers from all other WTO countries unless an exemption has been taken. Under national treatment, foreign service suppliers established in a country must be treated identically to a national service supplier, unless, again, a limitation on national treatment has been scheduled.

2. Reference Paper

Concerns related to establishing a regulatory environment conducive to market entry were discussed at length during the negotiations. Many participants suggested that regulatory disciplines might be inscribed as additional commitments in schedules as a way of safeguarding the value of market access commitments undertaken. Many countries therefore signed up, in a commonly negotiated text called the Reference Paper, to some or all of a set of regulatory principles on competition safeguards, interconnection guarantees, transparent licensing processes and the independence of regulators, designed to ensure that market access commitments were not nullified by an incumbent's anti-competitive behaviour. They also agreed that each would use the text as a tool in deciding what regulatory disciplines to undertake as additional commitments. By the February 1997 deadline, 63 of the 69 governments submitting schedules included commitments on regulatory disciplines, with 57 of these committing to the Reference Paper in whole or with a few modifications

3. WTO dispute resolution

The WTO has a dispute resolution mechanism to enforce the trade agreements signed up by Member countries. Under European law, complaints may be submitted in writing to the European Commission and a formal examination procedure may be invoked prior to the decision to pursue a dispute.[304]

The European Union has pursued formal proceedings against both Korea and Japan in respect of preferential trade practices favouring US suppliers of telecommunications equipment, which were resolved by agreement.[305] The US is currently threatening proceedings against Belgium regarding the licensing practices and conditions imposed by Belgium on the publishing of telephone directories.

It is the ability to suspend trade concessions or obligations not only in the sector of dispute (eg, telecommunications), but also, where appropriate, in other sectors under the same agreements (eg, GATS), or even another covered agreement, which is the real stick under the WTO's dispute settlement procedure.

F. CONCLUSION

The dramatic advances in networking technologies and communications in the latter half of the twentieth century are leading to a restructuring of the rules and principles that govern the telecommunications industry on a national and international level. The abandonment of old regulatory approaches, new market demands, the growing influence of the new trade in services regime negotiated at the World Trade Organisation (WTO), and the rise of the Internet, is transforming the historical telecommunications regime. To the extent that multilateral telecommunications rules will be needed in a privatised and liberalised global telecommunications market, they are being provided by the WTO and other trade institutions and a diverse range of private sector-led standards bodies.

---

304 Council Regulation 3286/94/EC of 22 December 1994 ([1994] OJ L349/71), laying down Community procedures in the field of the common commercial policy in order to ensure the exercise of the Community's rights under international trade rules, in particular those established under the auspices of the World Trade Organisation.
305 See WTO Report, 'Overview of the State-of-Play of WTO Disputes', 10 August 2000, www.wto.org.

Appendices

DIRECTIVE 2002/19/EC OF THE EUROPEAN PARLIAMENT AND OF THE COUNCIL

of 7 March 2002

on access to, and interconnection of, electronic communications networks and associated facilities
(Access Directive)

THE EUROPEAN PARLIAMENT AND THE COUNCIL OF THE EUROPEAN UNION,

Having regard to the Treaty establishing the European Community, and in particular Article 95 thereof,

Having regard to the proposal from the Commission ([1]),

Having regard to the opinion of the Economic and Social Committee ([2]),

Acting in accordance with the procedure laid down in Article 251 of the Treaty ([3]),

Whereas:

(1) Directive 2002/21/EC of the European Parliament and of the Council of 7 March 2002 on a common regulatory framework for electronic communications networks and services (Framework Directive) ([4]) lays down the objectives of a regulatory framework to cover electronic communications networks and services in the Community, including fixed and mobile telecommunications networks, cable television networks, networks used for terrestrial broadcasting, satellite networks and Internet networks, whether used for voice, fax, data or images. Such networks may have been authorised by Member States under Directive 2002/20/EC of the European Parliament and of the Council of 7 March 2002 on the authorisation of electronic communications networks and services (Authorisation Directive) ([5]) or have been authorised under previous regulatory measures. The provisions of this Directive apply to those networks that are used for the provision of publicly available electronic communications services. This Directive covers access and interconnection arrangements between service suppliers. Non-public networks do not have obligations

under this Directive except where, in benefiting from access to public networks, they may be subject to conditions laid down by Member States.

(2) Services providing content such as the offer for sale of a package of sound or television broadcasting content are not covered by the common regulatory framework for electronic communications networks and services.

(3) The term 'access' has a wide range of meanings, and it is therefore necessary to define precisely how that term is used in this Directive, without prejudice to how it may be used in other Community measures. An operator may own the underlying network or facilities or may rent some or all of them.

(4) Directive 95/47/EC of the European Parliament and of the Council of 24 October 1995 on the use of standards for the transmission of television signals ([6]) did not mandate any specific digital television transmission system or service requirement, and this opened up an opportunity for the market actors to take the initiative and develop suitable systems. Through the Digital Video Broadcasting Group, European market actors have developed a family of television transmission systems that have been adopted by broadcasters throughout the world. These transmissions systems have been standardised by the European Telecommunications Standards Institute (ETSI) and have become International Telecommunication Union recommendations. In relation to wide-screen digital television, the 16:9 aspect ratio is the reference format for wide-format television services and programmes, and is now established in Member States' markets as a result of Council Decision 93/424/EEC of 22 July 1993 on an action plan for the introduction of advanced television services in Europe ([7]).

(5) In an open and competitive market, there should be no restrictions that prevent undertakings from negotiating access and interconnection arrangements between themselves, in particular on cross-border agreements,

---

([1]) OJ C 365 E, 19.12.2000, p. 215 and OJ C 270 E, 25.9.2001, p. 161.
([2]) OJ C 123, 25.4.2001, p. 50.
([3]) Opinion of the European Parliament of 1 March 2001 (OJ C 277, 1.10.2001, p. 72), Council Common Position of 17 September 2001 (OJ C 337, 30.11.2001, p. 1) and Decision of the European Parliament of 12 December 2001 (not yet published in the Official Journal). Council Decision of 14 February 2002.
([4]) See page 33 of this Official Journal.
([5]) See page 21 of this Official Journal.

([6]) OJ L 281, 23.11.1995, p. 51.
([7]) OJ L 196, 5.8.1993, p. 48.

subject to the competition rules of the Treaty. In the context of achieving a more efficient, truly pan-European market, with effective competition, more choice and competitive services to consumers, undertakings which receive requests for access or interconnection should in principle conclude such agreements on a commercial basis, and negotiate in good faith.

(6) In markets where there continue to be large differences in negotiating power between undertakings, and where some undertakings rely on infrastructure provided by others for delivery of their services, it is appropriate to establish a framework to ensure that the market functions effectively. National regulatory authorities should have the power to secure, where commercial negotiation fails, adequate access and interconnection and interoperability of services in the interest of end-users. In particular, they may ensure end-to-end connectivity by imposing proportionate obligations on undertakings that control access to end-users. Control of means of access may entail ownership or control of the physical link to the end-user (either fixed or mobile), and/or the ability to change or withdraw the national number or numbers needed to access an end-user's network termination point. This would be the case for example if network operators were to restrict unreasonably end-user choice for access to Internet portals and services.

(7) National legal or administrative measures that link the terms and conditions for access or interconnection to the activities of the party seeking interconnection, and specifically to the degree of its investment in network infrastructure, and not to the interconnection or access services provided, may cause market distortion and may therefore not be compatible with competition rules.

(8) Network operators who control access to their own customers do so on the basis of unique numbers or addresses from a published numbering or addressing range. Other network operators need to be able to deliver traffic to those customers, and so need to be able to interconnect directly or indirectly to each other. The existing rights and obligations to negotiate interconnection should therefore be maintained. It is also appropriate to maintain the obligations formerly laid down in Directive 95/47/EC requiring fully digital electronic communications networks used for the distribution of television services and open to the public to be capable of distributing wide-screen television services and programmes, so that users are able to receive such programmes in the format in which they were transmitted.

(9) Interoperability is of benefit to end-users and is an important aim of this regulatory framework. Encouraging interoperability is one of the objectives for national regulatory authorities as set out in this framework, which also provides for the Commission to publish a list of standards and/or specifications covering the provision of services, technical interfaces and/or network functions, as the basis for encouraging harmonisation in electronic communications. Member States should encourage the use of published standards and/or specifications to the extent strictly necessary to ensure interoperability of services and to improve freedom of choice for users.

(10) Competition rules alone may not be sufficient to ensure cultural diversity and media pluralism in the area of digital television. Directive 95/47/EC provided an initial regulatory framework for the nascent digital television industry which should be maintained, including in particular the obligation to provide conditional access on fair, reasonable and non-discriminatory terms, in order to make sure that a wide variety of programming and services is available. Technological and market developments make it necessary to review these obligations on a regular basis, either by a Member State for its national market or the Commission for the Community, in particular to determine whether there is justification for extending obligations to new gateways, such as electronic programme guides (EPGs) and application program interfaces (APIs), to the extent that is necessary to ensure accessibility for end-users to specified digital broadcasting services. Member States may specify the digital broadcasting services to which access by end-users must be ensured by any legislative, regulatory or administrative means that they deem necessary.

(11) Member States may also permit their national regulatory authority to review obligations in relation to conditional access to digital broadcasting services in order to assess through a market analysis whether to withdraw or amend conditions for operators that do not have significant market power on the relevant market. Such withdrawal or amendment should not adversely affect access for end-users to such services or the prospects for effective competition.

(12) In order to ensure continuity of existing agreements and to avoid a legal vacuum, it is necessary to ensure that obligations for access and interconnection imposed under Articles 4, 6, 7, 8, 11, 12, and 14 of Directive 97/33/EC of the European Parliament and of the Council of 30 June 1997 on interconnection in telecommunications with regard to ensuring universal service and interoperability through application of the

principles of open network provision (ONP) (^{1}), obligations on special access imposed under Article 16 of Directive 98/10/EC of the European Parliament and of the Council of 26 February 1998 on the application of open network provision (ONP) to voice telephony and on universal service for telecommunications in a competitive environment (^{2}), and obligations concerning the provision of leased line transmission capacity under Council Directive 92/44/EEC of 5 June 1992 on the application of open network provision to leased lines (^{3}), are initially carried over into the new regulatory framework, but are subject to immediate review in the light of prevailing market conditions. Such a review should also extend to those organisations covered by Regulation (EC) No 2887/2000 of the European Parliament and of the Council of 18 December 2000 on unbundled access to the local loop (^{4}).

(13) The review should be carried out using an economic market analysis based on competition law methodology. The aim is to reduce *ex ante* sector specific rules progressively as competition in the market develops. However the procedure also takes account of transitional problems in the market such as those related to international roaming and of the possibility of new bottlenecks arising as a result of technological development, which may require *ex ante* regulation, for example in the area of broadband access networks. It may well be the case that competition develops at different speeds in different market segments and in different Member States, and national regulatory authorities should be able to relax regulatory obligations in those markets where competition is delivering the desired results. In order to ensure that market players in similar circumstances are treated in similar ways in different Member States, the Commission should be able to ensure harmonised application of the provisions of this Directive. National regulatory authorities and national authorities entrusted with the implementation of competition law should, where appropriate, coordinate their actions to ensure that the most appropriate remedy is applied. The Community and its Member States have entered into commitments on interconnection of telecommunications networks in the context of the World Trade Organisation agreement on basic telecommunications and these commitments need to be respected.

(14) Directive 97/33/EC laid down a range of obligations to be imposed on undertakings with significant market power, namely transparency, non-discrimination, accounting separation, access, and price control including cost orientation. This range of possible

obligations should be maintained but, in addition, they should be established as a set of maximum obligations that can be applied to undertakings, in order to avoid over-regulation. Exceptionally, in order to comply with international commitments or Community law, it may be appropriate to impose obligations for access or interconnection on all market players, as is currently the case for conditional access systems for digital television services.

(15) The imposition of a specific obligation on an undertaking with significant market power does not require an additional market analysis but a justification that the obligation in question is appropriate and proportionate in relation to the nature of the problem identified.

(16) Transparency of terms and conditions for access and interconnection, including prices, serve to speed-up negotiation, avoid disputes and give confidence to market players that a service is not being provided on discriminatory terms. Openness and transparency of technical interfaces can be particularly important in ensuring interoperability. Where a national regulatory authority imposes obligations to make information public, it may also specify the manner in which the information is to be made available, covering for example the type of publication (paper and/or electronic) and whether or not it is free of charge, taking into account the nature and purpose of the information concerned.

(17) The principle of non-discrimination ensures that undertakings with market power do not distort competition, in particular where they are vertically integrated undertakings that supply services to undertakings with whom they compete on downstream markets.

(18) Accounting separation allows internal price transfers to be rendered visible, and allows national regulatory authorities to check compliance with obligations for non-discrimination where applicable. In this regard the Commission published Recommendation 98/322/EC of 8 April 1998 on interconnection in a liberalised telecommunications market (Part 2 — accounting separation and cost accounting) (^{5}).

(19) Mandating access to network infrastructure can be justified as a means of increasing competition, but national regulatory authorities need to balance the rights of an infrastructure owner to exploit its infrastructure forits own benefit, and the rights of other service

---

(^{1}) OJ L 199, 26.7.1997, p. 32. Directive as last amended by Directive 98/61/EC (OJ L 268, 3.10.1998, p. 37).
(^{2}) OJ L 101, 1.4.1998, p. 24.
(^{3}) OJ L 165, 19.6.1992, p. 27. Directive as last amended by Commission Decision No 98/80/EC (OJ L 14, 20.1.1998, p. 27).
(^{4}) OJ L 366, 30.12.2000, p. 4.

(^{5}) OJ L 141, 13.5.1998, p. 6.

providers to access facilities that are essential for the provision of competing services. Where obligations are imposed on operators that require them to meet reasonable requests for access to and use of networks elements and associated facilities, such requests should only be refused on the basis of objective criteria such as technical feasibility or the need to maintain network integrity. Where access is refused, the aggrieved party may submit the case to the dispute resolutions procedure referred to in Articles 20 and 21 of Directive 2002/21/EC (Framework Directive). An operator with mandated access obligations cannot be required to provide types of access which are not within its powers to provide. The imposition by national regulatory authorities of mandated access that increases competition in the short-term should not reduce incentives for competitors to invest in alternative facilities that will secure more competition in the long-term. The Commission has published a Notice on the application of the competition rules to access agreements in the telecommunications sector ([1]) which addresses these issues. National regulatory authorities may impose technical and operational conditions on the provider and/or beneficiaries of mandated access in accordance with Community law. In particular the imposition of technical standards should comply with Directive 98/34/EC of the European Parliament and of the Council of 22 June 1998 laying down a procedure for the provision of information in the field of technical standards and regulations and of rules of Information Society Services ([2]).

(20) Price control may be necessary when market analysis in a particular market reveals inefficient competition. The regulatory intervention may be relatively light, such as an obligation that prices for carrier selection are reasonable as laid down in Directive 97/33/EC, or much heavier such as an obligation that prices are cost oriented to provide full justification for those prices where competition is not sufficiently strong to prevent excessive pricing. In particular, operators with significant market power should avoid a price squeeze whereby the difference between their retail prices and the interconnection prices charged to competitors who provide similar retail services is not adequate to ensure sustainable competition. When a national regulatory authority calculates costs incurred in establishing a service mandated under this Directive, it is appropriate to allow a reasonable return on the capital employed including appropriate labour and building costs, with the value of capital adjusted where necessary to reflect the current valuation of assets and efficiency of operations. The method of cost recovery should be appropriate to the circumstances taking account of the need to promote efficiency and sustainable competition and maximise consumer benefits.

(21) Where a national regulatory authority imposes obligations to implement a cost accounting system in order to support price controls, it may itself undertake an annual audit to ensure compliance with that cost accounting system, provided that it has the necessary qualified staff, or it may require the audit to be carried out by another qualified body, independent of the operator concerned.

(22) Publication of information by Member States will ensure that market players and potential market entrants understand their rights and obligations, and know where to find the relevant detailed information. Publication in the national gazette helps interested parties in other Member States to find the relevant information.

(23) In order to ensure that the pan-European electronic communications market is effective and efficient, the Commission should monitor and publish information on charges which contribute to determining prices to end-users.

(24) The development of the electronic communications market, with its associated infrastructure, could have adverse effects on the environment and the landscape. Member States should therefore monitor this process and, if necessary, take action to minimise any such effects by means of appropriate agreements and other arrangements with the relevant authorities.

(25) In order to determine the correct application of Community law, the Commission needs to know which undertakings have been designated as having significant market power and what obligations have been placed upon market players by national regulatory authorities. In addition to national publication of this information, it is therefore necessary for Member States to send this information to the Commission. Where Member States are required to send information to the Commission, this may be in electronic form, subject to appropriate authentication procedures being agreed.

(26) Given the pace of technological and market developments, the implementation of this Directive

---

([1]) OJ C 265, 22.8.1998, p. 2.
([2]) OJ L 204, 21.7.1998, p. 37. Directive as amended by Directive 98/48/EC (OJ L 217, 5.8.1998, p. 18).

should be reviewed within three years of its date of application to determine if it is meeting its objectives.

(27) The measures necessary for the implementation of this Directive should be adopted in accordance with Council Decision 1999/468/EC of 28 June 1999 laying down the procedures for the exercise of implementing powers conferred on the Commission (¹).

(28) Since the objectives of the proposed action, namely establishing a harmonised framework for the regulation of access to and interconnection of electronic communications networks and associated facilities, cannot be sufficiently achieved by the Member States and can therefore, by reason of the scale and effects of the action, be better achieved at Community level, the Community may adopt measures, in accordance with the principle of subsidiarity as set out in Article 5 of the Treaty. In accordance with the principle of proportionality, as set out in that Article, this Directive does not go beyond what is necessary in order to achieve those objectives,

HAVE ADOPTED THIS DIRECTIVE:

CHAPTER I

SCOPE, AIM AND DEFINITIONS

Article 1

Scope and aim

1. Within the framework set out in Directive 2002/21/EC (Framework Directive), this Directive harmonises the way in which Member States regulate access to, and interconnection of, electronic communications networks and associated facilities. The aim is to establish a regulatory framework, in accordance with internal market principles, for the relationships between suppliers of networks and services that will result in sustainable competition, interoperability of electronic communications services and consumer benefits.

2. This Directive establishes rights and obligations for operators and for undertakings seeking interconnection and/or access to their networks or associated facilities. It sets out objectives for national regulatory authorities with regard to access and interconnection, and lays down procedures to ensure that obligations imposed by national regulatory authorities are reviewed and, where appropriate, withdrawn

(¹) OJ L 184, 17.7.1999, p. 23.

once the desired objectives have been achieved. Access in this Directive does not refer to access by end-users.

Article 2

Definitions

For the purposes of this Directive the definitions set out in Article 2 of Directive 2002/21/EC (Framework Directive) shall apply.

The following definitions shall also apply:

(a) 'access' means the making available of facilities and/or services, to another undertaking, under defined conditions, on either an exclusive or non-exclusive basis, for the purpose of providing electronic communications services. It covers *inter alia*: access to network elements and associated facilities, which may involve the connection of equipment, by fixed or non-fixed means (in particular this includes access to the local loop and to facilities and services necessary to provide services over the local loop), access to physical infrastructure including buildings, ducts and masts; access to relevant software systems including operational support systems, access to number translation or systems offering equivalent functionality, access to fixed and mobile networks, in particular for roaming, access to conditional access systems for digital television services; access to virtual network services;

(b) 'interconnection' means the physical and logical linking of public communications networks used by the same or a different undertaking in order to allow the users of one undertaking to communicate with users of the same or another undertaking, or to access services provided by another undertaking. Services may be provided by the parties involved or other parties who have access to the network. Interconnection is a specific type of access implemented between public network operators;

(c) 'operator' means an undertaking providing or authorised to provide a public communications network or an associated facility;

(d) 'wide-screen television service' means a television service that consists wholly or partially of programmes produced and edited to be displayed in a full height wide-screen format. The 16:9 format is the reference format for wide-screen television services;

(e) 'local loop' means the physical circuit connecting the network termination point at the subscriber's premises to the main distribution frame or equivalent facility in the fixed public telephone network.

CHAPTER II

GENERAL PROVISIONS

Article 3

General framework for access and interconnection

1.   Member States shall ensure that there are no restrictions which prevent undertakings in the same Member State or in different Member States from negotiating between themselves agreements on technical and commercial arrangements for access and/or interconnection, in accordance with Community law. The undertaking requesting access or interconnection does not need to be authorised to operate in the Member State where access or interconnection is requested, if it is not providing services and does not operate a network in that Member State.

2.   Without prejudice to Article 31 of Directive 2002/22/EC of the European Parliament and of the Council of 7 March 2002 on universal service and users' rights relating to electronic communications networks and services (Universal Service Directive) (¹), Member States shall not maintain legal or administrative measures which oblige operators, when granting access or interconnection, to offer different terms and conditions to different undertakings for equivalent services and/or imposing obligations that are not related to the actual access and interconnection services provided without prejudice to the conditions fixed in the Annex of Directive 2002/20/EC (Authorisation Directive).

Article 4

Rights and obligations for undertakings

1.   Operators of public communications networks shall have a right and, when requested by other undertakings so authorised, an obligation to negotiate interconnection with each other for the purpose of providing publicly available electronic communications services, in order to ensure provision and interoperability of services throughout the Community. Operators shall offer access and interconnection to other undertakings on terms and conditions consistent with obligations imposed by the national regulatory authority pursuant to Articles 5, 6, 7 and 8.

2.   Public electronic communications networks established for the distribution of digital television services shall be capable of distributing wide-screen television services and programmes. Network operators that receive and redistribute wide-screen television services or programmes shall maintain that wide-screen format.

3.   Without prejudice to Article 11 of Directive 2002/20/EC (Authorisation Directive), Member States shall require that undertakings which acquire information from another undertaking before, during or after the process of negotiating

(¹) See page 51 of this Official Journal.

access or interconnection arrangements use that information solely for the purpose for which it was supplied and respect at all times the confidentiality of information transmitted or stored. The received information shall not be passed on to any other party, in particular other departments, subsidiaries or partners, for whom such information could provide a competitive advantage.

Article 5

Powers and responsibilities of the national regulatory authorities with regard to access and interconnection

1.   National regulatory authorities shall, acting in pursuit of the objectives set out in Article 8 of Directive 2002/21/EC (Framework Directive), encourage and where appropriate ensure, in accordance with the provisions of this Directive, adequate access and interconnection, and interoperability of services, exercising their responsibility in a way that promotes efficiency, sustainable competition, and gives the maximum benefit to end-users.

In particular, without prejudice to measures that may be taken regarding undertakings with significant market power in accordance with Article 8, national regulatory authorities shall be able to impose:

(a) to the extent that is necessary to ensure end-to-end connectivity, obligations on undertakings that control access to end-users, including in justified cases the obligation to interconnect their networks where this is not already the case;

(b) to the extent that is necessary to ensure accessibility for end-users to digital radio and television broadcasting services specified by the Member State, obligations on operators to provide access to the other facilities referred to in Annex I, Part II on fair, reasonable and non-discriminatory terms.

2.   When imposing obligations on an operator to provide access in accordance with Article 12, national regulatory authorities may lay down technical or operational conditions to be met by the provider and/or beneficiaries of such access, in accordance with Community law, where necessary to ensure normal operation of the network. Conditions that refer to implementation of specific technical standards or specifications shall respect Article 17 of Directive 2002/21/EC (Framework Directive).

3.   Obligations and conditions imposed in accordance with paragraphs 1 and 2 shall be objective, transparent, proportionate and non-discriminatory, and shall be implemented in accordance with the procedures referred to in Articles 6 and 7 of Directive 2002/21/EC (Framework Directive).

4. With regard to access and interconnection, Member States shall ensure that the national regulatory authority is empowered to intervene at its own initiative where justified or, in the absence of agreement between undertakings, at the request of either of the parties involved, in order to secure the policy objectives of Article 8 of Directive 2002/21/EC (Framework Directive), in accordance with the provisions of this Directive and the procedures referred to in Articles 6 and 7, 20 and 21 of Directive 2002/21/EC (Framework Directive).

CHAPTER III

OBLIGATIONS ON OPERATORS AND MARKET REVIEW PROCEDURES

Article 6

Conditional access systems and other facilities

1. Member States shall ensure that, in relation to conditional access to digital television and radio services broadcast to viewers and listeners in the Community, irrespective of the means of transmission, the conditions laid down in Annex I, Part I apply.

2. In the light of market and technological developments, Annex I may be amended in accordance with the procedure referred to in Article 14(3).

3. Notwithstanding the provisions of paragraph 1, Member States may permit their national regulatory authority, as soon as possible after the entry into force of this Directive and periodically thereafter, to review the conditions applied in accordance with this Article, by undertaking a market analysis in accordance with the first paragraph of Article 16 of Directive 2002/21/EC (Framework Directive) to determine whether to maintain, amend or withdraw the conditions applied.

Where, as a result of this market analysis, a national regulatory authority finds that one or more operators do not have significant market power on the relevant market, it may amend or withdraw the conditions with respect to those operators, in accordance with the procedures referred to in Articles 6 and 7 of Directive 2002/21/EC (Framework Directive), only to the extent that:

(a) accessibility for end-users to radio and television broadcasts and broadcasting channels and services specified in accordance with Article 31 of Directive 2002/22/EC (Universal Service Directive) would not be adversely affected by such amendment or withdrawal, and

(b) the prospects for effective competition in the markets for:

(i) retail digital television and radio broadcasting services, and

(ii) conditional access systems and other associated facilities,

would not be adversely affected by such amendment or withdrawal.

An appropriate period of notice shall be given to parties affected by such amendment or withdrawal of conditions.

4. Conditions applied in accordance with this Article are without prejudice to the ability of Member States to impose obligations in relation to the presentational aspect of electronic programme guides and similar listing and navigation facilities.

Article 7

Review of former obligations for access and interconnection

1. Member States shall maintain all obligations on undertakings providing public communications networks and/or services concerning access and interconnection that were in force prior to the date of entry into force of this Directive under Articles 4, 6, 7, 8, 11, 12, and 14 of Directive 97/33/EC, Article 16 of Directive 98/10/EC, and Articles 7 and 8 of Directive 92/44/EC, until such time as these obligations have been reviewed and a determination made in accordance with paragraph 3.

2. The Commission will indicate relevant markets for the obligations referred to in paragraph 1 in the initial recommendation on relevant product and service markets and the Decision identifying transnational markets to be adopted in accordance with Article 15 of Directive 2002/21/EC (Framework Directive).

3. Member States shall ensure that, as soon as possible after the entry into force of this Directive, and periodically thereafter, national regulatory authorities undertake a market analysis, in accordance with Article 16 of Directive 2002/21/EC (Framework Directive) to determine whether to maintain, amend or withdraw these obligations. An appropriate period of notice shall be given to parties affected by such amendment or withdrawal of obligations.

Article 8

Imposition, amendment or withdrawal of obligations

1. Member States shall ensure that national regulatory authorities are empowered to impose the obligations identified in Articles 9 to 13.

2. Where an operator is designated as having significant market power on a specific market as a result of a market analysis carried out in accordance with Article 16 of Directive 2002/21/EC (Framework Directive), national regulatory

authorities shall impose the obligations set out in Articles 9 to 13 of this Directive as appropriate.

3.   Without prejudice to:

— the provisions of Articles 5(1), 5(2) and 6,

— the provisions of Articles 12 and 13 of Directive 2002/21/EC (Framework Directive), Condition 7 in Part B of the Annex to Directive 2002/20/EC (Authorisation Directive) as applied by virtue of Article 6(1) of that Directive, Articles 27, 28 and 30 of Directive 2002/22/EC (Universal Service Directive) and the relevant provisions of Directive 97/66/EC of the European Parliament and of the Council of 15 December 1997 concerning the processing of personal data and the protection of privacy in the telecommunications sector (¹) containing obligations on undertakings other than those designated as having significant market power, or

— the need to comply with international commitments,

national regulatory authorities shall not impose the obligations set out in Articles 9 to 13 on operators that have not been designated in accordance with paragraph 2.

In exceptional circumstances, when a national regulatory authority intends to impose on operators with significant market power other obligations for access or interconnection than those set out in Articles 9 to 13 in this Directive it shall submit this request to the Commission. The Commission, acting in accordance with Article 14(2), shall take a decision authorising or preventing the national regulatory authority from taking such measures.

4.   Obligations imposed in accordance with this Article shall be based on the nature of the problem identified, proportionate and justified in the light of the objectives laid down in Article 8 of Directive 2002/21/EC (Framework Directive). Such obligations shall only be imposed following consultation in accordance with Articles 6 and 7 of that Directive.

5.   In relation to the third indent of the first subparagraph of paragraph 3, national regulatory authorities shall notify decisions to impose, amend or withdraw obligations on market players to the Commission, in accordance with the procedure referred to in Article 7 of Directive 2002/21/EC (Framework Directive).

Article 9

Obligation of transparency

1.   National regulatory authorities may, in accordance with the provisions of Article 8, impose obligations for

(¹) OJ L 24, 30.1.1998, p. 1.

transparency in relation to interconnection and/or access, requiring operators to make public specified information, such as accounting information, technical specifications, network characteristics, terms and conditions for supply and use, and prices.

2.   In particular where an operator has obligations of non-discrimination, national regulatory authorities may require that operator to publish a reference offer, which shall be sufficiently unbundled to ensure that undertakings are not required to pay for facilities which are not necessary for the service requested, giving a description of the relevant offerings broken down into components according to market needs, and the associated terms and conditions including prices. The national regulatory authority shall, *inter alia*, be able to impose changes to reference offers to give effect to obligations imposed under this Directive.

3.   National regulatory authorities may specify the precise information to be made available, the level of detail required and the manner of publication.

4.   Notwithstanding paragraph 3, where an operator has obligations under Article 12 concerning unbundled access to the twisted metallic pair local loop, national regulatory authorities shall ensure the publication of a reference offer containing at least the elements set out in Annex II.

5.   In the light of market and technological developments, Annex II may be amended in accordance with the procedure referred to in Article 14(3).

Article 10

Obligation of non-discrimination

1.   A national regulatory authority may, in accordance with the provisions of Article 8, impose obligations of non-discrimination, in relation to interconnection and/or access.

2.   Obligations of non-discrimination shall ensure, in particular, that the operator applies equivalent conditions in equivalent circumstances to other undertakings providing equivalent services, and provides services and information to others under the same conditions and of the same quality as it provides for its own services, or those of it subsidiaries or partners.

Article 11

Obligation of accounting separation

1.   A national regulatory authority may, in accordance with the provisions of Article 8, impose obligations for accounting separation in relation to specified activities related to interconnection and/or access.

In particular, a national regulatory authority may require a vertically integrated company to make transparent its wholesale prices and its internal transfer prices *inter alia* to ensure compliance where there is a requirement for non-discrimination under Article 10 or, where necessary, to prevent unfair cross-subsidy. National regulatory authorities may specify the format and accounting methodology to be used.

2. Without prejudice to Article 5 of Directive 2002/21/EC (Framework Directive), to facilitate the verification of compliance with obligations of transparency and non-discrimination, national regulatory authorities shall have the power to require that accounting records, including data on revenues received from third parties, are provided on request. National regulatory authorities may publish such information as would contribute to an open and competitive market, while respecting national and Community rules on commercial confidentiality.

Article 12

Obligations of access to, and use of, specific network facilities

1. A national regulatory authority may, in accordance with the provisions of Article 8, impose obligations on operators to meet reasonable requests for access to, and use of, specific network elements and associated facilities, *inter alia* in situations where the national regulatory authority considers that denial of access or unreasonable terms and conditions having a similar effect would hinder the emergence of a sustainable competitive market at the retail level, or would not be in the end-user's interest.

Operators may be required *inter alia*:

(a) to give third parties access to specified network elements and/or facilities, including unbundled access to the local loop;

(b) to negotiate in good faith with undertakings requesting access;

(c) not to withdraw access to facilities already granted;

(d) to provide specified services on a wholesale basis for resale by third parties;

(e) to grant open access to technical interfaces, protocols or other key technologies that are indispensable for the interoperability of services or virtual network services;

(f) to provide co-location or other forms of facility sharing, including duct, building or mast sharing;

(g) to provide specified services needed to ensure interoperability of end-to-end services to users, including facilities for intelligent network services or roaming on mobile networks;

(h) to provide access to operational support systems or similar software systems necessary to ensure fair competition in the provision of services;

(i) to interconnect networks or network facilities.

National regulatory authorities may attach to those obligations conditions covering fairness, reasonableness and timeliness.

2. When national regulatory authorities are considering whether to impose the obligations referred in paragraph 1, and in particular when assessing whether such obligations would be proportionate to the objectives set out in Article 8 of Directive 2002/21/EC (Framework Directive), they shall take account in particular of the following factors:

(a) the technical and economic viability of using or installing competing facilities, in the light of the rate of market development, taking into account the nature and type of interconnection and access involved;

(b) the feasibility of providing the access proposed, in relation to the capacity available;

(c) the initial investment by the facility owner, bearing in mind the risks involved in making the investment;

(d) the need to safeguard competition in the long term;

(e) where appropriate, any relevant intellectual property rights;

(f) the provision of pan-European services.

Article 13

Price control and cost accounting obligations

1. A national regulatory authority may, in accordance with the provisions of Article 8, impose obligations relating to cost recovery and price controls, including obligations for cost orientation of prices and obligations concerning cost accounting systems, for the provision of specific types of interconnection and/or access, in situations where a market analysis indicates that a lack of effective competition means

that the operator concerned might sustain prices at an excessively high level, or apply a price squeeze, to the detriment of end-users. National regulatory authorities shall take into account the investment made by the operator and allow him a reasonable rate of return on adequate capital employed, taking into account the risks involved.

2. National regulatory authorities shall ensure that any cost recovery mechanism or pricing methodology that is mandated serves to promote efficiency and sustainable competition and maximise consumer benefits. In this regard national regulatory authorities may also take account of prices available in comparable competitive markets.

3. Where an operator has an obligation regarding the cost orientation of its prices, the burden of proof that charges are derived from costs including a reasonable rate of return on investment shall lie with the operator concerned. For the purpose of calculating the cost of efficient provision of services, national regulatory authorities may use cost accounting methods independent of those used by the undertaking. National regulatory authorities may require an operator to provide full justification for its prices, and may, where appropriate, require prices to be adjusted.

4. National regulatory authorities shall ensure that, where implementation of a cost accounting system is mandated in order to support price controls, a description of the cost accounting system is made publicly available, showing at least the main categories under which costs are grouped and the rules used for the allocation of costs. Compliance with the cost accounting system shall be verified by a qualified independent body. A statement concerning compliance shall be published annually.

CHAPTER IV

PROCEDURAL PROVISIONS

Article 14

Committee

1. The Commission shall be assisted by the Communications Committee set up by Article 22 of Directive 2002/21/EC (Framework Directive).

2. Where reference is made to this paragraph, Articles 3 and 7 of Decision 1999/468/EC shall apply, having regard to the provisions of Article 8 thereof.

3. Where reference is made to this paragraph, Articles 5 and 7 of Decision 1999/468/EC shall apply, having regard to the provisions of Article 8 thereof.

The period laid down in Article 5(6) of Decision 1999/468/EC shall be set at three months.

4. The Committee shall adopt its rules of procedure.

Article 15

Publication of, and access to, information

1. Member States shall ensure that the specific obligations imposed on undertakings under this Directive are published and that the specific product/service and geographical markets are identified. They shall ensure that up-to-date information, provided that the information is not confidential and, in particular, does not comprise business secrets, is made publicly available in a manner that guarantees all interested parties easy access to that information.

2. Member States shall send to the Commission a copy of all such information published. The Commission shall make this information available in a readily accessible form, and shall distribute the information to the Communications Committee as appropriate.

Article 16

Notification

1. Member States shall notify to the Commission by at the latest the date of application referred to in Article 18(1) second subparagraph the national regulatory authorities responsible for the tasks set out in this Directive.

2. National regulatory authorities shall notify to the Commission the names of operators deemed to have significant market power for the purposes of this Directive, and the obligations imposed upon them under this Directive. Any changes affecting the obligations imposed upon undertakings or of the undertakings affected under the provisions of this Directive shall be notified to the Commission without delay.

Article 17

Review procedures

The Commission shall periodically review the functioning of this Directive and report to the European Parliament and to the Council, on the first occasion not later than three years after the date of application referred to in Article 18(1), second subparagraph. For this purpose, the Commission may request from the Member States information, which shall be supplied without undue delay.

Article 18

Transposition

1. Member States shall adopt and publish the laws, regulations and administrative provisions necessary to comply with this Directive by not later than 24 July 2003. They shall forthwith inform the Commission thereof.

They shall apply those measures from 25 July 2003.

When Member States adopt these measures, they shall contain a reference to this Directive or be accompanied by such a reference on the occasion of their official publication. The methods of making such reference shall be laid down by Member States.

2. Member States shall communicate to the Commission the text of the provisions of national law which they adopt in the field governed by this Directive and of any subsequent amendments to those provisions.

Article 19

Entry into force

This Directive shall enter into force on the day of its publication in the *Official Journal of the European Communities*.

Article 20

Addressees

This Directive is addressed to the Member States.

Done at Brussels, 7 March 2002.

For the European Parliament	*For the Council*
The President	*The President*
P. COX	J. C. APARICIO

———

ANNEX I

CONDITIONS FOR ACCESS TO DIGITAL TELEVISION AND RADIO SERVICES BROADCAST TO VIEWERS AND LISTENERS IN THE COMMUNITY

Part I: Conditions for conditional access systems to be applied in accordance with Article 6(1)

In relation to conditional access to digital television and radio services broadcast to viewers and listeners in the Community, irrespective of the means of transmission, Member States must ensure in accordance with Article 6 that the following conditions apply:

(a) conditional access systems operated on the market in the Community are to have the necessary technical capability for cost-effective transcontrol allowing the possibility for full control by network operators at local or regional level of the services using such conditional access systems;

(b) all operators of conditional access services, irrespective of the means of transmission, who provide access services to digital television and radio services and whose access services broadcasters depend on to reach any group of potential viewers or listeners are to:

— offer to all broadcasters, on a fair, reasonable and non-discriminatory basis compatible with Community competition law, technical services enabling the broadcasters' digitally-transmitted services to be received by viewers or listeners authorised by means of decoders administered by the service operators, and comply with Community competition law,

— keep separate financial accounts regarding their activity as conditional access providers.

(c) when granting licences to manufacturers of consumer equipment, holders of industrial property rights to conditional access products and systems are to ensure that this is done on fair, reasonable and non-discriminatory terms. Taking into account technical and commercial factors, holders of rights are not to subject the granting of licences to conditions prohibiting, deterring or discouraging the inclusion in the same product of:

— a common interface allowing connection with several other access systems, or

— means specific to another access system, provided that the licensee complies with the relevant and reasonable conditions ensuring, as far as he is concerned, the security of transactions of conditional access system operators.

Part II: Other facilities to which conditions may be applied under Article 5(1)(b)

(a) Access to application program interfaces (APIs);

(b) Access to electronic programme guides (EPGs).

ANNEX II

MINIMUM LIST OF ITEMS TO BE INCLUDED IN A REFERENCE OFFER FOR UNBUNDLED ACCESS TO THE TWISTED METALLIC PAIR LOCAL LOOP TO BE PUBLISHED BY NOTIFIED OPERATORS

For the purposes of this Annex the following definitions apply:

(a) 'local sub-loop' means a partial local loop connecting the network termination point at the subscriber's premises to a concentration point or a specified intermediate access point in the fixed public telephone network;

(b) 'unbundled access to the local loop' means full unbundled access to the local loop and shared access to the local loop; it does not entail a change in ownership of the local loop;

(c) 'full unbundled access to the local loop' means the provision to a beneficiary of access to the local loop or local sub-loop of the notified operator authorising the use of the full frequency spectrum of the twisted metallic pair;

(d) 'shared access to the local loop' means the provision to a beneficiary of access to the local loop or local sub-loop of the notified operator, authorising the use of the non-voice band frequency spectrum of the twisted metallic pair; the local loop continues to be used by the notified operator to provide the telephone service to the public;

A. **Conditions for unbundled access to the local loop**

1. Network elements to which access is offered covering in particular the following elements:

(a) access to local loops;

(b) access to non-voice band frequency spectrum of a local loop, in the case of shared access to the local loop;

2. Information concerning the locations of physical access sites ([1]), availability of local loops in specific parts of the access network;

3. Technical conditions related to access and use of local loops, including the technical characteristics of the twisted metallic pair in the local loop;

4. Ordering and provisioning procedures, usage restrictions.

B. **Co-location services**

1. Information on the notified operator's relevant sites ([1]).

2. Co-location options at the sites indicated under point 1 (including physical co-location and, as appropriate, distant co-location and virtual co-location).

3. Equipment characteristics: restrictions, if any, on equipment that can be co-located.

4. Security issues: measures put in place by notified operators to ensure the security of their locations.

5. Access conditions for staff of competitive operators.

6. Safety standards.

7. Rules for the allocation of space where co-location space is limited.

8. Conditions for beneficiaries to inspect the locations at which physical co-location is available, or sites where co-location has been refused on grounds of lack of capacity.

([1]) Availability of this information may be restricted to interested parties only, in order to avoid public security concerns.

C. Information systems

Conditions for access to notified operator's operational support systems, information systems or databases for pre-ordering, provisioning, ordering, maintenance and repair requests and billing.

D. Supply conditions

1. Lead time for responding to requests for supply of services and facilities; service level agreements, fault resolution, procedures to return to a normal level of service and quality of service parameters.

2. Standard contract terms, including, where appropriate, compensation provided for failure to meet lead times.

3. Prices or pricing formulae for each feature, function and facility listed above.

DIRECTIVE 2002/20/EC OF THE EUROPEAN PARLIAMENT AND OF THE COUNCIL

of 7 March 2002

on the authorisation of electronic communications networks and services
(Authorisation Directive)

THE EUROPEAN PARLIAMENT AND THE COUNCIL OF THE EUROPEAN UNION,

Having regard to the Treaty establishing the European Community, and in particular Article 95 thereof,

Having regard to the proposal from the Commission (¹),

Having regard to the opinion of the Economic and Social Committee (²),

Acting in accordance with the procedure laid down in Article 251 of the Treaty (³),

Whereas:

(1) The outcome of the public consultation on the 1999 review of the regulatory framework for electronic communications, as reflected in the Commission communication of 26 April 2000, and the findings reported by the Commission in its communications on the fifth and sixth reports on the implementation of the telecommunications regulatory package, has confirmed the need for a more harmonised and less onerous market access regulation for electronic communications networks and services throughout the Community.

(2) Convergence between different electronic communications networks and services and their technologies requires the establishment of an authorisation system covering all comparable services in a similar way regardless of the technologies used.

(3) The objective of this Directive is to create a legal framework to ensure the freedom to provide electronic communications networks and services, subject only to the conditions laid down in this Directive and to any restrictions in conformity with Article 46(1) of the Treaty, in particular measures regarding public policy, public security and public health.

(4) This Directive covers authorisation of all electronic communications networks and services whether they are provided to the public or not. This is important to ensure that both categories of providers may benefit

from objective, transparent, non-discriminatory and proportionate rights, conditions and procedures.

(5) This Directive only applies to the granting of rights to use radio frequencies where such use involves the provision of an electronic communications network or service, normally for remuneration. The self-use of radio terminal equipment, based on the non-exclusive use of specific radio frequencies by a user and not related to an economic activity, such as use of a citizen's band by radio amateurs, does not consist of the provision of an electronic communications network or service and is therefore not covered by this Directive. Such use is covered by the Directive 1999/5/EC of the European Parliament and of the Council of 9 March 1999 on radio equipment and telecommunications terminal equipment and the mutual recognition of their conformity (⁴).

(6) Provisions regarding the free movement of conditional access systems and the free provision of protected services based on such systems are laid down in Directive 98/84/EC of the European Parliament and of the Council of 20 November 1998 on the legal protection of services based on, or consisting of, conditional access (⁵). The authorisation of such systems and services therefore does not need to be covered by this Directive.

(7) The least onerous authorisation system possible should be used to allow the provision of electronic communications networks and services in order to stimulate the development of new electronic communications services and pan-European communications networks and services and to allow service providers and consumers to benefit from the economies of scale of the single market.

(8) Those aims can be best achieved by general authorisation of all electronic communications networks and services without requiring any explicit decision or administrative act by the national regulatory authority and by limiting any procedural requirements to notification only. Where Member States require notification by providers of electronic communication networks or services when they start their activities,

---

(¹) OJ C 365 E, 19.12.2000, p. 230 and OJ C 270 E, 25.9.2001, p. 182.

(²) OJ C 123, 25.4.2001, p. 55.

(³) Opinion of the European Parliament of 1 March 2001 (OJ C 277, 1.10.2001, p. 116), Council Common Position of 17 September 2001 (OJ C 337, 30.11.2001, p. 18) and Decision of the European Parliament of 12 December 2001(not yet published in the Official Journal). Council Decision of 14 February 2002.

(⁴) OJ L 91, 7.4.1999, p. 10.

(⁵) OJ L 320, 28.11.1998, p. 54.

they may also require proof of such notification having been made by means of any legally recognised postal or electronic acknowledgement of receipt of the notification. Such acknowledgement should in any case not consist of or require an administrative act by the national regulatory authority to which the notification must be made.

(9) It is necessary to include the rights and obligations of undertakings under general authorisations explicitly in such authorisations in order to ensure a level playing field throughout the Community and to facilitate cross-border negotiation of interconnection between public communications networks.

(10) The general authorisation entitles undertakings providing electronic communications networks and services to the public to negotiate interconnection under the conditions of Directive 2002/19/EC of the European Parliament and of the Council of 7 March 2002 on access to, and interconnection of, electronic communication networks and associated facilities (Access Directive) (¹). Undertakings providing electronic communications networks and services other than to the public can negotiate interconnection on commercial terms.

(11) The granting of specific rights may continue to be necessary for the use of radio frequencies and numbers, including short codes, from the national numbering plan. Rights to numbers may also be allocated from a European numbering plan, including for example the virtual country code '3883' which has been attributed to member countries of the European Conference of Post and Telecommunications (CEPT). Those rights of use should not be restricted except where this is unavoidable in view of the scarcity of radio frequencies and the need to ensure the efficient use thereof.

(12) This Directive does not prejudice whether radio frequencies are assigned directly to providers of electronic communication networks or services or to entities that use these networks or services. Such entities may be radio or television broadcast content providers. Without prejudice to specific criteria and procedures adopted by Member States to grant rights of use for radio frequencies to providers of radio or television broadcast content services, to pursue general interest objectives in conformity with Community law, the procedure for assignment of radio frequencies should in any event be objective, transparent, non-discriminatory and proportionate. In accordance with case law of the Court of Justice, any national restrictions on the rights guaranteed by Article 49 of the Treaty should be objectively justified, proportionate and not exceed what is necessary to achieve general interest objectives as defined by Member States in conformity with Community law. The responsibility for compliance with the conditions attached to the right to use a radio frequency and the relevant conditions attached to the general authorisation should in any case lie with the undertaking to whom the right of use for the radio frequency has been granted.

(13) As part of the application procedure for granting rights to use a radio frequency, Member States may verify whether the applicant will be able to comply with the conditions attached to such rights. For this purpose the applicant may be requested to submit the necessary information to prove his ability to comply with these conditions. Where such information is not provided, the application for the right to use a radio frequency may be rejected.

(14) Member States are neither obliged to grant nor prevented from granting rights to use numbers from the national numbering plan or rights to install facilities to undertakings other than providers of electronic communications networks or services.

(15) The conditions, which may be attached to the general authorisation and to the specific rights of use, should be limited to what is strictly necessary to ensure compliance with requirements and obligations under Community law and national law in accordance with Community law.

(16) In the case of electronic communications networks and services not provided to the public it is appropriate to impose fewer and lighter conditions than are justified for electronic communications networks and services provided to the public.

(17) Specific obligations which may be imposed on providers of electronic communications networks and services in accordance with Community law by virtue of their significant market power as defined in Directive 2002/21/EC of the European Parliament and of the Council of 7 March 2002 on a common regulatory framework for electronic communications networks and services (Framework Directive) (²) should be imposed separately from the general rights and obligations under the general authorisation.

(18) The general authorisation should only contain conditions which are specific to the electronic communications sector. It should not be made subject

---

(¹) See page 7 of this Official Journal.

(²) See page 33 of this Official Journal.

to conditions which are already applicable by virtue of other existing national law which is not specific to the electronic communications sector. Nevertheless, the national regulatory authorities may inform network operators and service providers about other legislation concerning their business, for instance through references on their websites.

(19) The requirement to publish decisions on the granting of rights to use frequencies or numbers may be fulfilled by making these decisions publicly accessible via a website.

(20) The same undertaking, for example a cable operator, can offer both an electronic communications service, such as the conveyance of television signals, and services not covered under this Directive, such as the commercialisation of an offer of sound or television broadcasting content services, and therefore additional obligations can be imposed on this undertaking in relation to its activity as a content provider or distributor, according to provisions other than those of this Directive, without prejudice to the list of conditions laid in the Annex to this Directive.

(21) When granting rights of use for radio frequencies, numbers or rights to install facilities, the relevant authorities may inform the undertakings to whom they grant such rights of the relevant conditions in the general authorisation.

(22) Where the demand for radio frequencies in a specific range exceeds their availability, appropriate and transparent procedures should be followed for the assignment of such frequencies in order to avoid any discrimination and optimise use of those scarce resources.

(23) National regulatory authorities should ensure, in establishing criteria for competitive or comparative selection procedures, that the objectives in Article 8 of Directive 2002/21/EC (Framework Directive) are met. It would therefore not be contrary to this Directive if the application of objective, non-discriminatory and proportionate selection criteria to promote the development of competition would have the effect of excluding certain undertakings from a competitive or comparative selection procedure for a particular radio frequency.

(24) Where the harmonised assignment of radio frequencies to particular undertakings has been agreed at European level, Member States should strictly implement such agreements in the granting of rights of use of radio frequencies from the national frequency usage plan.

(25) Providers of electronic communications networks and services may need a confirmation of their rights under the general authorisation with respect to interconnection and rights of way, in particular to facilitate negotiations with other, regional or local, levels of government or with service providers in other Member States. For this purpose the national regulatory authorities should provide declarations to undertakings either upon request or alternatively as an automatic response to a notification under the general authorisation. Such declarations should not by themselves constitute entitlements to rights nor should any rights under the general authorisation or rights of use or the exercise of such rights depend upon a declaration.

(26) Where undertakings find that their applications for rights to install facilities have not been dealt with in accordance with the principles set out in Directive 2002/21/EC (Framework Directive) or where such decisions are unduly delayed, they should have the right to appeal against decisions or delays in such decisions in accordance with that Directive.

(27) The penalties for non-compliance with conditions under the general authorisation should be commensurate with the infringement. Save in exceptional circumstances, it would not be proportionate to suspend or withdraw the right to provide electronic communications services or the right to use radio frequencies or numbers where an undertaking did not comply with one or more of the conditions under the general authorisation. This is without prejudice to urgent measures which the relevant authorities of the Member States may need to take in case of serious threats to public safety, security or health or to economic and operational interests of other undertakings. This Directive should also be without prejudice to any claims between undertakings for compensation for damages under national law.

(28) Subjecting service providers to reporting and information obligations can be cumbersome, both for the undertaking and for the national regulatory authority concerned. Such obligations should therefore be proportionate, objectively justified and limited to what is strictly necessary. It is not necessary to require systematic and regular proof of compliance with all conditions under the general authorisation or attached to rights of use. Undertakings have a right to know the purposes for which the information they should provide will be used. The provision of information should not be a condition for market access. For statistical purposes a notification may be required from providers of electronic communication networks or services when they cease activities.

(29) This Directive should be without prejudice to Member States' obligations to provide any information necessary for the defence of Community interests within the context of international agreements. This Directive should also be without prejudice to any reporting obligations under legislation which is not specific to the electronic communications sector such as competition law.

(30) Administrative charges may be imposed on providers of electronic communications services in order to finance the activities of the national regulatory authority in managing the authorisation system and for the granting of rights of use. Such charges should be limited to cover the actual administrative costs for those activities. For this purpose transparency should be created in the income and expenditure of national regulatory authorities by means of annual reporting about the total sum of charges collected and the administrative costs incurred. This will allow undertakings to verify that administrative costs and charges are in balance.

(31) Systems for administrative charges should not distort competition or create barriers for entry into the market. With a general authorisation system it will no longer be possible to attribute administrative costs and hence charges to individual undertakings except for the granting of rights to use numbers, radio frequencies and for rights to install facilities. Any applicable administrative charges should be in line with the principles of a general authorisation system. An example of a fair, simple and transparent alternative for these charge attribution criteria could be a turnover related distribution key. Where administrative charges are very low, flat rate charges, or charges combining a flat rate basis with a turnover related element could also be appropriate.

(32) In addition to administrative charges, usage fees may be levied for the use of radio frequencies and numbers as an instrument to ensure the optimal use of such resources. Such fees should not hinder the development of innovative services and competition in the market. This Directive is without prejudice to the purpose for which fees for rights of use are employed. Such fees may for instance be used to finance activities of national regulatory authorities that cannot be covered by administrative charges. Where, in the case of competitive or comparative selection procedures, fees for rights of use for radio frequencies consist entirely or partly of a one-off amount, payment arrangements should ensure that such fees do not in practice lead to selection on the basis of criteria unrelated to the objective of ensuring optimal use of radio frequencies. The Commission may publish on a regular basis

benchmark studies with regard to best practices for the assignment of radio frequencies, the assignment of numbers or the granting of rights of way.

(33) Member States may need to amend rights, conditions, procedures, charges and fees relating to general authorisations and rights of use where this is objectively justified. Such changes should be duly notified to all interested parties in good time, giving them adequate opportunity to express their views on any such amendments.

(34) The objective of transparency requires that service providers, consumers and other interested parties have easy access to any information regarding rights, conditions, procedures, charges, fees and decisions concerning the provision of electronic communications services, rights of use of radio frequencies and numbers, rights to install facilities, national frequency usage plans and national numbering plans. The national regulatory authorities have an important task in providing such information and keeping it up to date. Where such rights are administered by other levels of government the national regulatory authorities should endeavour to create a user-friendly instrument for access to information regarding such rights.

(35) The proper functioning of the single market on the basis of the national authorisation regimes under this Directive should be monitored by the Commission.

(36) In order to arrive at a single date of application of all elements of the new regulatory framework for the electronic communications sector, it is important that the process of national transposition of this Directive and of alignment of the existing licences with the new rules take place in parallel. However, in specific cases where the replacement of authorisations existing on the date of entry into force of this Directive by the general authorisation and the individual rights of use in accordance with this Directive would lead to an increase in the obligations for service providers operating under an existing authorisation or to a reduction of their rights, Member States may avail themselves of an additional nine months after the date of application of this Directive for alignment of such licences, unless this would have a negative effect on the rights and obligations of other undertakings.

(37) There may be circumstances under which the abolition of an authorisation condition regarding access to electronic communications networks would create serious hardship for one or more undertakings that have benefited from the condition. In such cases further transitional arrangements may be granted by the Commission, upon request by a Member State.

(38) Since the objectives of the proposed action, namely the harmonisation and simplification of electronic communications rules and conditions for the authorisation of networks and services cannot be sufficiently achieved by the Member States and can therefore, by reason of the scale and effects of the action, be better achieved at Community level, the Community may adopt measures in accordance with the principle of subsidiarity as set out in Article 5 of the Treaty. In accordance with the principle of proportionality, as set out in that Article, this Directive does not go beyond what is necessary for those objectives,

HAVE ADOPTED THIS DIRECTIVE:

Article 1

Objective and scope

1. The aim of this Directive is to implement an internal market in electronic communications networks and services through the harmonisation and simplification of authorisation rules and conditions in order to facilitate their provision throughout the Community.

2. This Directive shall apply to authorisations for the provision of electronic communications networks and services.

Article 2

Definitions

1. For the purposes of this Directive, the definitions set out in Article 2 of Directive 2002/21/EC (Framework Directive) shall apply.

2. The following definitions shall also apply:

(a) 'general authorisation' means a legal framework established by the Member State ensuring rights for the provision of electronic communications networks or services and laying down sector specific obligations that may apply to all or to specific types of electronic communications networks and services, in accordance with this Directive;

(b) 'harmful interference' means interference which endangers the functioning of a radionavigation service or of other safety services or which otherwise seriously degrades, obstructs or repeatedly interrupts a radiocommunications service operating in accordance with the applicable Community or national regulations.

Article 3

General authorisation of electronic communications networks and services

1. Member States shall ensure the freedom to provide electronic communications networks and services, subject to the conditions set out in this Directive. To this end, Member States shall not prevent an undertaking from providing electronic communications networks or services, except where this is necessary for the reasons set out in Article 46(1) of the Treaty.

2. The provision of electronic communications networks or the provision of electronic communications services may, without prejudice to the specific obligations referred to in Article 6(2) or rights of use referred to in Article 5, only be subject to a general authorisation. The undertaking concerned may be required to submit a notification but may not be required to obtain an explicit decision or any other administrative act by the national regulatory authority before exercising the rights stemming from the authorisation. Upon notification, when required, an undertaking may begin activity, where necessary subject to the provisions on rights of use in Articles 5, 6 and 7.

3. The notification referred to in paragraph 2 shall not entail more than a declaration by a legal or natural person to the national regulatory authority of the intention to commence the provision of electronic communication networks or services and the submission of the minimal information which is required to allow the national regulatory authority to keep a register or list of providers of electronic communications networks and services. This information must be limited to what is necessary for the identification of the provider, such as company registration numbers, and the provider's contact persons, the provider's address, a short description of the network or service, and an estimated date for starting the activity.

Article 4

Minimum list of rights derived from the general authorisation

1. Undertakings authorised pursuant to Article 3, shall have the right to:

(a) provide electronic communications networks and services;

(b) have their application for the necessary rights to install facilities considered in accordance with Article 11 of Directive 2002/21/EC (Framework Directive).

2. When such undertakings provide electronic communications networks or services to the public the general authorisation shall also give them the right to:

(a) negotiate interconnection with and where applicable obtain access to or interconnection from other providers of publicly available communications networks and services covered by a general authorisation anywhere in the Community under the conditions of and in accordance with Directive 2002/19/EC (Access Directive);

(b) be given an opportunity to be designated to provide different elements of a universal service and/or to cover different parts of the national territory in accordance with Directive 2002/22/EC of the European Parliament and of the Council of 7 March 2002 on universal service and users' rights relating to electronic communications networks and services (Universal Service Directive) (¹).

Article 5

Rights of use for radio frequencies and numbers

1.   Member States shall, where possible, in particular where the risk of harmful interference is negligible, not make the use of radio frequencies subject to the grant of individual rights of use but shall include the conditions for usage of such radio frequencies in the general authorisation.

2.   Where it is necessary to grant individual rights of use for radio frequencies and numbers, Member States shall grant such rights, upon request, to any undertaking providing or using networks or services under the general authorisation, subject to the provisions of Articles 6, 7 and 11(1)(c) of this Directive and any other rules ensuring the efficient use of those resources in accordance with Directive 2002/21/EC (Framework Directive).

Without prejudice to specific criteria and procedures adopted by Member States to grant rights of use of radio frequencies to providers of radio or television broadcast content services with a view to pursuing general interest objectives in conformity with Community law, such rights of use shall be granted through open, transparent and non-discriminatory procedures. When granting rights of use, Member States shall specify whether those rights can be transferred at the initiative of the right holder, and under which conditions, in the case of radio frequencies, in accordance with Article 9 of Directive 2002/21/EC (Framework Directive). Where Member States grant rights of use for a limited period of time, the duration shall be appropriate for the service concerned.

3.   Decisions on rights of use shall be taken, communicated and made public as soon as possible after receipt of the complete application by the national regulatory authority, within three weeks in the case of numbers that have been allocated for specific purposes within the national numbering plan and within six weeks in the case of radio frequencies that have been allocated for specific purposes within the national

(¹) See page 51 of this Official Journal.

frequency plan. The latter time limit shall be without prejudice to any applicable international agreements relating to the use of radio frequencies or of orbital positions.

4.   Where it has been decided, after consultation with interested parties in accordance with Article 6 of Directive 2002/21/EC (Framework Directive), that rights for use of numbers of exceptional economic value are to be granted through competitive or comparative selection procedures, Member States may extend the maximum period of three weeks by up to three weeks.

With regard to competitive or comparative selection procedures for radio frequencies Article 7 shall apply.

5.   Member States shall not limit the number of rights of use to be granted except where this is necessary to ensure the efficient use of radio frequencies in accordance with Article 7.

Article 6

Conditions attached to the general authorisation and to the rights of use for radio frequencies and for numbers, and specific obligations

1.   The general authorisation for the provision of electronic communications networks or services and the rights of use for radio frequencies and rights of use for numbers may be subject only to the conditions listed respectively in parts A, B and C of the Annex. Such conditions shall be objectively justified in relation to the network or service concerned, non-discriminatory, proportionate and transparent.

2.   Specific obligations which may be imposed on providers of electronic communications networks and services under Articles 5(1), 5(2), 6 and 8 of Directive 2002/19/EC (Access Directive) and Articles 16, 17, 18 and 19 of Directive 2002/22/EC (Universal Service Directive) or on those designated to provide universal service under the said Directive shall be legally separate from the rights and obligations under the general authorisation. In order to achieve transparency for undertakings, the criteria and procedures for imposing such specific obligations on individual undertakings shall be referred to in the general authorisation.

3.   The general authorisation shall only contain conditions which are specific for that sector and are set out in Part A of the Annex and shall not duplicate conditions which are applicable to undertakings by virtue of other national legislation.

4.   Member States shall not duplicate the conditions of the general authorisation where they grant the right of use for radio frequencies or numbers.

Article 7

Procedure for limiting the number of rights of use to be granted for radio frequencies

1. Where a Member State is considering whether to limit the number of rights of use to be granted for radio frequencies, it shall *inter alia*:

(a) give due weight to the need to maximise benefits for users and to facilitate the development of competition;

(b) give all interested parties, including users and consumers, the opportunity to express their views on any limitation in accordance with Article 6 of Directive 2002/21/EC (Framework Directive);

(c) publish any decision to limit the granting of rights of use, stating the reasons therefor;

(d) after having determined the procedure, invite applications for rights of use; and

(e) review the limitation at reasonable intervals or at the reasonable request of affected undertakings.

2. Where a Member State concludes that further rights of use for radio frequencies can be granted, it shall publish that conclusion and invite applications for such rights.

3. Where the granting of rights of use for radio frequencies needs to be limited, Member States shall grant such rights on the basis of selection criteria which must be objective, transparent, non-discriminatory and proportionate. Any such selection criteria must give due weight to the achievement of the objectives of Article 8 of Directive 2002/21/EC (Framework Directive).

4. Where competitive or comparative selection procedures are to be used, Member States may extend the maximum period of six weeks referred to in Article 5(3) for as long as necessary to ensure that such procedures are fair, reasonable, open and transparent to all interested parties, but by no longer than eight months.

These time limits shall be without prejudice to any applicable international agreements relating to the use of radio frequencies and satellite coordination.

5. This Article is without prejudice to the transfer of rights of use for radio frequencies in accordance with Article 9 of Directive 2002/21/EC (Framework Directive).

Article 8

Harmonised assignment of radio frequencies

Where the usage of radio frequencies has been harmonised, access conditions and procedures have been agreed, and

undertakings to which the radio frequencies shall be assigned have been selected in accordance with international agreements and Community rules, Member States shall grant the right of use for such radio frequencies in accordance therewith. Provided that all national conditions attached to the right to use the radio frequencies concerned have been satisfied in the case of a common selection procedure, Member States shall not impose any further conditions, additional criteria or procedures which would restrict, alter or delay the correct implementation of the common assignment of such radio frequencies.

Article 9

Declarations to facilitate the exercise of rights to install facilities and rights of interconnection

At the request of an undertaking, national regulatory authorities shall, within one week, issue standardised declarations, confirming, where applicable, that the undertaking has submitted a notification under Article 3(2) and detailing under what circumstances any undertaking providing electronic communications networks or services under the general authorisation has the right to apply for rights to install facilities, negotiate interconnection, and/or obtain access or interconnection in order to facilitate the exercise of those rights for instance at other levels of government or in relation to other undertakings. Where appropriate such declarations may also be issued as an automatic reply following the notification referred to in Article 3(2).

Article 10

Compliance with the conditions of the general authorisation or of rights of use and with specific obligations

1. National regulatory authorities may require undertakings providing electronic communications networks or services covered by the general authorisation or enjoying rights of use for radio frequencies or numbers to provide information necessary to verify compliance with the conditions of the general authorisation or of rights of use or with the specific obligations referred to in Article 6(2), in accordance with Article 11.

2. Where a national regulatory authority finds that an undertaking does not comply with one or more of the conditions of the general authorisation, or of rights of use or with the specific obligations referred to in Article 6(2), it shall notify the undertaking of those findings and give the undertaking a reasonable opportunity to state its views or remedy any breaches within:

— one month after notification, or

— a shorter period agreed by the undertaking or stipulated by the national regulatory authority in case of repeated breaches, or

— a longer period decided by the national regulatory authority.

3. If the undertaking concerned does not remedy the breaches within the period as referred to in paragraph 2, the relevant authority shall take appropriate and proportionate measures aimed at ensuring compliance. In this regard, Member States may empower the relevant authorities to impose financial penalties where appropriate. The measures and the reasons on which they are based shall be communicated to the undertaking concerned within one week of their adoption and shall stipulate a reasonable period for the undertaking to comply with the measure.

4. Notwithstanding the provisions of paragraphs 2 and 3, Member States may empower the relevant authority to impose financial penalties where appropriate on undertakings for failure to provide information in accordance with obligations imposed under Article 11(1)(a) or (b) of this Directive or Article 9 of Directive 2002/19/EC (Access Directive) within a reasonable period stipulated by the national regulatory authority.

5. In cases of serious and repeated breaches of the conditions of the general authorisation, the rights of use or specific obligations referred to in Article 6(2), where measures aimed at ensuring compliance as referred to in paragraph 3 of this Article have failed, national regulatory authorities may prevent an undertaking from continuing to provide electronic communications networks or services or suspend or withdraw rights of use.

6. Irrespective of the provisions of paragraphs 2, 3 and 5, where the relevant authority has evidence of a breach of the conditions of the general authorisation, rights of use or specific obligations referred to in Article 6(2) that represents an immediate and serious threat to public safety, public security or public health or will create serious economic or operational problems for other providers or users of electronic communications networks or services, it may take urgent interim measures to remedy the situation in advance of reaching a final decision. The undertaking concerned shall thereafter be given a reasonable opportunity to state its view and propose any remedies. Where appropriate, the relevant authority may confirm the interim measures.

7. Undertakings shall have the right to appeal against measures taken under this Article in accordance with the procedure referred to in Article 4 of Directive 2002/21/EC (Framework Directive).

Article 11

Information required under the general authorisation, for rights of use and for the specific obligations

1. Without prejudice to information and reporting obligations under national legislation other than the general authorisation, national regulatory authorities may only require undertakings to provide information under the general authorisation, for rights of use or the specific obligations referred to in Article 6(2) that is proportionate and objectively justified for:

(a) systematic or case-by-case verification of compliance with conditions 1 and 2 of Part A, condition 6 of Part B and condition 7 of Part C of the Annex and of compliance with obligations as referred to in Article 6(2);

(b) case-by-case verification of compliance with conditions as set out in the Annex where a complaint has been received or where the national regulatory authority has other reasons to believe that a condition is not complied with or in case of an investigation by the national regulatory authority on its own initiative;

(c) procedures for and assessment of requests for granting rights of use;

(d) publication of comparative overviews of quality and price of services for the benefit of consumers;

(e) clearly defined statistical purposes;

(f) market analysis for the purposes of Directive 2002/19/EC (Access Directive) or Directive 2002/22/EC (Universal Service Directive).

The information referred to in points (a), (b), (d), (e) and (f) of the first subparagraph may not be required prior to or as a condition for market access.

2. Where national regulatory authorities require undertakings to provide information as referred to in paragraph 1, they shall inform them of the specific purpose for which this information is to be used.

Article 12

Administrative charges

1. Any administrative charges imposed on undertakings providing a service or a network under the general authorisation or to whom a right of use has been granted shall:

(a) in total, cover only the administrative costs which will be incurred in the management, control and enforcement of the general authorisation scheme and of rights of use and of specific obligations as referred to in Article 6(2), which may include costs for international cooperation, harmonisation and standardisation, market analysis, monitoring compliance and other market control, as well as regulatory work involving preparation and enforcement of secondary legislation and administrative decisions, such as decisions on access and interconnection; and

(b) be imposed upon the individual undertakings in an objective, transparent and proportionate manner which minimises additional administrative costs and attendant charges.

2. Where national regulatory authorities impose administrative charges, they shall publish a yearly overview of their administrative costs and of the total sum of the charges collected. In the light of the difference between the total sum of the charges and the administrative costs, appropriate adjustments shall be made.

Article 13

Fees for rights of use and rights to install facilities

Member States may allow the relevant authority to impose fees for the rights of use for radio frequencies or numbers or rights to install facilities on, over or under public or private property which reflect the need to ensure the optimal use of these resources. Member States shall ensure that such fees shall be objectively justified, transparent, non-discriminatory and proportionate in relation to their intended purpose and shall take into account the objectives in Article 8 of Directive 2002/21/EC (Framework Directive).

Article 14

Amendment of rights and obligations

1. Member States shall ensure that the rights, conditions and procedures concerning general authorisations and rights of use or rights to install facilities may only be amended in objectively justified cases and in a proportionate manner. Notice shall be given in an appropriate manner of the intention to make such amendments and interested parties, including users and consumers, shall be allowed a sufficient period of time to express their views on the proposed amendments, which shall be no less than four weeks except in exceptional circumstances.

2. Member States shall not restrict or withdraw rights to install facilities before expiry of the period for which they were granted except where justified and where applicable in conformity with relevant national provisions regarding compensation for withdrawal of rights.

Article 15

Publication of information

1. Member States shall ensure that all relevant information on rights, conditions, procedures, charges, fees and decisions concerning general authorisations and rights of use is published and kept up to date in an appropriate manner so as to provide easy access to that information for all interested parties.

2. Where information as referred to in paragraph 1 is held at different levels of government, in particular information regarding procedures and conditions on rights to install facilities, the national regulatory authority shall make all reasonable efforts, bearing in mind the costs involved, to create a user-friendly overview of all such information, including information on the relevant levels of government and the responsible authorities, in order to facilitate applications for rights to install facilities.

Article 16

Review procedures

The Commission shall periodically review the functioning of the national authorisation systems and the development of cross-border service provision within the Community and report to the European Parliament and to the Council on the first occasion not later than three years after the date of application of this Directive referred to in Article 18(1), second subparagraph. For this purpose, the Commission may request from the Member States information, which shall be supplied without undue delay.

Article 17

Existing authorisations

1. Member States shall bring authorisations already in existence on the date of entry into force of this Directive into line with the provisions of this Directive by at the latest the date of application referred to in Article 18(1), second subparagraph.

2. Where application of paragraph 1 results in a reduction of the rights or an extension of the obligations under authorisations already in existence, Member States may extend the validity of those rights and obligations until at the latest nine months after the date of application referred to in Article 18(1), second subparagraph, provided that the rights of other undertakings under Community law are not affected thereby. Member States shall notify such extensions to the Commission and state the reasons therefor.

3. Where the Member State concerned can prove that the abolition of an authorisation condition regarding access to electronic communications networks, which was in force before the date of entry into force of this Directive, creates excessive difficulties for undertakings that have benefited from mandated access to another network, and where it is not possible for these undertakings to negotiate new agreements on reasonable commercial terms before the date of application referred to in Article 18(1), second subparagraph, Member States may request a temporary prolongation of the relevant condition(s). Such requests shall be submitted by the date of application referred to in Article 18(1), second subparagraph,

at the latest, and shall specify the condition(s) and period for which the temporary prolongation is requested.

The Member State shall inform the Commission of the reasons for requesting a prolongation. The Commission shall consider such a request, taking into account the particular situation in that Member State and of the undertaking(s) concerned, and the need to ensure a coherent regulatory environment at a Community level. It shall take a decision on whether to grant or reject the request, and where it decides to grant the request, on the scope and duration of the prolongation to be granted. The Commission shall communicate its decision to the Member State concerned within six months after receipt of the application for a prolongation. Such decisions shall be published in the *Official Journal of the European Communities*.

Article 18

Transposition

1.   Member States shall adopt and publish the laws, regulations and administrative provisions necessary to comply with this Directive by 24 July 2003 at the latest. They shall forthwith inform the Commission thereof.

They shall apply those measures from 25 July 2003.

When Member States adopt these measures, they shall contain a reference to this Directive or be accompanied by such reference on the occasion of their official publication. The methods of making such reference shall be laid down by Member States.

2.   Member States shall communicate to the Commission the text of the provisions of national law which they adopt in the field governed by this Directive and of any subsequent amendments to those provisions.

Article 19

Entry into force

This Directive shall enter into force on the day of its publication in the *Official Journal of the European Communities*.

Article 20

Addressees

This Directive is addressed to the Member States.

Done at Brussels, 7 March 2002.

For the European Parliament	*For the Council*
The President	*The President*
P. COX	J. C. APARICIO

ANNEX

The conditions listed in this Annex provide the maximum list of conditions which may be attached to general authorisations (Part A), rights to use radio frequencies (Part B) and rights to use numbers (Part C) as referred to in Article 6(1) and Article 11(1)(a).

A. **Conditions which may be attached to a general authorisation**

1. Financial contributions to the funding of universal service in conformity with Directive 2002/22/EC (Universal Service Directive).

2. Administrative charges in accordance with Article 12 of this Directive.

3. Interoperability of services and interconnection of networks in conformity with Directive 2002/19/EC (Access Directive).

4. Accessibility of numbers from the national numbering plan to end-users including conditions in conformity with Directive 2002/22/EC (Universal Service Directive).

5. Environmental and town and country planning requirements, as well as requirements and conditions linked to the granting of access to or use of public or private land and conditions linked to co-location and facility sharing in conformity with Directive 2002/22/EC (Framework Directive) and including, where applicable, any financial or technical guarantees necessary to ensure the proper execution of infrastructure works.

6. 'Must carry' obligations in conformity with Directive 2002/22/EC (Universal Service Directive).

7. Personal data and privacy protection specific to the electronic communications sector in conformity with Directive 97/66/EC of the European Parliament and of the Council of 15 December 1997 concerning the processing of personal data and the protection of privacy in the telecommunications sector [1].

8. Consumer protection rules specific to the electronic communications sector including conditions in conformity with Directive 2002/22/EC (Universal Service Directive).

9. Restrictions in relation to the transmission of illegal content, in accordance with Directive 2000/31/EC of the European Parliament and of the Council of 8 June 2000 on certain legal aspects of information society services, in particular electronic commerce, in the internal market [2] and restrictions in relation to the transmission of harmful content in accordance with Article 2a(2) of Council Directive 89/552/EEC of 3 October 1989 on the coordination of certain provisions laid down by law, regulation or administrative action in Member States concerning the pursuit of television broadcasting activities [3].

10. Information to be provided under a notification procedure in accordance with Article 3(3) of this Directive and for other purposes as included in Article 11 of this Directive.

11. Enabling of legal interception by competent national authorities in conformity with Directive 97/66/EC and Directive 95/46/EC of the European Parliament and of the Council of 24 October 1995 on the protection of individuals with regard to the processing of personal data and on the free movement of such data [4].

12. Terms of use during major disasters to ensure communications between emergency services and authorities and broadcasts to the general public.

13. Measures regarding the limitation of exposure of the general public to electromagnetic fields caused by electronic communications networks in accordance with Community law.

14. Access obligations other than those provided for in Article 6(2) of this Directive applying to undertakings providing electronic communications networks or services, in conformity with Directive 2002/19/EC (Access Directive).

---

[1] OJ L 24, 30.1.1998, p. 1.
[2] OJ L 178, 17.7.2000, p. 1.
[3] OJ L 298, 17.10.1989, p. 23. Directive as amended by Directive 97/36/EC of the European Parliament and of the Council (OJ L 202, 30.7.1997, p. 60).
[4] OJ L 281, 23.11.1995, p. 31.

15. Maintenance of the integrity of public communications networks in accordance with Directive 2002/19/EC (Access Directive) and Directive 2002/22/EC (Universal Service Directive) including by conditions to prevent electromagnetic interference between electronic communications networks and/or services in accordance with Council Directive 89/336/EEC of 3 May 1989 on the approximation of the laws of the Member States relating to electromagnetic compatibility ([1]).

16. Security of public networks against unauthorised access according to Directive 97/66/EC.

17. Conditions for the use of radio frequencies, in conformity with Article 7(2) of Directive 1999/5/EC, where such use is not made subject to the granting of individual rights of use in accordance with Article 5(1) of this Directive.

18. Measures designed to ensure compliance with the standards and/or specifications referred to in Article 17 of Directive 2002/21/EC (Framework Directive).

B. **Conditions which may be attached to rights of use for radio frequencies**

1. Designation of service or type of network or technology for which the rights of use for the frequency has been granted, including, where applicable, the exclusive use of a frequency for the transmission of specific content or specific audiovisual services.

2. Effective and efficient use of frequencies in conformity with Directive 2002/21/EC (Framework Directive), including, where appropriate, coverage requirements.

3. Technical and operational conditions necessary for the avoidance of harmful interference and for the limitation of exposure of the general public to electromagnetic fields, where such conditions are different from those included in the general authorisation.

4. Maximum duration in conformity with Article 5 of this Directive, subject to any changes in the national frequency plan.

5. Transfer of rights at the initiative of the right holder and conditions for such transfer in conformity with Directive 2002/21/EC (Framework Directive).

6. Usage fees in accordance with Article 13 of this Directive.

7. Any commitments which the undertaking obtaining the usage right has made in the course of a competitive or comparative selection procedure.

8. Obligations under relevant international agreements relating to the use of frequencies.

C. **Conditions which may be attached to rights of use for numbers**

1. Designation of service for which the number shall be used, including any requirements linked to the provision of that service.

2. Effective and efficient use of numbers in conformity with Directive 2002/21/EC (Framework Directive).

3. Number portability requirements in conformity with Directive 2002/22/EC (Universal Service Directive).

4. Obligation to provide public directory subscriber information for the purposes of Articles 5 and 25 of Directive 2002/22/EC (Universal Service Directive).

5. Maximum duration in conformity with Article 5 of this Directive, subject to any changes in the national numbering plan.

6. Transfer of rights at the initiative of the right holder and conditions for such transfer in conformity with Directive 2002/21/EC (Framework Directive).

7. Usage fees in accordance with Article 13 of this Directive.

8. Any commitments which the undertaking obtaining the usage right has made in the course of a competitive or comparative selection procedure.

9. Obligations under relevant international agreements relating to the use of numbers.

([1]) OJ L 139, 23.5.1989, p. 19. Directive as last amended by Directive 93/68/EEC (OJ L 220, 30.8.1993, p. 1).

COMMISSION DIRECTIVE 2002/77/EC

of 16 September 2002

on competition in the markets for electronic communications networks and services

(Text with EEA relevance)

THE COMMISSION OF THE EUROPEAN COMMUNITIES,

Having regard to the Treaty establishing the European Community, and in particular Article 86(3) thereof,

Whereas:

(1) Commission Directive 90/388/EEC of 28 June 1990 on competition in the markets for telecommunications services (^{1}), as last amended by Directive 1999/64/EC (^{2}), has been substantially amended several times. Since further amendments are to be made, it should be recast in the interest of clarity.

(2) Article 86 of the Treaty entrusts the Commission with the task of ensuring that, in the case of public undertakings and undertakings enjoying special or exclusive rights, Member States comply with their obligations under Community law. Pursuant to Article 86(3), the Commission can specify and clarify the obligations arising from that Article and, in that framework, set out the conditions which are necessary to allow the Commission to perform effectively the duty of surveillance imposed upon it by that paragraph.

(3) Directive 90/388/EEC required Member States to abolish special and exclusive rights for the provision of telecommunications services, initially for other services than voice telephony, satellite services and mobile radiocommunications, and then it gradually established full competition in the telecommunications market.

(4) A number of other Directives in this field have also been adopted under Article 95 of the Treaty by the European Parliament and the Council aiming, principally, at the establishment of an internal market for telecommunications services through the implementation of open network provision and the provision of a universal service in an environment of open and competitive markets. Those Directives should be repealed with effect from 25 July 2003 when the new regulatory framework for electronic communications networks and services is applied.

(5) The new electronic communications regulatory framework consists of one general Directive, Directive 2002/21/EC of the European Parliament and of the Council of

7 March 2002 on a common regulatory framework for electronic communications networks and services (Framework Directive) (^{3}) and four specific Directives: Directive 2002/20/EC of the European Parliament and of the Council of 7 March 2002 on the authorisation of electronic communications networks and services (Authorisation Directive) (^{4}), Directive 2002/19/EC of the European Parliament and of the Council of 7 March 2002 on access to, and interconnection of, electronic communications networks and associated facilities (Access Directive) (^{5}), Directive 2002/22/EC of the European Parliament and of the Council of 7 March 2002 on universal service and users' rights relating to electronic communications networks and services (Universal Service Directive) (^{6}), and Directive 2002/58/EC of the European Parliament and of the Council of 12 July 2002 concerning the processing of personal data and the protection of privacy in the electronic communications (Directive on privacy and electronic communications) sector (^{7}).

(6) In the light of the developments which have marked the liberalisation process and the gradual opening of the telecommunications markets in Europe since 1990, certain definitions used in Directive 90/388/EEC and its amending acts should be adjusted in order to reflect the latest technological developments in the telecommunications field, or replaced in order to take account of the convergence phenomenon which has shaped the information technology, media and telecommunications industries over recent years. The wording of certain provisions should, where possible, be clarified in order to facilitate their application, taking into account, where appropriate, the relevant Directives adopted under Article 95 of the Treaty, and the experience acquired through the implementation of Directive 90/388/EEC as amended.

(7) This Directive makes reference to 'electronic communications services' and 'electronic communications networks' rather than the previously used terms 'telecommunications services' and 'telecommunications networks'. These new definitions are indispensable in order to take account of the convergence phenomenon by bringing together under one single definition all electronic communications services and/or networks which are concerned with the conveyance of signals by wire, radio, optical or other electromagnetic means (i.e. fixed, wireless, cable television, satellite networks). Thus, the transmission and broadcasting of radio and television

(^{1}) OJ L 192, 24.7.1990, p. 10.
(^{2}) OJ L 175, 10.7.1999, p. 39.
(^{3}) OJ L 108, 24.4.2002, p. 33.
(^{4}) OJ L 108, 24.4.2002, p. 21.
(^{5}) OJ L 108, 24.4.2002, p. 7.
(^{6}) OJ L 108, 24.4.2002, p. 51.
(^{7}) OJ L 201, 31.7.2002, p. 37.

programmes should be recognised as an electronic communication service and networks used for such transmission and broadcasting should likewise be recognised as electronic communications networks. Furthermore, it should be made clear that the new definition of electronic communications networks also covers fibre networks which enable third parties, using their own switching or routing equipment, to convey signals.

(8) In this context, it should be made clear that Member States must remove (if they have not already done so) exclusive and special rights for the provision of all electronic communications networks, not just those for the provision of electronic communications services and should ensure that undertakings are entitled to provide such services without prejudice to the provisions of Directives 2002/19/EC, 2002/20/EC, 2002/21/EC and 2002/22/EC. The definition of electronic communications networks should also mean that Member States are not permitted to restrict the right of an operator to establish, extend and/or provide a cable network on the ground that such network could also be used for the transmission of radio and television programming. In particular, special or exclusive rights which amount to restricting the use of electronic communications networks for the transmission and distribution of television signals are contrary to Article 86(1), read in conjunction with Article 43 (right of establishment) and/or Article 82(b) of the EC Treaty insofar as they have the effect of permitting a dominant undertaking to limit 'production, markets or technical development to the prejudice of consumers'. This is, however, without prejudice to the specific rules adopted by the Member States in accordance with Community law, and, in particular, in accordance with Council Directive 89/552/EEC of 3 October 1989 (¹), on the coordination of certain provisions laid down by law, regulation or administrative action in Member States concerning the pursuit of television broadcasting activities, as amended by Directive 97/36/EC of the European Parliament and of the Council (²), governing the distribution of audiovisual programmes intended for the general public.

(9) Pursuant to the principle of proportionality, Member States should no longer make the provision of electronic communications services and the establishment and provision of electronic communications networks subject to a licensing regime but to a general authorisation regime. This is also required by Directive 2002/20/EC, according to which electronic communications services or networks should be provided on the basis of a general authorisation and not on the basis of a license. An aggrieved party should have the right to challenge a decision preventing him from providing electronic communications services or networks before an independent body and, ultimately, before a court or a tribunal. It is a fundamental principle of Community law that an individual is entitled to effective judicial protection whenever a State measure violates rights conferred upon him by the provisions of a Directive.

(10) Public authorities may exercise a dominant influence on the behaviour of public undertakings, as a result either of the rules governing the undertaking or of the manner in which the shareholdings are distributed. Therefore, where Member States control vertically integrated network operators which operate networks which have been established under special or exclusive rights, those Member States should ensure that, in order to avoid potential breaches of the Treaty competition rules, such operators, when they enjoy a dominant position in the relevant market, do not discriminate in favour of their own activities. It follows that Member States should take all measures necessary to prevent any discrimination between such vertically integrated operators and their competitors.

(11) This Directive should also clarify the principle derived from Commission Directive 96/2/EC of 16 January 1996 amending Directive 90/388/EC with regard to mobile and personal communications (³), by providing that Member States should not grant exclusive or special rights of use of radio frequencies and that the rights of use of those frequencies should be assigned according to objective, non-discriminatory and transparent procedures. This should be without prejudice to specific criteria and procedures adopted by Member States to grant such rights to providers of radio or television broadcast content services with a view to pursuing general interest objectives in conformity with Community law.

(12) Any national scheme pursuant to Directive 2002/22/EC, serving to share the net cost of the provision of universal service obligations shall be based on objective, transparent and non-discriminatory criteria and shall be consistent with the principles of proportionality and of least market distortion. Least market distortion means that contributions should be recovered in a way that as far as possible minimises the impact of the financial burden falling on end-users, for example by spreading contributions as widely as possible.

(13) Where rights and obligations arising from international conventions setting up international satellite organisations are not compatible with the competition rules of the Treaty, Member States should take, in accordance with Article 307 of the EC Treaty, all appropriate steps to eliminate such incompatibilities. This Directive should clarify this obligation because Article 3 of Directive 94/46/EC (⁴), merely required Member States to 'communicate to the Commission' the information they possessed on such incompatibilities. Article 11 of this Directive should clarify the obligation on Member States to remove any restrictions which could still be in force because of those international conventions.

(¹) OJ L 298, 17.10.1989, p. 23.
(²) OJ L 202, 30.7.1997, p. 60.

(³) OJ L 20, 26.1.1996, p. 59.
(⁴) OJ L 268, 19.10.1994, p. 15.

(14) This Directive should maintain the obligation imposed on Member States by Directive 1999/64/EC, so as to ensure that dominant providers of electronic communications networks and publicly available telephone services operate their public electronic communication network and cable television network as separate legal entities.

(15) This Directive should be without prejudice to obligations of the Member States concerning the time limits set out in Annex I, Part B, within which the Member States are to comply with the preceding Directives.

(16) Member States should supply to the Commission any information which is necessary to demonstrate that existing national implementing legislation reflects the clarifications provided for in this Directive as compared with Directives 90/388/EC, 94/46/EC, 95/51/EC (¹), 96/2/EC, 96/19/EC (²) and 1999/64/EC.

(17) In the light of the above, Directive 90/388/EC should be repealed,

HAS ADOPTED THIS DIRECTIVE:

Article 1

Definitions

For the purposes of this Directive the following definitions shall apply:

1. 'electronic communications network' shall mean transmission systems and, where applicable, switching or routing equipment and other resources which permit the conveyance of signals by wire, by radio, by optical or by other electromagnetic means, including satellite networks, fixed (circuit — and packet — switched, including Internet) and mobile terrestrial networks, and electricity cable systems, to the extent that they are used for the purpose of transmitting signals, networks used for radio and television broadcasting, and cable television networks, irrespective of the type of information conveyed;

2. 'public communications network' shall mean an electronic communications network used wholly or mainly for the provision of public electronic communications services;

3. 'electronic communications services' shall mean a service normally provided for remuneration which consists wholly or mainly in the conveyance of signals on electronic communications networks, including telecommunications services and transmission services in networks used for broadcasting but exclude services providing or exercising editorial control over, content transmitted using electronic communications networks and services; it does not include information society services as defined in Article 1 of Directive 98/34/EC which do not consist wholly or mainly in the conveyance of signals on electronic communications networks;

(¹) OJ L 256, 26.10.1995, p. 49.
(²) OJ L 74, 22.3.1996, p. 13.

4. 'publicly available electronic communications services' shall mean electronic communications services available to the public;

5. 'exclusive rights' shall mean the rights that are granted by a Member State to one undertaking through any legislative, regulatory or administrative instrument, reserving it the right to provide an electronic communications service or to undertake an electronic communications activity within a given geographical area;

6. 'special rights' shall mean the rights that are granted by a Member State to a limited number of undertakings through any legislative, regulatory or administrative instrument which, within a given geographical area:

  (a) designates or limits to two or more the number of such undertakings authorised to provide an electronic communications service or undertake an electronic communications activity, otherwise than according to objective, proportional and non-discriminatory criteria, or

  (b) confers on undertakings, otherwise than according to such criteria, legal or regulatory advantages which substantially affect the ability of any other undertaking to provide the same electronic communications service or to undertake the same electronic communications activity in the same geographical area under substantially equivalent conditions;

7. 'satellite earth station network' shall mean a configuration of two or more earth stations which interwork by means of a satellite;

8. 'cable television networks' shall mean any mainly wire-based infrastructure established primarily for the delivery or distribution of radio or television broadcast to the public.

Article 2

Exclusive and special rights for electronic communications networks and electronic communications services

1. Member States shall not grant or maintain in force exclusive or special rights for the establishment and/or the provision of electronic communications networks, or for the provision of publicly available electronic communications services.

2. Member States shall take all measures necessary to ensure that any undertaking is entitled to provide electronic communications services or to establish, extend or provide electronic communications networks.

3. Member States shall ensure that no restrictions are imposed or maintained on the provision of electronic communications services over electronic communications networks established by the providers of electronic communications services, over infrastructures provided by third parties, or by means of sharing networks, other facilities or sites without prejudice to the provisions of Directives 2002/19/EC, 2002/20/EC, 2002/21/EC and 2002/22/EC.

4.   Member States shall ensure that a general authorisation granted to an undertaking to provide electronic communications services or to establish and/or provide electronic communications networks, as well as the conditions attached thereto, shall be based on objective, non-discriminatory, proportionate and transparent criteria.

5.   Reasons shall be given for any decision taken on the grounds set out in Article 3(1) of Directive 2002/20/EC preventing an undertaking from providing electronic communications services or networks.

Any aggrieved party should have the possibility to challenge such a decision before a body that is independent of the parties involved and ultimately before a court or a tribunal.

Article 3

Vertically integrated public undertakings

In addition to the requirements set out in Article 2(2), and without prejudice to Article 14 of Directive 2002/21/EC, Member States, shall ensure that vertically integrated public undertakings which provide electronic communications networks and which are in a dominant position do not discriminate in favour of their own activities.

Article 4

Rights of use of frequencies

Without prejudice to specific criteria and procedures adopted by Member States to grant rights of use of radio frequencies to providers of radio or television broadcast content services with a view to pursuing general interest objectives in conformity with Community law:

1. Member States shall not grant exclusive or special rights of use of radio frequencies for the provision of electronic communications services.

2. The assignment of radio frequencies for electronic communication services shall be based on objective, transparent, non-discriminatory and proportionate criteria.

Article 5

Directory services

Member States shall ensure that all exclusive and/or special rights with regard to the establishment and provision of directory services on their territory, including both the publication of directories and directory enquiry services, are abolished.

Article 6

Universal service obligations

1.   Any national scheme pursuant to Directive 2002/22/EC, serving to share the net cost of the provision of universal service obligations shall be based on objective, transparent and non-discriminatory criteria and shall be consistent with the principle of proportionality and of least market distortion. In particular, where universal service obligations are imposed in whole or in part on public undertakings providing electronic communications services, this shall be taken into consideration in calculating any contribution to the net cost of universal service obligations.

2.   Member States shall communicate any scheme of the kind referred to in paragraph 1 to the Commission.

Article 7

Satellites

1.   Member States shall ensure that any regulatory prohibition or restriction on the offer of space segment capacity to any authorised satellite earth station network operator are abolished, and shall authorise within their territory any space-segment supplier to verify that the satellite earth station network for use in connection with the space segment of the supplier in question is in conformity with the published conditions for access to such person's space segment capacity.

2.   Member States which are party to international conventions setting up international satellite organisations shall, where such conventions are not compatible with the competition rules of the EC Treaty, take all appropriate steps to eliminate such incompatibilities.

Article 8

Cable television networks

1.   Each Member State shall ensure that no undertaking providing public electronic communications networks operates its cable television network using the same legal entity as it uses for its other public electronic communications network, when such undertaking:

(a) is controlled by that Member State or benefits from special rights; and

(b) is dominant in a substantial part of the common market in the provision of public electronic communications networks and publicly available telephone services; and

(c) operates a cable television network which has been established under special or exclusive right in the same geographic area.

2.   The term 'publicly available telephone services' shall be considered synonymous with the term 'public voice telephony services' referred to in Article 1 of Directive 1999/64/EC.

3.   Member States which consider that there is sufficient competition in the provision of local loop infrastructure and services in their territory shall inform the Commission accordingly.

Such information shall include a detailed description of the market structure. The information provided shall be made available to any interested party on demand, regard being had to the legitimate interest of undertakings in the protection of their business secrets.

4.   The Commission shall decide within a reasonable period, after having heard the comments of these parties, whether the obligation of legal separation may be ended in the Member State concerned.

5.   The Commission shall review the application of this Article not later than 31 December 2004.

Article 9

Member States shall supply to the Commission not later than 24 July 2003 such information as will allow the Commission to confirm that the provisions of this Directive have been complied with.

Article 10

Repeal

Directive 90/388/EC, as amended by the Directives listed in Annex I, Part A, is repealed with effect from 25 July 2003, without prejudice to the obligations of the Member States in respect of the time limits for transposition laid down in Annex I, Part B.

References to the repealed Directives shall be construed as references to this Directive and shall be read in accordance with the correlation table in Annex II.

Article 11

This Directive shall enter into force on the 20th day following that of its publication in the *Official Journal of the European Communities*.

Article 12

This Directive is addressed to the Member States.

Done at Brussels, 16 September 2002.

For the Commission

Mario MONTI

Member of the Commission

ANNEX I

PART A

List of Directives to be repealed

Directive 90/388/EEC (OJ L 192, 24.7.1990, p. 10)

Articles 2 and 3 of Directive 94/46/EC (OJ L 268, 19.1.1994, p. 15)

Directive 95/51/EC (OJ L 256, 26.10.1995, p. 49)

Directive 96/2/EC (OJ L 20, 26.1.1996, p. 59)

Directive 96/19/EC (OJ L 74, 22.3.1996, p. 13)

Directive 1999/64/EC (OJ L 175, 10.7.1999, p. 39)

PART B

Transposition dates for the above Directives

Directive 90/388/EEC: transposition date:	31 December 1990
Directive 94/46/EC: transposition date:	8 August 1995
Directive 95/51/EC: transposition date:	1 October 1996
Directive 96/2/EC: transposition date:	15 November 1996
Directive 96/19/EC: transposition date:	11 January 1997
Directive 1999/64/EC: transposition date:	30 April 2000

———

ANNEX II

Correlation table

This Directive	Directive 90/388/EEC
Article 1 (Definitions)	Article 1
Article 2 (withdrawal of exclusive/special rights)	Article 2
Article 3 (vertically integrated public undertakings)	Article 3(a)(ii)
Article 4 (rights of use of radio frequencies)	Article 3(b)
Article 5 (directory services)	Article 4(b)
Article 6 (universal service obligations)	Article 4(c)
Article 7 (satellites)	Article 3 of Directive 94/46/EC
Article 8 (cable networks)	Article 9

DIRECTIVE 2002/58/EC OF THE EUROPEAN PARLIAMENT AND OF THE COUNCIL

of 12 July 2002

concerning the processing of personal data and the protection of privacy in the electronic communications sector (Directive on privacy and electronic communications)

THE EUROPEAN PARLIAMENT AND THE COUNCIL OF THE EUROPEAN UNION,

Having regard to the Treaty establishing the European Community, and in particular Article 95 thereof,

Having regard to the proposal from the Commission (¹),

Having regard to the opinion of the Economic and Social Committee (²),

Having consulted the Committee of the Regions,

Acting in accordance with the procedure laid down in Article 251 of the Treaty (³),

Whereas:

(1) Directive 95/46/EC of the European Parliament and of the Council of 24 October 1995 on the protection of individuals with regard to the processing of personal data and on the free movement of such data (⁴) requires Member States to ensure the rights and freedoms of natural persons with regard to the processing of personal data, and in particular their right to privacy, in order to ensure the free flow of personal data in the Community.

(2) This Directive seeks to respect the fundamental rights and observes the principles recognised in particular by the Charter of fundamental rights of the European Union. In particular, this Directive seeks to ensure full respect for the rights set out in Articles 7 and 8 of that Charter.

(3) Confidentiality of communications is guaranteed in accordance with the international instruments relating to human rights, in particular the European Convention for the Protection of Human Rights and Fundamental Freedoms, and the constitutions of the Member States.

(4) Directive 97/66/EC of the European Parliament and of the Council of 15 December 1997 concerning the processing of personal data and the protection of privacy in the telecommunications sector (⁵) translated the principles set out in Directive 95/46/EC into specific rules for the telecommunications sector. Directive 97/66/EC has to be adapted to developments in the markets and technologies for electronic communications services in order to provide an equal level of protection of personal data and privacy for users of publicly available electronic communications services, regardless of the technologies used. That Directive should therefore be repealed and replaced by this Directive.

(5) New advanced digital technologies are currently being introduced in public communications networks in the Community, which give rise to specific requirements concerning the protection of personal data and privacy of the user. The development of the information society is characterised by the introduction of new electronic communications services. Access to digital mobile networks has become available and affordable for a large public. These digital networks have large capacities and possibilities for processing personal data. The successful cross-border development of these services is partly dependent on the confidence of users that their privacy will not be at risk.

(6) The Internet is overturning traditional market structures by providing a common, global infrastructure for the delivery of a wide range of electronic communications services. Publicly available electronic communications services over the Internet open new possibilities for users but also new risks for their personal data and privacy.

(7) In the case of public communications networks, specific legal, regulatory and technical provisions should be made in order to protect fundamental rights and freedoms of natural persons and legitimate interests of legal persons, in particular with regard to the increasing capacity for automated storage and processing of data relating to subscribers and users.

(8) Legal, regulatory and technical provisions adopted by the Member States concerning the protection of personal data, privacy and the legitimate interest of legal persons, in the electronic communication sector, should be harmonised in order to avoid obstacles to the internal market for electronic communication in accordance with Article 14 of the Treaty. Harmonisation should be limited to requirements necessary to guarantee that the promotion and development of new electronic communications services and networks between Member States are not hindered.

(¹) OJ C 365 E, 19.12.2000, p. 223.
(²) OJ C 123, 25.4.2001, p. 53.
(³) Opinion of the European Parliament of 13 November 2001 (not yet published in the Official Journal), Council Common Position of 28 January 2002 (OJ C 113 E, 14.5.2002, p. 39) and Decision of the European Parliament of 30 May 2002 (not yet published in the Official Journal). Council Decision of 25 June 2002.
(⁴) OJ L 281, 23.11.1995, p. 31.
(⁵) OJ L 24, 30.1.1998, p. 1.

(9) The Member States, providers and users concerned, together with the competent Community bodies, should cooperate in introducing and developing the relevant technologies where this is necessary to apply the guarantees provided for by this Directive and taking particular account of the objectives of minimising the processing of personal data and of using anonymous or pseudonymous data where possible.

(10) In the electronic communications sector, Directive 95/46/EC applies in particular to all matters concerning protection of fundamental rights and freedoms, which are not specifically covered by the provisions of this Directive, including the obligations on the controller and the rights of individuals. Directive 95/46/EC applies to non-public communications services.

(11) Like Directive 95/46/EC, this Directive does not address issues of protection of fundamental rights and freedoms related to activities which are not governed by Community law. Therefore it does not alter the existing balance between the individual's right to privacy and the possibility for Member States to take the measures referred to in Article 15(1) of this Directive, necessary for the protection of public security, defence, State security (including the economic well-being of the State when the activities relate to State security matters) and the enforcement of criminal law. Consequently, this Directive does not affect the ability of Member States to carry out lawful interception of electronic communications, or take other measures, if necessary for any of these purposes and in accordance with the European Convention for the Protection of Human Rights and Fundamental Freedoms, as interpreted by the rulings of the European Court of Human Rights. Such measures must be appropriate, strictly proportionate to the intended purpose and necessary within a democratic society and should be subject to adequate safeguards in accordance with the European Convention for the Protection of Human Rights and Fundamental Freedoms.

(12) Subscribers to a publicly available electronic communications service may be natural or legal persons. By supplementing Directive 95/46/EC, this Directive is aimed at protecting the fundamental rights of natural persons and particularly their right to privacy, as well as the legitimate interests of legal persons. This Directive does not entail an obligation for Member States to extend the application of Directive 95/46/EC to the protection of the legitimate interests of legal persons, which is ensured within the framework of the applicable Community and national legislation.

(13) The contractual relation between a subscriber and a service provider may entail a periodic or a one-off payment for the service provided or to be provided. Prepaid cards are also considered as a contract.

(14) Location data may refer to the latitude, longitude and altitude of the user's terminal equipment, to the direction of travel, to the level of accuracy of the location information, to the identification of the network cell in which the terminal equipment is located at a certain point in time and to the time the location information was recorded.

(15) A communication may include any naming, numbering or addressing information provided by the sender of a communication or the user of a connection to carry out the communication. Traffic data may include any translation of this information by the network over which the communication is transmitted for the purpose of carrying out the transmission. Traffic data may, *inter alia*, consist of data referring to the routing, duration, time or volume of a communication, to the protocol used, to the location of the terminal equipment of the sender or recipient, to the network on which the communication originates or terminates, to the beginning, end or duration of a connection. They may also consist of the format in which the communication is conveyed by the network.

(16) Information that is part of a broadcasting service provided over a public communications network is intended for a potentially unlimited audience and does not constitute a communication in the sense of this Directive. However, in cases where the individual subscriber or user receiving such information can be identified, for example with video-on-demand services, the information conveyed is covered within the meaning of a communication for the purposes of this Directive.

(17) For the purposes of this Directive, consent of a user or subscriber, regardless of whether the latter is a natural or a legal person, should have the same meaning as the data subject's consent as defined and further specified in Directive 95/46/EC. Consent may be given by any appropriate method enabling a freely given specific and informed indication of the user's wishes, including by ticking a box when visiting an Internet website.

(18) Value added services may, for example, consist of advice on least expensive tariff packages, route guidance, traffic information, weather forecasts and tourist information.

(19) The application of certain requirements relating to presentation and restriction of calling and connected line identification and to automatic call forwarding to subscriber lines connected to analogue exchanges should not be made mandatory in specific cases where such application would prove to be technically impossible or would require a disproportionate economic effort. It is important for interested parties to be informed of such cases and the Member States should therefore notify them to the Commission.

(20) Service providers should take appropriate measures to safeguard the security of their services, if necessary in conjunction with the provider of the network, and inform subscribers of any special risks of a breach of the security of the network. Such risks may especially occur for electronic communications services over an open network such as the Internet or analogue mobile telephony. It is particularly important for subscribers and users of such services to be fully informed by their service provider of the existing security risks which lie outside the scope of possible remedies by the service provider. Service providers who offer publicly available electronic communications services over the Internet should inform users and subscribers of measures they can take to protect the security of their communications for instance by using specific types of software or encryption technologies. The requirement to inform subscribers of particular security risks does not discharge a service provider from the obligation to take, at its own costs, appropriate and immediate measures to remedy any new, unforeseen security risks and restore the normal security level of the service. The provision of information about security risks to the subscriber should be free of charge except for any nominal costs which the subscriber may incur while receiving or collecting the information, for instance by downloading an electronic mail message. Security is appraised in the light of Article 17 of Directive 95/46/EC.

(21) Measures should be taken to prevent unauthorised access to communications in order to protect the confidentiality of communications, including both the contents and any data related to such communications, by means of public communications networks and publicly available electronic communications services. National legislation in some Member States only prohibits intentional unauthorised access to communications.

(22) The prohibition of storage of communications and the related traffic data by persons other than the users or without their consent is not intended to prohibit any automatic, intermediate and transient storage of this information in so far as this takes place for the sole purpose of carrying out the transmission in the electronic communications network and provided that the information is not stored for any period longer than is necessary for the transmission and for traffic management purposes, and that during the period of storage the confidentiality remains guaranteed. Where this is necessary for making more efficient the onward transmission of any publicly accessible information to other recipients of the service upon their request, this Directive should not prevent such information from being further stored, provided that this information would in any case be accessible to the public without restriction and that any data referring to the individual subscribers or users requesting such information are erased.

(23) Confidentiality of communications should also be ensured in the course of lawful business practice. Where necessary and legally authorised, communications can be recorded for the purpose of providing evidence of a commercial transaction. Directive 95/46/EC applies to such processing. Parties to the communications should be informed prior to the recording about the recording, its purpose and the duration of its storage. The recorded communication should be erased as soon as possible and in any case at the latest by the end of the period during which the transaction can be lawfully challenged.

(24) Terminal equipment of users of electronic communications networks and any information stored on such equipment are part of the private sphere of the users requiring protection under the European Convention for the Protection of Human Rights and Fundamental Freedoms. So-called spyware, web bugs, hidden identifiers and other similar devices can enter the user's terminal without their knowledge in order to gain access to information, to store hidden information or to trace the activities of the user and may seriously intrude upon the privacy of these users. The use of such devices should be allowed only for legitimate purposes, with the knowledge of the users concerned.

(25) However, such devices, for instance so-called 'cookies', can be a legitimate and useful tool, for example, in analysing the effectiveness of website design and advertising, and in verifying the identity of users engaged in on-line transactions. Where such devices, for instance cookies, are intended for a legitimate purpose, such as to facilitate the provision of information society services, their use should be allowed on condition that users are provided with clear and precise information in accordance with Directive 95/46/EC about the purposes of cookies or similar devices so as to ensure that users are made aware of information being placed on the terminal equipment they are using. Users should have the opportunity to refuse to have a cookie or similar device stored on their terminal equipment. This is particularly important where users other than the original user have access to the terminal equipment and thereby to any data containing privacy-sensitive information stored on such equipment. Information and the right to refuse may be offered once for the use of various devices to be installed on the user's terminal equipment during the same connection and also covering any further use that may be made of those devices during subsequent connections. The methods for giving information, offering a right to refuse or requesting consent should be made as user-friendly as possible. Access to specific website content may still be made conditional on the well-informed acceptance of a cookie or similar device, if it is used for a legitimate purpose.

(26) The data relating to subscribers processed within electronic communications networks to establish connections and to transmit information contain information on the private life of natural persons and concern the right to respect for their correspondence or concern the legitimate interests of legal persons. Such data may only be stored to the extent that is necessary for the provision of the service for the purpose of billing and for interconnection payments, and for a limited time. Any further processing of such data which the provider of the publicly available electronic communications services may want to perform, for the marketing of electronic communications services or for the provision of value added services, may only be allowed if the subscriber has agreed to this on the basis of accurate and full information given by the provider of the publicly available electronic communications services about the types of further processing it intends to perform and about the subscriber's right not to give or to withdraw his/her consent to such processing. Traffic data used for marketing communications services or for the provision of value added services should also be erased or made anonymous after the provision of the service. Service providers should always keep subscribers informed of the types of data they are processing and the purposes and duration for which this is done.

(27) The exact moment of the completion of the transmission of a communication, after which traffic data should be erased except for billing purposes, may depend on the type of electronic communications service that is provided. For instance for a voice telephony call the transmission will be completed as soon as either of the users terminates the connection. For electronic mail the transmission is completed as soon as the addressee collects the message, typically from the server of his service provider.

(28) The obligation to erase traffic data or to make such data anonymous when it is no longer needed for the purpose of the transmission of a communication does not conflict with such procedures on the Internet as the caching in the domain name system of IP addresses or the caching of IP addresses to physical address bindings or the use of log-in information to control the right of access to networks or services.

(29) The service provider may process traffic data relating to subscribers and users where necessary in individual cases in order to detect technical failure or errors in the transmission of communications. Traffic data necessary for billing purposes may also be processed by the provider in order to detect and stop fraud consisting of unpaid use of the electronic communications service.

(30) Systems for the provision of electronic communications networks and services should be designed to limit the amount of personal data necessary to a strict minimum. Any activities related to the provision of the electronic communications service that go beyond the transmission of a communication and the billing thereof should be based on aggregated, traffic data that cannot be related to subscribers or users. Where such activities cannot be based on aggregated data, they should be considered as value added services for which the consent of the subscriber is required.

(31) Whether the consent to be obtained for the processing of personal data with a view to providing a particular value added service should be that of the user or of the subscriber, will depend on the data to be processed and on the type of service to be provided and on whether it is technically, procedurally and contractually possible to distinguish the individual using an electronic communications service from the legal or natural person having subscribed to it.

(32) Where the provider of an electronic communications service or of a value added service subcontracts the processing of personal data necessary for the provision of these services to another entity, such subcontracting and subsequent data processing should be in full compliance with the requirements regarding controllers and processors of personal data as set out in Directive 95/46/EC. Where the provision of a value added service requires that traffic or location data are forwarded from an electronic communications service provider to a provider of value added services, the subscribers or users to whom the data are related should also be fully informed of this forwarding before giving their consent for the processing of the data.

(33) The introduction of itemised bills has improved the possibilities for the subscriber to check the accuracy of the fees charged by the service provider but, at the same time, it may jeopardise the privacy of the users of publicly available electronic communications services. Therefore, in order to preserve the privacy of the user, Member States should encourage the development of electronic communication service options such as alternative payment facilities which allow anonymous or strictly private access to publicly available electronic communications services, for example calling cards and facilities for payment by credit card. To the same end, Member States may ask the operators to offer their subscribers a different type of detailed bill in which a certain number of digits of the called number have been deleted.

(34) It is necessary, as regards calling line identification, to protect the right of the calling party to withhold the presentation of the identification of the line from which the call is being made and the right of the called party to reject calls from unidentified lines. There is justification for overriding the elimination of calling line identification presentation in specific cases. Certain subscribers, in particular help lines and similar organisations, have an interest in guaranteeing the anonymity of their callers. It is necessary, as regards connected line identification, to protect the right and the legitimate interest of the called party to withhold the presentation of the identification of the line to which the calling party is actually connected, in particular in the case of forwarded calls. The providers of publicly available electronic communications services should inform their subscribers of the existence of calling and connected line identification in the network and of all services which are offered on the basis of calling and connected line identification as well as the privacy options which are available. This will allow the subscribers to make an informed choice about the privacy facilities they may want to use. The privacy options which are offered on a per-line basis do not necessarily have to be available as an automatic network service but may be obtainable through a simple request to the provider of the publicly available electronic communications service.

(35) In digital mobile networks, location data giving the geographic position of the terminal equipment of the mobile user are processed to enable the transmission of communications. Such data are traffic data covered by Article 6 of this Directive. However, in addition, digital mobile networks may have the capacity to process location data which are more precise than is necessary for the transmission of communications and which are used for the provision of value added services such as services providing individualised traffic information and guidance to drivers. The processing of such data for value added services should only be allowed where subscribers have given their consent. Even in cases where subscribers have given their consent, they should have a simple means to temporarily deny the processing of location data, free of charge.

(36) Member States may restrict the users' and subscribers' rights to privacy with regard to calling line identification where this is necessary to trace nuisance calls and with regard to calling line identification and location data where this is necessary to allow emergency services to carry out their tasks as effectively as possible. For these purposes, Member States may adopt specific provisions to entitle providers of electronic communications services to provide access to calling line identification and location data without the prior consent of the users or subscribers concerned.

(37) Safeguards should be provided for subscribers against the nuisance which may be caused by automatic call forwarding by others. Moreover, in such cases, it must be possible for subscribers to stop the forwarded calls being passed on to their terminals by simple request to the provider of the publicly available electronic communications service.

(38) Directories of subscribers to electronic communications services are widely distributed and public. The right to privacy of natural persons and the legitimate interest of legal persons require that subscribers are able to determine whether their personal data are published in a directory and if so, which. Providers of public directories should inform the subscribers to be included in such directories of the purposes of the directory and of any particular usage which may be made of electronic versions of public directories especially through search functions embedded in the software, such as reverse search functions enabling users of the directory to discover the name and address of the subscriber on the basis of a telephone number only.

(39) The obligation to inform subscribers of the purpose(s) of public directories in which their personal data are to be included should be imposed on the party collecting the data for such inclusion. Where the data may be transmitted to one or more third parties, the subscriber should be informed of this possibility and of the recipient or the categories of possible recipients. Any transmission should be subject to the condition that the data may not be used for other purposes than those for which they were collected. If the party collecting the data from the subscriber or any third party to whom the data have been transmitted wishes to use the data for an additional purpose, the renewed consent of the subscriber is to be obtained either by the initial party collecting the data or by the third party to whom the data have been transmitted.

(40) Safeguards should be provided for subscribers against intrusion of their privacy by unsolicited communications for direct marketing purposes in particular by means of automated calling machines, telefaxes, and e-mails, including SMS messages. These forms of unsolicited commercial communications may on the one hand be relatively easy and cheap to send and on the other may impose a burden and/or cost on the recipient. Moreover, in some cases their volume may also cause difficulties for electronic communications networks and terminal equipment. For such forms of unsolicited communications for direct marketing, it is justified to require that prior explicit consent of the recipients is obtained before such communications are addressed to them. The single market requires a harmonised approach to ensure simple, Community-wide rules for businesses and users.

(41) Within the context of an existing customer relationship, it is reasonable to allow the use of electronic contact details for the offering of similar products or services, but only by the same company that has obtained the electronic contact details in accordance with Directive 95/46/EC. When electronic contact details are obtained, the customer should be informed about their further use for direct marketing in a clear and distinct manner, and be given the opportunity to refuse such usage. This opportunity should continue to be offered with each subsequent direct marketing message, free of charge, except for any costs for the transmission of this refusal.

(42) Other forms of direct marketing that are more costly for the sender and impose no financial costs on subscribers and users, such as person-to-person voice telephony calls, may justify the maintenance of a system giving subscribers or users the possibility to indicate that they do not want to receive such calls. Nevertheless, in order not to decrease existing levels of privacy protection, Member States should be entitled to uphold national systems, only allowing such calls to subscribers and users who have given their prior consent.

(43) To facilitate effective enforcement of Community rules on unsolicited messages for direct marketing, it is necessary to prohibit the use of false identities or false return addresses or numbers while sending unsolicited messages for direct marketing purposes.

(44) Certain electronic mail systems allow subscribers to view the sender and subject line of an electronic mail, and also to delete the message, without having to download the rest of the electronic mail's content or any attachments, thereby reducing costs which could arise from downloading unsolicited electronic mails or attachments. These arrangements may continue to be useful in certain cases as an additional tool to the general obligations established in this Directive.

(45) This Directive is without prejudice to the arrangements which Member States make to protect the legitimate interests of legal persons with regard to unsolicited communications for direct marketing purposes. Where Member States establish an opt-out register for such communications to legal persons, mostly business users, the provisions of Article 7 of Directive 2000/31/EC of the European Parliament and of the Council of 8 June 2000 on certain legal aspects of information society services, in particular electronic commerce, in the internal market (Directive on electronic commerce) (¹) are fully applicable.

(46) The functionalities for the provision of electronic communications services may be integrated in the network or in any part of the terminal equipment of the user, including the software. The protection of the personal data and the privacy of the user of publicly available electronic communications services should be independent of the configuration of the various compo-

nents necessary to provide the service and of the distribution of the necessary functionalities between these components. Directive 95/46/EC covers any form of processing of personal data regardless of the technology used. The existence of specific rules for electronic communications services alongside general rules for other components necessary for the provision of such services may not facilitate the protection of personal data and privacy in a technologically neutral way. It may therefore be necessary to adopt measures requiring manufacturers of certain types of equipment used for electronic communications services to construct their product in such a way as to incorporate safeguards to ensure that the personal data and privacy of the user and subscriber are protected. The adoption of such measures in accordance with Directive 1999/5/EC of the European Parliament and of the Council of 9 March 1999 on radio equipment and telecommunications terminal equipment and the mutual recognition of their conformity (²) will ensure that the introduction of technical features of electronic communication equipment including software for data protection purposes is harmonised in order to be compatible with the implementation of the internal market.

(47) Where the rights of the users and subscribers are not respected, national legislation should provide for judicial remedies. Penalties should be imposed on any person, whether governed by private or public law, who fails to comply with the national measures taken under this Directive.

(48) It is useful, in the field of application of this Directive, to draw on the experience of the Working Party on the Protection of Individuals with regard to the Processing of Personal Data composed of representatives of the supervisory authorities of the Member States, set up by Article 29 of Directive 95/46/EC.

(49) To facilitate compliance with the provisions of this Directive, certain specific arrangements are needed for processing of data already under way on the date that national implementing legislation pursuant to this Directive enters into force,

HAVE ADOPTED THIS DIRECTIVE:

Article 1

Scope and aim

1. This Directive harmonises the provisions of the Member States required to ensure an equivalent level of protection of fundamental rights and freedoms, and in particular the right to privacy, with respect to the processing of personal data in the electronic communication sector and to ensure the free movement of such data and of electronic communication equipment and services in the Community.

(¹) OJ L 178, 17.7.2000, p. 1.

(²) OJ L 91, 7.4.1999, p. 10.

2. The provisions of this Directive particularise and complement Directive 95/46/EC for the purposes mentioned in paragraph 1. Moreover, they provide for protection of the legitimate interests of subscribers who are legal persons.

3. This Directive shall not apply to activities which fall outside the scope of the Treaty establishing the European Community, such as those covered by Titles V and VI of the Treaty on European Union, and in any case to activities concerning public security, defence, State security (including the economic well-being of the State when the activities relate to State security matters) and the activities of the State in areas of criminal law.

Article 2

Definitions

Save as otherwise provided, the definitions in Directive 95/46/EC and in Directive 2002/21/EC of the European Parliament and of the Council of 7 March 2002 on a common regulatory framework for electronic communications networks and services (Framework Directive) (¹) shall apply.

The following definitions shall also apply:

(a) 'user' means any natural person using a publicly available electronic communications service, for private or business purposes, without necessarily having subscribed to this service;

(b) 'traffic data' means any data processed for the purpose of the conveyance of a communication on an electronic communications network or for the billing thereof;

(c) 'location data' means any data processed in an electronic communications network, indicating the geographic position of the terminal equipment of a user of a publicly available electronic communications service;

(d) 'communication' means any information exchanged or conveyed between a finite number of parties by means of a publicly available electronic communications service. This does not include any information conveyed as part of a broadcasting service to the public over an electronic communications network except to the extent that the information can be related to the identifiable subscriber or user receiving the information;

(e) 'call' means a connection established by means of a publicly available telephone service allowing two-way communication in real time;

(f) 'consent' by a user or subscriber corresponds to the data subject's consent in Directive 95/46/EC;

(g) 'value added service' means any service which requires the processing of traffic data or location data other than traffic data beyond what is necessary for the transmission of a communication or the billing thereof;

(h) 'electronic mail' means any text, voice, sound or image message sent over a public communications network which

(¹) OJ L 108, 24.4.2002, p. 33.

can be stored in the network or in the recipient's terminal equipment until it is collected by the recipient.

Article 3

Services concerned

1. This Directive shall apply to the processing of personal data in connection with the provision of publicly available electronic communications services in public communications networks in the Community.

2. Articles 8, 10 and 11 shall apply to subscriber lines connected to digital exchanges and, where technically possible and if it does not require a disproportionate economic effort, to subscriber lines connected to analogue exchanges.

3. Cases where it would be technically impossible or require a disproportionate economic effort to fulfil the requirements of Articles 8, 10 and 11 shall be notified to the Commission by the Member States.

Article 4

Security

1. The provider of a publicly available electronic communications service must take appropriate technical and organisational measures to safeguard security of its services, if necessary in conjunction with the provider of the public communications network with respect to network security. Having regard to the state of the art and the cost of their implementation, these measures shall ensure a level of security appropriate to the risk presented.

2. In case of a particular risk of a breach of the security of the network, the provider of a publicly available electronic communications service must inform the subscribers concerning such risk and, where the risk lies outside the scope of the measures to be taken by the service provider, of any possible remedies, including an indication of the likely costs involved.

Article 5

Confidentiality of the communications

1. Member States shall ensure the confidentiality of communications and the related traffic data by means of a public communications network and publicly available electronic communications services, through national legislation. In particular, they shall prohibit listening, tapping, storage or other kinds of interception or surveillance of communications and the related traffic data by persons other than users, without the consent of the users concerned, except when legally authorised to do so in accordance with Article 15(1). This paragraph shall not prevent technical storage which is necessary for the conveyance of a communication without prejudice to the principle of confidentiality.

2.   Paragraph 1 shall not affect any legally authorised recording of communications and the related traffic data when carried out in the course of lawful business practice for the purpose of providing evidence of a commercial transaction or of any other business communication.

3.   Member States shall ensure that the use of electronic communications networks to store information or to gain access to information stored in the terminal equipment of a subscriber or user is only allowed on condition that the subscriber or user concerned is provided with clear and comprehensive information in accordance with Directive 95/46/EC, *inter alia* about the purposes of the processing, and is offered the right to refuse such processing by the data controller. This shall not prevent any technical storage or access for the sole purpose of carrying out or facilitating the transmission of a communication over an electronic communications network, or as strictly necessary in order to provide an information society service explicitly requested by the subscriber or user.

Article 6

Traffic data

1.   Traffic data relating to subscribers and users processed and stored by the provider of a public communications network or publicly available electronic communications service must be erased or made anonymous when it is no longer needed for the purpose of the transmission of a communication without prejudice to paragraphs 2, 3 and 5 of this Article and Article 15(1).

2.   Traffic data necessary for the purposes of subscriber billing and interconnection payments may be processed. Such processing is permissible only up to the end of the period during which the bill may lawfully be challenged or payment pursued.

3.   For the purpose of marketing electronic communications services or for the provision of value added services, the provider of a publicly available electronic communications service may process the data referred to in paragraph 1 to the extent and for the duration necessary for such services or marketing, if the subscriber or user to whom the data relate has given his/her consent. Users or subscribers shall be given the possibility to withdraw their consent for the processing of traffic data at any time.

4.   The service provider must inform the subscriber or user of the types of traffic data which are processed and of the duration of such processing for the purposes mentioned in paragraph 2 and, prior to obtaining consent, for the purposes mentioned in paragraph 3.

5.   Processing of traffic data, in accordance with paragraphs 1, 2, 3 and 4, must be restricted to persons acting under the authority of providers of the public communications networks and publicly available electronic communications services handling billing or traffic management, customer enquiries, fraud detection, marketing electronic communications services or providing a value added service, and must be restricted to what is necessary for the purposes of such activities.

6.   Paragraphs 1, 2, 3 and 5 shall apply without prejudice to the possibility for competent bodies to be informed of traffic data in conformity with applicable legislation with a view to settling disputes, in particular interconnection or billing disputes.

Article 7

Itemised billing

1.   Subscribers shall have the right to receive non-itemised bills.

2.   Member States shall apply national provisions in order to reconcile the rights of subscribers receiving itemised bills with the right to privacy of calling users and called subscribers, for example by ensuring that sufficient alternative privacy enhancing methods of communications or payments are available to such users and subscribers.

Article 8

Presentation and restriction of calling and connected line identification

1.   Where presentation of calling line identification is offered, the service provider must offer the calling user the possibility, using a simple means and free of charge, of preventing the presentation of the calling line identification on a per-call basis. The calling subscriber must have this possibility on a per-line basis.

2.   Where presentation of calling line identification is offered, the service provider must offer the called subscriber the possibility, using a simple means and free of charge for reasonable use of this function, of preventing the presentation of the calling line identification of incoming calls.

3.   Where presentation of calling line identification is offered and where the calling line identification is presented prior to the call being established, the service provider must offer the called subscriber the possibility, using a simple means, of rejecting incoming calls where the presentation of the calling line identification has been prevented by the calling user or subscriber.

4.   Where presentation of connected line identification is offered, the service provider must offer the called subscriber the possibility, using a simple means and free of charge, of preventing the presentation of the connected line identification to the calling user.

5.   Paragraph 1 shall also apply with regard to calls to third countries originating in the Community. Paragraphs 2, 3 and 4 shall also apply to incoming calls originating in third countries.

6.   Member States shall ensure that where presentation of calling and/or connected line identification is offered, the providers of publicly available electronic communications services inform the public thereof and of the possibilities set out in paragraphs 1, 2, 3 and 4.

Article 9

Location data other than traffic data

1.   Where location data other than traffic data, relating to users or subscribers of public communications networks or publicly available electronic communications services, can be processed, such data may only be processed when they are made anonymous, or with the consent of the users or subscribers to the extent and for the duration necessary for the provision of a value added service. The service provider must inform the users or subscribers, prior to obtaining their consent, of the type of location data other than traffic data which will be processed, of the purposes and duration of the processing and whether the data will be transmitted to a third party for the purpose of providing the value added service. Users or subscribers shall be given the possibility to withdraw their consent for the processing of location data other than traffic data at any time.

2.   Where consent of the users or subscribers has been obtained for the processing of location data other than traffic data, the user or subscriber must continue to have the possibility, using a simple means and free of charge, of temporarily refusing the processing of such data for each connection to the network or for each transmission of a communication.

3.   Processing of location data other than traffic data in accordance with paragraphs 1 and 2 must be restricted to persons acting under the authority of the provider of the public communications network or publicly available communications service or of the third party providing the value added service, and must be restricted to what is necessary for the purposes of providing the value added service.

Article 10

Exceptions

Member States shall ensure that there are transparent procedures governing the way in which a provider of a public communications network and/or a publicly available electronic communications service may override:

(a)   the elimination of the presentation of calling line identification, on a temporary basis, upon application of a subscriber requesting the tracing of malicious or nuisance calls. In this case, in accordance with national law, the data containing the identification of the calling subscriber will be stored and be made available by the provider of a public communications network and/or publicly available electronic communications service;

(b)   the elimination of the presentation of calling line identification and the temporary denial or absence of consent of a subscriber or user for the processing of location data, on a per-line basis for organisations dealing with emergency calls and recognised as such by a Member State, including law enforcement agencies, ambulance services and fire brigades, for the purpose of responding to such calls.

Article 11

Automatic call forwarding

Member States shall ensure that any subscriber has the possibility, using a simple means and free of charge, of stopping automatic call forwarding by a third party to the subscriber's terminal.

Article 12

Directories of subscribers

1.   Member States shall ensure that subscribers are informed, free of charge and before they are included in the directory, about the purpose(s) of a printed or electronic directory of subscribers available to the public or obtainable through directory enquiry services, in which their personal data can be included and of any further usage possibilities based on search functions embedded in electronic versions of the directory.

2.   Member States shall ensure that subscribers are given the opportunity to determine whether their personal data are included in a public directory, and if so, which, to the extent that such data are relevant for the purpose of the directory as determined by the provider of the directory, and to verify, correct or withdraw such data. Not being included in a public subscriber directory, verifying, correcting or withdrawing personal data from it shall be free of charge.

3.   Member States may require that for any purpose of a public directory other than the search of contact details of persons on the basis of their name and, where necessary, a minimum of other identifiers, additional consent be asked of the subscribers.

4.   Paragraphs 1 and 2 shall apply to subscribers who are natural persons. Member States shall also ensure, in the framework of Community law and applicable national legislation, that the legitimate interests of subscribers other than natural persons with regard to their entry in public directories are sufficiently protected.

Article 13

Unsolicited communications

1.   The use of automated calling systems without human intervention (automatic calling machines), facsimile machines (fax) or electronic mail for the purposes of direct marketing may only be allowed in respect of subscribers who have given their prior consent.

2.   Notwithstanding paragraph 1, where a natural or legal person obtains from its customers their electronic contact details for electronic mail, in the context of the sale of a product or a service, in accordance with Directive 95/46/EC, the same natural or legal person may use these electronic contact details for direct marketing of its own similar products or services provided that customers clearly and distinctly are given the opportunity to object, free of charge and in an easy manner, to such use of electronic contact details when they are collected and on the occasion of each message in case the customer has not initially refused such use.

3. Member States shall take appropriate measures to ensure that, free of charge, unsolicited communications for purposes of direct marketing, in cases other than those referred to in paragraphs 1 and 2, are not allowed either without the consent of the subscribers concerned or in respect of subscribers who do not wish to receive these communications, the choice between these options to be determined by national legislation.

4. In any event, the practice of sending electronic mail for purposes of direct marketing disguising or concealing the identity of the sender on whose behalf the communication is made, or without a valid address to which the recipient may send a request that such communications cease, shall be prohibited.

5. Paragraphs 1 and 3 shall apply to subscribers who are natural persons. Member States shall also ensure, in the framework of Community law and applicable national legislation, that the legitimate interests of subscribers other than natural persons with regard to unsolicited communications are sufficiently protected.

Article 14

Technical features and standardisation

1. In implementing the provisions of this Directive, Member States shall ensure, subject to paragraphs 2 and 3, that no mandatory requirements for specific technical features are imposed on terminal or other electronic communication equipment which could impede the placing of equipment on the market and the free circulation of such equipment in and between Member States.

2. Where provisions of this Directive can be implemented only by requiring specific technical features in electronic communications networks, Member States shall inform the Commission in accordance with the procedure provided for by Directive 98/34/EC of the European Parliament and of the Council of 22 June 1998 laying down a procedure for the provision of information in the field of technical standards and regulations and of rules on information society services (¹).

3. Where required, measures may be adopted to ensure that terminal equipment is constructed in a way that is compatible with the right of users to protect and control the use of their personal data, in accordance with Directive 1999/5/EC and Council Decision 87/95/EEC of 22 December 1986 on standardisation in the field of information technology and communications (²).

Article 15

Application of certain provisions of Directive 95/46/EC

1. Member States may adopt legislative measures to restrict the scope of the rights and obligations provided for in Article 5, Article 6, Article 8(1), (2), (3) and (4), and Article 9 of this

---

(¹) OJ L 204, 21.7.1998, p. 37. Directive as amended by Directive 98/48/EC (OJ L 217, 5.8.1998, p. 18).
(²) OJ L 36, 7.2.1987, p. 31. Decision as last amended by the 1994 Act of Accession.

Directive when such restriction constitutes a necessary, appropriate and proportionate measure within a democratic society to safeguard national security (i.e. State security), defence, public security, and the prevention, investigation, detection and prosecution of criminal offences or of unauthorised use of the electronic communication system, as referred to in Article 13(1) of Directive 95/46/EC. To this end, Member States may, *inter alia*, adopt legislative measures providing for the retention of data for a limited period justified on the grounds laid down in this paragraph. All the measures referred to in this paragraph shall be in accordance with the general principles of Community law, including those referred to in Article 6(1) and (2) of the Treaty on European Union.

2. The provisions of Chapter III on judicial remedies, liability and sanctions of Directive 95/46/EC shall apply with regard to national provisions adopted pursuant to this Directive and with regard to the individual rights derived from this Directive.

3. The Working Party on the Protection of Individuals with regard to the Processing of Personal Data instituted by Article 29 of Directive 95/46/EC shall also carry out the tasks laid down in Article 30 of that Directive with regard to matters covered by this Directive, namely the protection of fundamental rights and freedoms and of legitimate interests in the electronic communications sector.

Article 16

Transitional arrangements

1. Article 12 shall not apply to editions of directories already produced or placed on the market in printed or off-line electronic form before the national provisions adopted pursuant to this Directive enter into force.

2. Where the personal data of subscribers to fixed or mobile public voice telephony services have been included in a public subscriber directory in conformity with the provisions of Directive 95/46/EC and of Article 11 of Directive 97/66/EC before the national provisions adopted in pursuance of this Directive enter into force, the personal data of such subscribers may remain included in this public directory in its printed or electronic versions, including versions with reverse search functions, unless subscribers indicate otherwise, after having received complete information about purposes and options in accordance with Article 12 of this Directive.

Article 17

Transposition

1. Before 31 October 2003 Member States shall bring into force the provisions necessary to comply with this Directive. They shall forthwith inform the Commission thereof.

When Member States adopt those provisions, they shall contain a reference to this Directive or be accompanied by such a reference on the occasion of their official publication. The methods of making such reference shall be laid down by the Member States.

2.   Member States shall communicate to the Commission the text of the provisions of national law which they adopt in the field governed by this Directive and of any subsequent amendments to those provisions.

Article 18

Review

The Commission shall submit to the European Parliament and the Council, not later than three years after the date referred to in Article 17(1), a report on the application of this Directive and its impact on economic operators and consumers, in particular as regards the provisions on unsolicited communications, taking into account the international environment. For this purpose, the Commission may request information from the Member States, which shall be supplied without undue delay. Where appropriate, the Commission shall submit proposals to amend this Directive, taking account of the results of that report, any changes in the sector and any other proposal it may deem necessary in order to improve the effectiveness of this Directive.

Article 19

Repeal

Directive 97/66/EC is hereby repealed with effect from the date referred to in Article 17(1).

References made to the repealed Directive shall be construed as being made to this Directive.

Article 20

Entry into force

This Directive shall enter into force on the day of its publication in the *Official Journal of the European Communities*.

Article 21

Addressees

This Directive is addressed to the Member States.

Done at Brussels, 12 July 2002.

For the European Parliament	For the Council
The President	The President
P. COX	T. PEDERSEN

Selected articles of the Treaty Establishing the European Community
(consolidated text)

(Official Journal C 325 of 24 December 2002)

Article 3

For the purposes set out in Article 2, the activities of the Community shall include, as provided in this Treaty and in accordance with the timetable set out therein:

(g)   a system ensuring that competition in the internal market is not distorted;

Article 49

Within the framework of the provisions set out below, restrictions on freedom to provide services within the Community shall be prohibited in respect of nationals of Member States who are established in a State of the Community other than that of the person for whom the services are intended.

The Council may, acting by a qualified majority on a proposal from the Commission, extend the provisions of the Chapter to nationals of a third country who provide services and who are established within the Community.

Article 50

Services shall be considered to be "services" within the meaning of this Treaty where they are normally provided for remuneration, in so far as they are not governed by the provisions relating to freedom of movement for goods, capital and persons.

"Services" shall in particular include:

(a)   activities of an industrial character;

(b)   activities of a commercial character;

(c)   activities of craftsmen;

(d)   activities of the professions.

Without prejudice to the provisions of the chapter relating to the right of establishment, the person providing a service may, in order to do so, temporarily pursue his activity in the State where the service is provided, under the same conditions as are imposed by that State on its own nationals.

Article 51

1.   Freedom to provide services in the field of transport shall be governed by the provisions of the title relating to transport.

2.   The liberalisation of banking and insurance services connected with movements of capital shall be effected in step with the liberalisation of movement of capital.

Article 52

1.   In order to achieve the liberalisation of a specific service, the Council shall, on a proposal from the Commission and after consulting the Economic and Social Committee and the European Parliament, issue directives acting by a qualified majority.

2.   As regards the directives referred to in paragraph 1, priority shall as a general rule be given to those services which directly affect production costs or the liberalisation of which helps to promote trade in goods.

Article 53

The Member States declare their readiness to undertake the liberalisation of services beyond the extent required by the directives issued pursuant to Article 52(1), if their general economic situation and the situation of the economic sector concerned so permit.

To this end, the Commission shall make recommendations to the Member States concerned.

Article 54

As long as restrictions on freedom to provide services have not been abolished, each Member State shall apply such restrictions without distinction on grounds of nationality or residence to all persons providing services within the meaning of the first paragraph of Article 49.

Article 55

The provisions of Articles 45 to 48 shall apply to the matters covered by this chapter.

Article 81

1.   The following shall be prohibited as incompatible with the common market: all agreements between undertakings, decisions by associations of undertakings and concerted practices which may affect trade between Member States and which have as their object or effect the prevention, restriction or distortion of competition within the common market, and in particular those which:

(a)   directly or indirectly fix purchase or selling prices or any other trading conditions;

(b)   limit or control production, markets, technical development, or investment;

(c)   share markets or sources of supply;

(d)   apply dissimilar conditions to equivalent transactions with other trading parties, thereby placing them at a competitive disadvantage;

(e)   make the conclusion of contracts subject to acceptance by the other parties of supplementary obligations which, by their nature or according to commercial usage, have no connection with the subject of such contracts.

2.   Any agreements or decisions prohibited pursuant to this article shall be automatically void.

3.   The provisions of paragraph 1 may, however, be declared inapplicable in the case of:

—   any agreement or category of agreements between undertakings,

— any decision or category of decisions by associations of undertakings,

— any concerted practice or category of concerted practices,

which contributes to improving the production or distribution of goods or to promoting technical or economic progress, while allowing consumers a fair share of the resulting benefit, and which does not:

(a) impose on the undertakings concerned restrictions which are not indispensable to the attainment of these objectives;

(b) afford such undertakings the possibility of eliminating competition in respect of a substantial part of the products in question.

Article 82

Any abuse by one or more undertakings of a dominant position within the common market or in a substantial part of it shall be prohibited as incompatible with the common market in so far as it may affect trade between Member States.

Such abuse may, in particular, consist in:

(a) directly or indirectly imposing unfair purchase or selling prices or other unfair trading conditions;

(b) limiting production, markets or technical development to the prejudice of consumers;

(c) applying dissimilar conditions to equivalent transactions with other trading parties, thereby placing them at a competitive disadvantage;

(d) making the conclusion of contracts subject to acceptance by the other parties of supplementary obligations which, by their nature or according to commercial usage, have no connection with the subject of such contracts.

Article 86

1. In the case of public undertakings and undertakings to which Member States grant special or exclusive rights, Member States shall neither enact nor maintain in force any measure contrary to the rules contained in this Treaty, in particular to those rules provided for in Article 12 and Articles 81 to 89.

2. Undertakings entrusted with the operation of services of general economic interest or having the character of a revenue-producing monopoly shall be subject to the rules contained in this Treaty, in particular to the rules on competition, in so far as the application of such rules does not obstruct the performance, in law or in fact, of the particular tasks assigned to them. The development of trade must not be affected to such an extent as would be contrary to the interests of the Community.

3. The Commission shall ensure the application of the provisions of this Article and shall, where necessary, address appropriate directives or decisions to Member States.

DIRECTIVE 2002/21/EC OF THE EUROPEAN PARLIAMENT AND OF THE COUNCIL

of 7 March 2002

on a common regulatory framework for electronic communications networks and services (Framework Directive)

THE EUROPEAN PARLIAMENT AND THE COUNCIL OF THE EUROPEAN UNION,

Having regard to the Treaty establishing the European Community, and in particular Article 95 thereof,

Having regard to the proposal from the Commission (¹),

Having regard to the opinion of the Economic and Social Committee (²),

Acting in accordance with the procedure laid down in Article 251 of the Treaty (³),

Whereas:

(1) The current regulatory framework for telecommunications has been successful in creating the conditions for effective competition in the telecommunications sector during the transition from monopoly to full competition.

(2) On 10 November 1999, the Commission presented a communication to the European Parliament, the Council, the Economic and Social Committee and the Committee of the Regions entitled 'Towards a new framework for electronic communications infrastructure and associated services – the 1999 communications review'. In that communication, the Commission reviewed the existing regulatory framework for telecommunications, in accordance with its obligation under Article 8 of Council Directive 90/387/EEC of 28 June 1990 on the establishment of the internal market for telecommunications services through the implementation of open network provision (⁴). It also presented a series of policy proposals for a new regulatory framework for electronic communications infrastructure and associated services for public consultation.

(3) On 26 April 2000 the Commission presented a communication to the European Parliament, the Council, the Economic and Social Committee and the Committee of the Regions on the results of the public

consultation on the 1999 communications review and orientations for the new regulatory framework. The communication summarised the public consultation and set out certain key orientations for the preparation of a new framework for electronic communications infrastructure and associated services.

(4) The Lisbon European Council of 23 and 24 March 2000 highlighted the potential for growth, competitiveness and job creation of the shift to a digital, knowledge-based economy. In particular, it emphasised the importance for Europe's businesses and citizens of access to an inexpensive, world-class communications infrastructure and a wide range of services.

(5) The convergence of the telecommunications, media and information technology sectors means all transmission networks and services should be covered by a single regulatory framework. That regulatory framework consists of this Directive and four specific Directives: Directive 2002/20/EC of the European Parliament and of the Council of 7 March 2002 on the authorisation of electronic communications networks and services (Authorisation Directive) (⁵), Directive 2002/19/EC of the European Parliament and of the Council of 7 March 2002 on access to, and interconnection of, electronic communications networks and associated facilities (Access Directive) (⁶), Directive 2002/22/EC of the European Parliament and of the Council of 7 March 2002 on universal service and users' rights relating to electronic communications networks and services (Universal Service Directive) (⁷), Directive 97/66/EC of the European Parliament and of the Council of 15 December 1997 concerning the processing of personal data and the protection of privacy in the telecommunications sector (⁸), (hereinafter referred to as 'the Specific Directives'). It is necessary to separate the regulation of transmission from the regulation of content. This framework does not therefore cover the content of services delivered over electronic communications networks using electronic communications services, such as broadcasting content, financial services and certain information society services, and is therefore without prejudice to measures taken at Community or national level in respect of such services, in compliance with Community law, in order to promote cultural and linguistic diversity and to ensure the defence of media pluralism. The content of

(¹) OJ C 365 E, 19.12.2000, p. 198 and OJ C 270 E, 25.9.2001, p. 199.

(²) OJ C 123, 25.4.2001, p. 56.

(³) Opinion of the European Parliament of 1 March 2001 (OJ C 277, 1.10.2001, p. 91), Council Common Position of 17 September 2001 (OJ C 337, 30.11.2001, p. 34) and Decision of the European Parliament of 12 December 2001 (not yet published in the Official Journal). Council Decision of 14 February 2002.

(⁴) OJ L 192, 24.7.1990, p. 1. Directive as amended by Directive 97/51/EC of the European Parliament and of the Council (OJ L 295, 29.10.1997, p. 23).

(⁵) See page 21 of this Official Journal.

(⁶) See page 7 of this Official Journal.

(⁷) See page 51 of this Official Journal.

(⁸) OJ L 24, 30.1.1998, p. 1.

television programmes is covered by Council Directive 89/552/EEC of 3 October 1989 on the coordination of certain provisions laid down by law, regulation or administrative action in Member States concerning the pursuit of television broadcasting activities (¹). The separation between the regulation of transmission and the regulation of content does not prejudice the taking into account of the links existing between them, in particular in order to guarantee media pluralism, cultural diversity and consumer protection.

(6) Audiovisual policy and content regulation are undertaken in pursuit of general interest objectives, such as freedom of expression, media pluralism, impartiality, cultural and linguistic diversity, social inclusion, consumer protection and the protection of minors. The Commission communication 'Principles and guidelines for the Community's audio-visual policy in the digital age', and the Council conclusions of 6 June 2000 welcoming this communication, set out the key actions to be taken by the Community to implement its audio-visual policy.

(7) The provisions of this Directive and the Specific Directives are without prejudice to the possibility for each Member State to take the necessary measures to ensure the protection of its essential security interests, to safeguard public policy and public security, and to permit the investigation, detection and prosecution of criminal offences, including the establishment by national regulatory authorities of specific and proportional obligations applicable to providers of electronic communications services.

(8) This Directive does not cover equipment within the scope of Directive 1999/5/EC of the European Parliament and of the Council of 9 March 1999 on radio equipment and telecommunications terminal equipment and the mutual recognition of their conformity (²), but does cover consumer equipment used for digital television. It is important for regulators to encourage network operators and terminal equipment manufacturers to cooperate in order to facilitate access by disabled users to electronic communications services.

(9) Information society services are covered by Directive 2000/31/EC of the European Parliament and of the Council of 8 June 2000 on certain legal aspects of information society services, in particular electronic commerce, in the internal market (Directive on electronic commerce) (³).

(10) The definition of 'information society service' in Article 1 of Directive 98/34/EC of the European Parliament and of the Council of 22 June 1998 laying down a procedure for the provision of information in the field of technical standards and regulations and of rules of information society services (⁴) spans a wide range of economic activities which take place on-line. Most of these activities are not covered by the scope of this Directive because they do not consist wholly or mainly in the conveyance of signals on electronic communications networks. Voice telephony and electronic mail conveyance services are covered by this Directive. The same undertaking, for example an Internet service provider, can offer both an electronic communications service, such as access to the Internet, and services not covered under this Directive, such as the provision of web-based content.

(11) In accordance with the principle of the separation of regulatory and operational functions, Member States should guarantee the independence of the national regulatory authority or authorities with a view to ensuring the impartiality of their decisions. This requirement of independence is without prejudice to the institutional autonomy and constitutional obligations of the Member States or to the principle of neutrality with regard to the rules in Member States governing the system of property ownership laid down in Article 295 of the Treaty. National regulatory authorities should be in possession of all the necessary resources, in terms of staffing, expertise, and financial means, for the performance of their tasks.

(12) Any party who is the subject of a decision by a national regulatory authority should have the right to appeal to a body that is independent of the parties involved. This body may be a court. Furthermore, any undertaking which considers that its applications for the granting of rights to install facilities have not been dealt with in accordance with the principles set out in this Directive should be entitled to appeal against such decisions. This appeal procedure is without prejudice to the division of competences within national judicial systems and to the rights of legal entities or natural persons under national law.

(13) National regulatory authorities need to gather information from market players in order to carry out their tasks effectively. Such information may also need to be gathered on behalf of the Commission, to allow it to fulfil its obligations under Community law. Requests for information should be proportionate and not impose an undue burden on undertakings. Information

---

(¹) OJ L 298, 17.10.1989, p. 23. Directive as amended by Directive 97/36/EC of the European Parliament and of the Council (OJ L 202, 30.7.1997, p. 60).
(²) OJ L 91, 7.4.1999, p. 10.
(³) OJ L 178, 17.7.2000, p. 1.

(⁴) OJ L 204, 21.7.1998, p. 37. Directive as amended by Directive 98/48/EC (OJ L 217, 5.8.1998, p. 18).

gathered by national regulatory authorities should be publicly available, except in so far as it is confidential in accordance with national rules on public access to information and subject to Community and national law on business confidentiality.

(14) Information that is considered confidential by a national regulatory authority, in accordance with Community and national rules on business confidentiality, may only be exchanged with the Commission and other national regulatory authorities where such exchange is strictly necessary for the application of the provisions of this Directive or the Specific Directives. The information exchanged should be limited to that which is relevant and proportionate to the purpose of such an exchange.

(15) It is important that national regulatory authorities consult all interested parties on proposed decisions and take account of their comments before adopting a final decision. In order to ensure that decisions at national level do not have an adverse effect on the single market or other Treaty objectives, national regulatory authorities should also notify certain draft decisions to the Commission and other national regulatory authorities to give them the opportunity to comment. It is appropriate for national regulatory authorities to consult interested parties on all draft measures which have an effect on trade between Member States. The cases where the procedures referred to in Articles 6 and 7 apply are defined in this Directive and in the Specific Directives. The Commission should be able, after consulting the Communications Committee, to require a national regulatory authority to withdraw a draft measure where it concerns definition of relevant markets or the designation or not of undertakings with significant market power, and where such decisions would create a barrier to the single market or would be incompatible with Community law and in particular the policy objectives that national regulatory authorities should follow. This procedure is without prejudice to the notification procedure provided for in Directive 98/34/EC and the Commission's prerogatives under the Treaty in respect of infringements of Community law.

(16) National regulatory authorities should have a harmonised set of objectives and principles to underpin, and should, where necessary, coordinate their actions with the regulatory authorities of other Member States in carrying out their tasks under this regulatory framework.

(17) The activities of national regulatory authorities established under this Directive and the Specific Directives contribute to the fulfilment of broader policies in the areas of culture, employment, the environment, social cohesion and town and country planning.

(18) The requirement for Member States to ensure that national regulatory authorities take the utmost account of the desirability of making regulation technologically neutral, that is to say that it neither imposes nor discriminates in favour of the use of a particular type of technology, does not preclude the taking of proportionate steps to promote certain specific services where this is justified, for example digital television as a means for increasing spectrum efficiency.

(19) Radio frequencies are an essential input for radio-based electronic communications services and, in so far as they relate to such services, should therefore be allocated and assigned by national regulatory authorities according to a set of harmonised objectives and principles governing their action as well as to objective, transparent and non-discriminatory criteria, taking into account the democratic, social, linguistic and cultural interests related to the use of frequency. It is important that the allocation and assignment of radio frequencies is managed as efficiently as possible. Transfer of radio frequencies can be an effective means of increasing efficient use of spectrum, as long as there are sufficient safeguards in place to protect the public interest, in particular the need to ensure transparency and regulatory supervision of such transfers. Decision No 676/2002/EC of the European Parliament and of the Council of 7 March 2002 on a regulatory framework for radio spectrum policy in the European Community (Radio Spectrum Decision) (¹) establishes a framework for harmonisation of radio frequencies, and action taken under this Directive should seek to facilitate the work under that Decision.

(20) Access to numbering resources on the basis of transparent, objective and non-discriminatory criteria is essential for undertakings to compete in the electronic communications sector. All elements of national numbering plans should be managed by national regulatory authorities, including point codes used in network addressing. Where there is a need for harmonisation of numbering resources in the Community to support the development of pan-European services, the Commission may take technical implementing measures using its executive powers. Where this is appropriate to ensure full global interoperability of services, Member States should coordinate their national positions in accordance with the Treaty in international organisations and fora where numbering decisions are taken. The provisions of this Directive do not establish any new areas of responsibility for the national regulatory authorities in the field of Internet naming and addressing.

(¹) See page 1 of this Official Journal.

(21) Member States may use, *inter alia*, competitive or comparative selection procedures for the assignment of radio frequencies as well as numbers with exceptional economic value. In administering such schemes, national regulatory authorities should take into account the provisions of Article 8.

(22) It should be ensured that procedures exist for the granting of rights to install facilities that are timely, non-discriminatory and transparent, in order to guarantee the conditions for fair and effective competition. This Directive is without prejudice to national provisions governing the expropriation or use of property, the normal exercise of property rights, the normal use of the public domain, or to the principle of neutrality with regard to the rules in Member States governing the system of property ownership.

(23) Facility sharing can be of benefit for town planning, public health or environmental reasons, and should be encouraged by national regulatory authorities on the basis of voluntary agreements. In cases where undertakings are deprived of access to viable alternatives, compulsory facility or property sharing may be appropriate. It covers *inter alia*: physical co-location and duct, building, mast, antenna or antenna system sharing. Compulsory facility or property sharing should be imposed on undertakings only after full public consultation.

(24) Where mobile operators are required to share towers or masts for environmental reasons, such mandated sharing may lead to a reduction in the maximum transmitted power levels allowed for each operator for reasons of public health, and this in turn may require operators to install more transmission sites to ensure national coverage.

(25) There is a need for *ex ante* obligations in certain circumstances in order to ensure the development of a competitive market. The definition of significant market power in the Directive 97/33/EC of the European Parliament and of the Council of 30 June 1997 on interconnection in telecommunications with regard to ensuring universal service and interoperability through application of the principles of open network provision (ONP) (¹) has proved effective in the initial stages of market opening as the threshold for *ex ante* obligations, but now needs to be adapted to suit more complex and dynamic markets. For this reason, the definition used in

this Directive is equivalent to the concept of dominance as defined in the case law of the Court of Justice and the Court of First Instance of the European Communities.

(26) Two or more undertakings can be found to enjoy a joint dominant position not only where there exist structural or other links between them but also where the structure of the relevant market is conducive to coordinated effects, that is, it encourages parallel or aligned anti-competitive behaviour on the market.

(27) It is essential that *ex ante* regulatory obligations should only be imposed where there is not effective competition, i.e. in markets where there are one or more undertakings with significant market power, and where national and Community competition law remedies are not sufficient to address the problem. It is necessary therefore for the Commission to draw up guidelines at Community level in accordance with the principles of competition law for national regulatory authorities to follow in assessing whether competition is effective in a given market and in assessing significant market power. National regulatory authorities should analyse whether a given product or service market is effectively competitive in a given geographical area, which could be the whole or a part of the territory of the Member State concerned or neighbouring parts of territories of Member States considered together. An analysis of effective competition should include an analysis as to whether the market is prospectively competitive, and thus whether any lack of effective competition is durable. Those guidelines will also address the issue of newly emerging markets, where de facto the market leader is likely to have a substantial market share but should not be subjected to inappropriate obligations. The Commission should review the guidelines regularly to ensure that they remain appropriate in a rapidly developing market. National regulatory authorities will need to cooperate with each other where the relevant market is found to be transnational.

(28) In determining whether an undertaking has significant market power in a specific market, national regulatory authorities should act in accordance with Community law and take into the utmost account the Commission guidelines.

(29) The Community and the Member States have entered into commitments in relation to standards and the regulatory framework of telecommunications networks and services in the World Trade Organisation.

(¹) OJ L 199, 26.7.1997, p. 32. Directive as amended by Directive 98/61/EC (OJ L 268, 3.10.1998, p. 37).

(30) Standardisation should remain primarily a market-driven process. However there may still be situations where it is appropriate to require compliance with specified standards at Community level to ensure interoperability in the single market. At national level, Member States are subject to the provisions of Directive 98/34/EC. Directive 95/47/EC of the European Parliament and of the Council of 24 October 1995 on the use of standards for the transmission of television signals (¹) did not mandate any specific digital television transmission system or service requirement. Through the Digital Video Broadcasting Group, European market players have developed a family of television transmission systems that have been standardised by the European Telecommunications Standards Institute (ETSI) and have become International Telecommunication Union recommendations. Any decision to make the implementation of such standards mandatory should follow a full public consultation. Standardisation procedures under this Directive are without prejudice to the provisions of Directive 1999/5/EC, Council Directive 73/23/EEC of 19 February 1973 on the harmonisation of the laws of Member States relating to electrical equipment designed for use within certain voltage limits (²) and Council Directive 89/336/EEC of 3 May 1989 on the approximation of the laws of the Member States relating to electromagnetic compatibility (³).

(31) Interoperability of digital interactive television services and enhanced digital television equipment, at the level of the consumer, should be encouraged in order to ensure the free flow of information, media pluralism and cultural diversity. It is desirable for consumers to have the capability of receiving, regardless of the transmission mode, all digital interactive television services, having regard to technological neutrality, future technological progress, the need to promote the take-up of digital television, and the state of competition in the markets for digital television services. Digital interactive television platform operators should strive to implement an open application program interface (API) which conforms to standards or specifications adopted by a European standards organisation. Migration from existing APIs to new open APIs should be encouraged and organised, for example by Memoranda of Understanding between all relevant market players. Open APIs facilitate interoperability, i.e. the portability of interactive content between delivery mechanisms, and full functionality of this content on enhanced digital television equipment. However, the need not to hinder the functioning of the receiving equipment and to protect it from malicious attacks, for example from viruses, should be taken into account.

(32) In the event of a dispute between undertakings in the same Member State in an area covered by this Directive or the Specific Directives, for example relating to obligations for access and interconnection or to the means of transferring subscriber lists, an aggrieved party that has negotiated in good faith but failed to reach agreement should be able to call on the national regulatory authority to resolve the dispute. National regulatory authorities should be able to impose a solution on the parties. The intervention of a national regulatory authority in the resolution of a dispute between undertakings providing electronic communications networks or services in a Member State should seek to ensure compliance with the obligations arising under this Directive or the Specific Directives.

(33) In addition to the rights of recourse granted under national or Community law, there is a need for a simple procedure to be initiated at the request of either party in a dispute, to resolve cross-border disputes which lie outside the competence of a single national regulatory authority.

(34) A single Committee should replace the 'ONP Committee' instituted by Article 9 of Directive 90/387/EEC and the Licensing Committee instituted by Article 14 of Directive 97/13/EC of the European Parliament and of the Council of 10 April 1997 on a common framework for general authorisations and individual licences in the field of telecommunications services (⁴).

(35) National regulatory authorities and national competition authorities should provide each other with the information necessary to apply the provisions of this Directive and the Specific Directives, in order to allow them to cooperate fully together. In respect of the information exchanged, the receiving authority should ensure the same level of confidentiality as the originating authority.

(36) The Commission has indicated its intention to set up a European regulators group for electronic communications networks and services which would constitute a suitable mechanism for encouraging cooperation and coordination of national regulatory authorities, in order to promote the development of the internal market for electronic communications networks and services, and to seek to achieve consistent application, in all Member States, of the provisions set out in this Directive and the Specific Directives, in particular in areas where national law implementing Community law gives national regulatory authorities considerable discretionary powers in application of the relevant rules.

(¹) OJ L 281, 23.11.1995, p. 51.
(²) OJ L 77, 26.3.1973, p. 29.
(³) OJ L 139, 23.5.1989, p. 19.

(⁴) OJ L 117, 7.5.1997, p. 15.

(37) National regulatory authorities should be required to cooperate with each other and with the Commission in a transparent manner to ensure consistent application, in all Member States, of the provisions of this Directive and the Specific Directives. This cooperation could take place, *inter alia*, in the Communications Committee or in a group comprising European regulators. Member States should decide which bodies are national regulatory authorities for the purposes of this Directive and the Specific Directives.

(38) Measures that could affect trade between Member States are measures that may have an influence, direct or indirect, actual or potential, on the pattern of trade between Member States in a manner which might create a barrier to the single market. They comprise measures that have a significant impact on operators or users in other Member States, which include, *inter alia*: measures which affect prices for users in other Member States; measures which affect the ability of an undertaking established in another Member State to provide an electronic communications service, and in particular measures which affect the ability to offer services on a transnational basis; and measures which affect market structure or access, leading to repercussions for undertakings in other Member States.

(39) The provisions of this Directive should be reviewed periodically, in particular with a view to determining the need for modification in the light of changing technological or market conditions.

(40) The measures necessary for the implementation of this Directive should be adopted in accordance with Council Decision 1999/468/EC of 28 June 1999 laying down the procedures for the exercise of implementing powers conferred on the Commission ([1]).

(41) Since the objectives of the proposed action, namely achieving a harmonised framework for the regulation of electronic communications services, electronic communications networks, associated facilities and associated services cannot be sufficiently achieved by the Member States and can therefore, by reason of the scale and effects of the action, be better achieved at Community level, the Community may adopt measures in accordance with the principle of subsidiarity as set out in Article 5 of the Treaty. In accordance with the principle of proportionality, as set out in that Article, this Directive does not go beyond what is necessary for those objectives.

(42) Certain directives and decisions in this field should be repealed.

(43) The Commission should monitor the transition from the existing framework to the new framework, and may in particular, at an appropriate time, bring forward a proposal to repeal Regulation (EC) No 2887/2000 of the European Parliament and of the Council of 18 December 2000 on unbundled access to the local loop ([2]),

HAVE ADOPTED THIS DIRECTIVE:

CHAPTER I

SCOPE, AIM AND DEFINITIONS

Article 1

Scope and aim

1. This Directive establishes a harmonised framework for the regulation of electronic communications services, electronic communications networks, associated facilities and associated services. It lays down tasks of national regulatory authorities and establishes a set of procedures to ensure the harmonised application of the regulatory framework throughout the Community.

2. This Directive as well as the Specific Directives are without prejudice to obligations imposed by national law in accordance with Community law or by Community law in respect of services provided using electronic communications networks and services.

3. This Directive as well as the Specific Directives are without prejudice to measures taken at Community or national level, in compliance with Community law, to pursue general interest objectives, in particular relating to content regulation and audio-visual policy.

4. This Directive and the Specific Directives are without prejudice to the provisions of Directive 1999/5/EC.

Article 2

Definitions

For the purposes of this Directive:

(a) 'electronic communications network' means transmission systems and, where applicable, switching or routing equipment and other resources which permit the conveyance of signals by wire, by radio, by optical or by other electromagnetic means, including satellite networks, fixed (circuit- and packet-switched, including Internet) and mobile terrestrial networks, electricity cable systems, to the extent that they are used for the purpose of transmitting

---

([1]) OJ L 184, 17.7.1999, p. 23.

([2]) OJ L 336, 30.12.2000, p. 4.

signals, networks used for radio and television broadcasting, and cable television networks, irrespective of the type of information conveyed;

(b) 'transnational markets' means markets identified in accordance with Article 15(4) covering the Community or a substantial part thereof;

(c) 'electronic communications service' means a service normally provided for remuneration which consists wholly or mainly in the conveyance of signals on electronic communications networks, including telecommunications services and transmission services in networks used for broadcasting, but exclude services providing, or exercising editorial control over, content transmitted using electronic communications networks and services; it does not include information society services, as defined in Article 1 of Directive 98/34/EC, which do not consist wholly or mainly in the conveyance of signals on electronic communications networks;

(d) 'public communications network' means an electronic communications network used wholly or mainly for the provision of publicly available electronic communications services;

(e) 'associated facilities' means those facilities associated with an electronic communications network and/or an electronic communications service which enable and/or support the provision of services via that network and/or service. It includes conditional access systems and electronic programme guides;

(f) 'conditional access system' means any technical measure and/or arrangement whereby access to a protected radio or television broadcasting service in intelligible form is made conditional upon subscription or other form of prior individual authorisation;

(g) 'national regulatory authority' means the body or bodies charged by a Member State with any of the regulatory tasks assigned in this Directive and the Specific Directives;

(h) 'user' means a legal entity or natural person using or requesting a publicly available electronic communications service;

(i) 'consumer' means any natural person who uses or requests a publicly available electronic communications service for purposes which are outside his or her trade, business or profession;

(j) 'universal service' means the minimum set of services, defined in Directive 2002/22/EC (Universal Service Directive), of specified quality which is available to all users regardless of their geographical location and, in the light of specific national conditions, at an affordable price;

(k) 'subscriber' means any natural person or legal entity who or which is party to a contract with the provider of publicly available electronic communications services for the supply of such services;

(l) 'Specific Directives' means Directive 2002/20/EC (Authorisation Directive), Directive 2002/19/EC (Access Directive), Directive 2002/22/EC (Universal Service Directive) and Directive 97/66/EC;

(m) 'provision of an electronic communications network' means the establishment, operation, control or making available of such a network;

(n) 'end-user' means a user not providing public communications networks or publicly available electronic communications services.

(o) 'enhanced digital television equipment' means set-top boxes intended for connection to television sets or integrated digital television sets, able to receive digital interactive television services;

(p) 'application program interface (API)' means the software interfaces between applications, made available by broadcasters or service providers, and the resources in the enhanced digital television equipment for digital television and radio services.

CHAPTER II

NATIONAL REGULATORY AUTHORITIES

Article 3

National regulatory authorities

1. Member States shall ensure that each of the tasks assigned to national regulatory authorities in this Directive and the Specific Directives is undertaken by a competent body.

2. Member States shall guarantee the independence of national regulatory authorities by ensuring that they are legally distinct from and functionally independent of all organisations providing electronic communications networks, equipment or services. Member States that retain ownership or control of undertakings providing electronic communications networks and/or services shall ensure effective structural separation of the regulatory function from activities associated with ownership or control.

3. Member States shall ensure that national regulatory authorities exercise their powers impartially and transparently.

4. Member States shall publish the tasks to be undertaken by national regulatory authorities in an easily accessible form, in particular where those tasks are assigned to more than one

body. Member States shall ensure, where appropriate, consultation and cooperation between those authorities, and between those authorities and national authorities entrusted with the implementation of competition law and national authorities entrusted with the implementation of consumer law, on matters of common interest. Where more than one authority has competence to address such matters, Member States shall ensure that the respective tasks of each authority are published in an easily accessible form.

5. National regulatory authorities and national competition authorities shall provide each other with the information necessary for the application of the provisions of this Directive and the Specific Directives. In respect of the information exchanged, the receiving authority shall ensure the same level of confidentiality as the originating authority.

6. Member States shall notify to the Commission all national regulatory authorities assigned tasks under this Directive and the Specific Directives, and their respective responsibilities.

Article 4

Right of appeal

1. Member States shall ensure that effective mechanisms exist at national level under which any user or undertaking providing electronic communications networks and/or services who is affected by a decision of a national regulatory authority has the right of appeal against the decision to an appeal body that is independent of the parties involved. This body, which may be a court, shall have the appropriate expertise available to it to enable it to carry out its functions. Member States shall ensure that the merits of the case are duly taken into account and that there is an effective appeal mechanism. Pending the outcome of any such appeal, the decision of the national regulatory authority shall stand, unless the appeal body decides otherwise.

2. Where the appeal body referred to in paragraph 1 is not judicial in character, written reasons for its decision shall always be given. Furthermore, in such a case, its decision shall be subject to review by a court or tribunal within the meaning of Article 234 of the Treaty.

Article 5

Provision of information

1. Member States shall ensure that undertakings providing electronic communications networks and services provide all the information, including financial information, necessary for national regulatory authorities to ensure conformity with the provisions of, or decisions made in accordance with, this Directive and the Specific Directives. These undertakings shall provide such information promptly on request and to the

timescales and level of detail required by the national regulatory authority. The information requested by the national regulatory authority shall be proportionate to the performance of that task. The national regulatory authority shall give the reasons justifying its request for information.

2. Member States shall ensure that national regulatory authorities provide the Commission, after a reasoned request, with the information necessary for it to carry out its tasks under the Treaty. The information requested by the Commission shall be proportionate to the performance of those tasks. Where the information provided refers to information previously provided by undertakings at the request of the national regulatory authority, such undertakings shall be informed thereof. To the extent necessary, and unless the authority that provides the information has made an explicit and reasoned request to the contrary, the Commission shall make the information provided available to another such authority in another Member State.

Subject to the requirements of paragraph 3, Member States shall ensure that the information submitted to one national regulatory authority can be made available to another such authority in the same or different Member State, after a substantiated request, where necessary to allow either authority to fulfil its responsibilities under Community law.

3. Where information is considered confidential by a national regulatory authority in accordance with Community and national rules on business confidentiality, the Commission and the national regulatory authorities concerned shall ensure such confidentiality.

4. Member States shall ensure that, acting in accordance with national rules on public access to information and subject to Community and national rules on business confidentiality, national regulatory authorities publish such information as would contribute to an open and competitive market.

5. National regulatory authorities shall publish the terms of public access to information as referred to in paragraph 4, including procedures for obtaining such access.

Article 6

Consultation and transparency mechanism

Except in cases falling within Articles 7(6), 20 or 21 Member States shall ensure that where national regulatory authorities intend to take measures in accordance with this Directive or the Specific Directives which have a significant impact on the relevant market, they give interested parties the opportunity to comment on the draft measure within a reasonable period. National regulatory authorities shall publish their national consultation procedures. Member States shall ensure the establishment of a single information point through which all current consultations can be accessed. The results of the consultation procedure shall be made publicly available by the national regulatory authority, except in the case of confidential information in accordance with Community and national law on business confidentiality.

Article 7

Consolidating the internal market for electronic communications

1.   In carrying out their tasks under this Directive and the Specific Directives, national regulatory authorities shall take the utmost account of the objectives set out in Article 8, including in so far as they relate to the functioning of the internal market.

2.   National regulatory authorities shall contribute to the development of the internal market by cooperating with each other and with the Commission in a transparent manner to ensure the consistent application, in all Member States, of the provisions of this Directive and the Specific Directives. To this end, they shall, in particular, seek to agree on the types of instruments and remedies best suited to address particular types of situations in the market place.

3.   In addition to the consultation referred to in Article 6, where a national regulatory authority intends to take a measure which:

(a) falls within the scope of Articles 15 or 16 of this Directive, Articles 5 or 8 of Directive 2002/19/EC (Access Directive) or Article 16 of Directive 2002/22/EC (Universal Service Directive), and

(b) would affect trade between Member States,

it shall at the same time make the draft measure accessible to the Commission and the national regulatory authorities in other Member States, together with the reasoning on which the measure is based, in accordance with Article 5(3), and inform the Commission and other national regulatory authorities thereof. National regulatory authorities and the Commission may make comments to the national regulatory authority concerned only within one month or within the period referred to in Article 6 if that period is longer. The one-month period may not be extended.

4.   Where an intended measure covered by paragraph 3 aims at:

(a) defining a relevant market which differs from those defined in the recommendation in accordance with Article 15(1), or

(b) deciding whether or not to designate an undertaking as having, either individually or jointly with others, significant market power, under Article 16(3), (4) or (5),

and would affect trade between Member States and the Commission has indicated to the national regulatory authority that it considers that the draft measure would create a barrier to the single market or if it has serious doubts as to its compatibility with Community law and in particular the objectives referred to in Article 8, then the draft measure shall not be adopted for a further two months. This period may not be extended. Within this period the Commission may, in accordance with the procedure referred to in Article 22(2), take a decision requiring the national regulatory authority concerned to withdraw the draft measure. This decision shall be accompanied by a detailed and objective analysis of why the Commission considers that the draft measure should not be adopted together with specific proposals for amending the draft measure.

5.   The national regulatory authority concerned shall take the utmost account of comments of other national regulatory authorities and the Commission and may, except in cases covered by paragraph 4, adopt the resulting draft measure and, where it does so, shall communicate it to the Commission.

6.   In exceptional circumstances, where a national regulatory authority considers that there is an urgent need to act, by way of derogation from the procedure set out in paragraphs 3 and 4, in order to safeguard competition and protect the interests of users, it may immediately adopt proportionate and provisional measures. It shall, without delay, communicate those measures, with full reasons, to the Commission and the other national regulatory authorities. A decision by the national regulatory authority to render such measures permanent or extend the time for which they are applicable shall be subject to the provisions of paragraphs 3 and 4.

CHAPTER III

TASKS OF NATIONAL REGULATORY AUTHORITIES

Article 8

Policy objectives and regulatory principles

1.   Member States shall ensure that in carrying out the regulatory tasks specified in this Directive and the Specific Directives, the national regulatory authorities take all reasonable measures which are aimed at achieving the objectives set out in paragraphs 2, 3 and 4. Such measures shall be proportionate to those objectives.

Member States shall ensure that in carrying out the regulatory tasks specified in this Directive and the Specific Directives, in particular those designed to ensure effective competition, national regulatory authorities take the utmost account of the desirability of making regulations technologically neutral.

National regulatory authorities may contribute within their competencies to ensuring the implementation of policies aimed at the promotion of cultural and linguistic diversity, as well as media pluralism.

2. The national regulatory authorities shall promote competition in the provision of electronic communications networks, electronic communications services and associated facilities and services by *inter alia*:

(a) ensuring that users, including disabled users, derive maximum benefit in terms of choice, price, and quality;

(b) ensuring that there is no distortion or restriction of competition in the electronic communications sector;

(c) encouraging efficient investment in infrastructure, and promoting innovation; and

(d) encouraging efficient use and ensuring the effective management of radio frequencies and numbering resources.

3. The national regulatory authorities shall contribute to the development of the internal market by *inter alia*:

(a) removing remaining obstacles to the provision of electronic communications networks, associated facilities and services and electronic communications services at European level;

(b) encouraging the establishment and development of trans-European networks and the interoperability of pan-European services, and end-to-end connectivity;

(c) ensuring that, in similar circumstances, there is no discrimination in the treatment of undertakings providing electronic communications networks and services;

(d) cooperating with each other and with the Commission in a transparent manner to ensure the development of consistent regulatory practice and the consistent application of this Directive and the Specific Directives.

4. The national regulatory authorities shall promote the interests of the citizens of the European Union by *inter alia*:

(a) ensuring all citizens have access to a universal service specified in Directive 2002/22/EC (Universal Service Directive);

(b) ensuring a high level of protection for consumers in their dealings with suppliers, in particular by ensuring the availability of simple and inexpensive dispute resolution procedures carried out by a body that is independent of the parties involved;

(c) contributing to ensuring a high level of protection of personal data and privacy;

(d) promoting the provision of clear information, in particular requiring transparency of tariffs and conditions for using publicly available electronic communications services;

(e) addressing the needs of specific social groups, in particular disabled users; and

(f) ensuring that the integrity and security of public communications networks are maintained.

Article 9

Management of radio frequencies for electronic communications services

1. Member States shall ensure the effective management of radio frequencies for electronic communication services in their territory in accordance with Article 8. They shall ensure that the allocation and assignment of such radio frequencies by national regulatory authorities are based on objective, transparent, non-discriminatory and proportionate criteria.

2. Member States shall promote the harmonisation of use of radio frequencies across the Community, consistent with the need to ensure effective and efficient use thereof and in accordance with the Decision No 676/2002/EC (Radio Spectrum Decision).

3. Member States may make provision for undertakings to transfer rights to use radio frequencies with other undertakings.

4. Member States shall ensure that an undertaking's intention to transfer rights to use radio frequencies is notified to the national regulatory authority responsible for spectrum assignment and that any transfer takes place in accordance with procedures laid down by the national regulatory authority and is made public. National regulatory authorities shall ensure that competition is not distorted as a result of any such transaction. Where radio frequency use has been harmonised through the application of Decision No 676/2002/EC (Radio Spectrum Decision) or other Community measures, any such transfer shall not result in change of use of that radio frequency.

Article 10

Numbering, naming and addressing

1. Member States shall ensure that national regulatory authorities control the assignment of all national numbering

resources and the management of the national numbering plans. Member States shall ensure that adequate numbers and numbering ranges are provided for all publicly available electronic communications services. National regulatory authorities shall establish objective, transparent and non-discriminatory assigning procedures for national numbering resources.

2. National regulatory authorities shall ensure that numbering plans and procedures are applied in a manner that gives equal treatment to all providers of publicly available electronic communications services. In particular, Member States shall ensure that an undertaking allocated a range of numbers does not discriminate against other providers of electronic communications services as regards the number sequences used to give access to their services.

3. Member States shall ensure that the national numbering plans, and all subsequent additions or amendments thereto, are published, subject only to limitations imposed on the grounds of national security.

4. Member States shall support the harmonisation of numbering resources within the Community where that is necessary to support the development of pan European services. The Commission may, in accordance with the procedure referred to in Article 22(3), take the appropriate technical implementing measures on this matter.

5. Where this is appropriate in order to ensure full global interoperability of services, Member States shall coordinate their positions in international organisations and forums in which decisions are taken on issues relating to the numbering, naming and addressing of electronic communications networks and services.

Article 11

Rights of way

1. Member States shall ensure that when a competent authority considers:

— an application for the granting of rights to install facilities on, over or under public or private property to an undertaking authorised to provide public communications networks, or

— an application for the granting of rights to install facilities on, over or under public property to an undertaking authorised to provide electronic communications networks other than to the public,

the competent authority:

— acts on the basis of transparent and publicly available procedures, applied without discrimination and without delay, and

— follows the principles of transparency and non-discrimination in attaching conditions to any such rights.

The abovementioned procedures can differ depending on whether the applicant is providing public communications networks or not.

2. Member States shall ensure that where public or local authorities retain ownership or control of undertakings operating electronic communications networks and/or services, there is effective structural separation of the function responsible for granting the rights referred to in paragraph 1 from activities associated with ownership or control.

3. Member States shall ensure that effective mechanisms exist to allow undertakings to appeal against decisions on the granting of rights to install facilities to a body that is independent of the parties involved.

Article 12

Co-location and facility sharing

1. Where an undertaking providing electronic communications networks has the right under national legislation to install facilities on, over or under public or private property, or may take advantage of a procedure for the expropriation or use of property, national regulatory authorities shall encourage the sharing of such facilities or property.

2. In particular where undertakings are deprived of access to viable alternatives because of the need to protect the environment, public health, public security or to meet town and country planning objectives, Member States may impose the sharing of facilities or property (including physical co-location) on an undertaking operating an electronic communications network or take measures to facilitate the coordination of public works only after an appropriate period of public consultation during which all interested parties must be given an opportunity to express their views. Such sharing or coordination arrangements may include rules for apportioning the costs of facility or property sharing.

Article 13

Accounting separation and financial reports

1. Member States shall require undertakings providing public communications networks or publicly available electronic communications services which have special or exclusive rights for the provision of services in other sectors in the same or another Member State to:

(a) keep separate accounts for the activities associated with the provision of electronic communications networks or services, to the extent that would be required if these activities were carried out by legally independent companies, so as to identify all elements of cost and revenue, with the basis of their calculation and the detailed attribution methods used, related to their activities associated with the provision of electronic communications networks or services including an itemised breakdown of fixed asset and structural costs, or

(b) have structural separation for the activities associated with the provision of electronic communications networks or services.

Member States may choose not to apply the requirements referred to in the first subparagraph to undertakings the annual turnover of which in activities associated with electronic communications networks or services in the Member States is less than EUR 50 million.

2. Where undertakings providing public communications networks or publicly available electronic communications services are not subject to the requirements of company law and do not satisfy the small and medium-sized enterprise criteria of Community law accounting rules, their financial reports shall be drawn up and submitted to independent audit and published. The audit shall be carried out in accordance with the relevant Community and national rules.

This requirement shall also apply to the separate accounts required under paragraph 1(a).

CHAPTER IV

GENERAL PROVISIONS

Article 14

Undertakings with significant market power

1. Where the Specific Directives require national regulatory authorities to determine whether operators have significant market power in accordance with the procedure referred to in Article 16, paragraphs 2 and 3 of this Article shall apply.

2. An undertaking shall be deemed to have significant market power if, either individually or jointly with others, it enjoys a position equivalent to dominance, that is to say a position of economic strength affording it the power to behave to an appreciable extent independently of competitors, customers and ultimately consumers.

In particular, national regulatory authorities shall, when assessing whether two or more undertakings are in a joint dominant position in a market, act in accordance with Community law and take into the utmost account the guidelines on market analysis and the assessment of significant market power published by the Commission pursuant to

Article 15. Criteria to be used in making such an assessment are set out in Annex II.

3. Where an undertaking has significant market power on a specific market, it may also be deemed to have significant market power on a closely related market, where the links between the two markets are such as to allow the market power held in one market to be leveraged into the other market, thereby strengthening the market power of the undertaking.

Article 15

Market definition procedure

1. After public consultation and consultation with national regulatory authorities the Commission shall adopt a recommendation on relevant product and service markets (hereinafter 'the recommendation'). The recommendation shall identify in accordance with Annex I hereto those product and service markets within the electronic communications sector, the characteristics of which may be such as to justify the imposition of regulatory obligations set out in the Specific Directives, without prejudice to markets that may be defined in specific cases under competition law. The Commission shall define markets in accordance with the principles of competition law.

The Commission shall regularly review the recommendation.

2. The Commission shall publish, at the latest on the date of entry into force of this Directive, guidelines for market analysis and the assessment of significant market power (hereinafter 'the guidelines') which shall be in accordance with the principles of competition law.

3. National regulatory authorities shall, taking the utmost account of the recommendation and the guidelines, define relevant markets appropriate to national circumstances, in particular relevant geographic markets within their territory, in accordance with the principles of competition law. National regulatory authorities shall follow the procedures referred to in Articles 6 and 7 before defining the markets that differ from those defined in the recommendation.

4. After consultation with national regulatory authorities the Commission may, acting in accordance with the procedure referred to in Article 22(3), adopt a Decision identifying transnational markets.

Article 16

Market analysis procedure

1. As soon as possible after the adoption of the recommendation or any updating thereof, national regulatory authorities shall carry out an analysis of the relevant markets,

taking the utmost account of the guidelines. Member States shall ensure that this analysis is carried out, where appropriate, in collaboration with the national competition authorities.

2.   Where a national regulatory authority is required under Articles 16, 17, 18 or 19 of Directive 2002/22/EC (Universal Service Directive), or Articles 7 or 8 of Directive 2002/19/EC (Access Directive) to determine whether to impose, maintain, amend or withdraw obligations on undertakings, it shall determine on the basis of its market analysis referred to in paragraph 1 of this Article whether a relevant market is effectively competitive.

3.   Where a national regulatory authority concludes that the market is effectively competitive, it shall not impose or maintain any of the specific regulatory obligations referred to in paragraph 2 of this Article. In cases where sector specific regulatory obligations already exist, it shall withdraw such obligations placed on undertakings in that relevant market. An appropriate period of notice shall be given to parties affected by such a withdrawal of obligations.

4.   Where a national regulatory authority determines that a relevant market is not effectively competitive, it shall identify undertakings with significant market power on that market in accordance with Article 14 and the national regulatory authority shall on such undertakings impose appropriate specific regulatory obligations referred to in paragraph 2 of this Article or maintain or amend such obligations where they already exist.

5.   In the case of transnational markets identified in the Decision referred to in Article 15(4), the national regulatory authorities concerned shall jointly conduct the market analysis taking the utmost account of the guidelines and decide on any imposition, maintenance, amendment or withdrawal of regulatory obligations referred to in paragraph 2 of this Article in a concerted fashion.

6.   Measures taken according to the provisions of paragraphs 3, 4 and 5 of this Article shall be subject to the procedures referred to in Articles 6 and 7.

Article 17

Standardisation

1.   The Commission, acting in accordance with the procedure referred to in Article 22(2), shall draw up and publish in the *Official Journal of the European Communities* a list of standards and/or specifications to serve as a basis for encouraging the harmonised provision of electronic communications networks, electronic communications services and associated facilities and services. Where necessary, the Commission may, acting in accordance with the procedure referred to in Article 22(2) and following consultation of the Committee established by Directive 98/34/EC, request that standards be drawn up by the European standards organisations (European Committee for Standardisation (CEN), European Committee for Electrotechnical Standardisation (CENELEC), and European Telecommunications Standards Institute (ETSI)).

2.   Member States shall encourage the use of the standards and/or specifications referred to in paragraph 1, for the provision of services, technical interfaces and/or network functions, to the extent strictly necessary to ensure interoperability of services and to improve freedom of choice for users.

As long as standards and/or specifications have not been published in accordance with paragraph 1, Member States shall encourage the implementation of standards and/or specifications adopted by the European standards organisations.

In the absence of such standards and/or specifications, Member States shall encourage the implementation of international standards or recommendations adopted by the International Telecommunication Union (ITU), the International Organisation for Standardisation (ISO) or the International Electrotechnical Commission (IEC).

Where international standards exist, Member States shall encourage the European standards organisations to use them, or the relevant parts of them, as a basis for the standards they develop, except where such international standards or relevant parts would be ineffective.

3.   If the standards and/or specifications referred to in paragraph 1 have not been adequately implemented so that interoperability of services in one or more Member States cannot be ensured, the implementation of such standards and/or specifications may be made compulsory under the procedure laid down in paragraph 4, to the extent strictly necessary to ensure such interoperability and to improve freedom of choice for users.

4.   Where the Commission intends to make the implementation of certain standards and/or specifications compulsory, it shall publish a notice in the *Official Journal of the European Communities* and invite public comment by all parties concerned. The Commission, acting in accordance with the procedure referred to in Article 22(3), shall make implementation of the relevant standards compulsory by making reference to them as compulsory standards in the list of standards and/or specifications published in the *Official Journal of the European Communities*.

5.   Where the Commission considers that standards and/or specifications referred to in paragraph 1 no longer contribute to the provision of harmonised electronic communications services, or that they no longer meet consumers' needs or are hampering technological development, it shall, acting in accordance with the procedure referred to in Article 22(2), remove them from the list of standards and/or specifications referred to in paragraph 1.

6.   Where the Commission considers that standards and/or specifications referred to in paragraph 4 no longer contribute to the provision of harmonised electronic communications services, or that they no longer meet consumers' needs or are hampering technological development, it shall, acting in

accordance with the procedure referred to in Article 22(3), remove them from this list of standards and/or specifications referred to in paragraph 1.

7.   This Article does not apply in respect of any of the essential requirements, interface specifications or harmonised standards to which the provisions of Directive 1999/5/EC apply.

Article 18

Interoperability of digital interactive television services

1.   In order to promote the free flow of information, media pluralism and cultural diversity, Member States shall encourage, in accordance with the provisions of Article 17(2):

(a) providers of digital interactive television services for distribution to the public in the Community on digital interactive television platforms, regardless of the transmission mode, to use an open API;

(b) providers of all enhanced digital television equipment deployed for the reception of digital interactive television services on interactive digital television platforms to comply with an open API in accordance with the minimum requirements of the relevant standards or specifications.

2.   Without prejudice to Article 5(1)(b) of Directive 2002/19/ EC (Access Directive), Member States shall encourage proprietors of APIs to make available on fair, reasonable and non-discriminatory terms, and against appropriate remuneration, all such information as is necessary to enable providers of digital interactive television services to provide all services supported by the API in a fully functional form.

3.   Within one year after the date of application referred to in Article 28(1), second subparagraph, the Commission shall examine the effects of this Article. If interoperability and freedom of choice for users have not been adequately achieved in one or more Member States, the Commission may take action in accordance with the procedure laid down in Article 17(3) and (4).

Article 19

Harmonisation procedures

1.   Where the Commission, acting in accordance with the procedure referred to in Article 22(2), issues recommendations to Member States on the harmonised application of the provisions in this Directive and the Specific Directives in order to further the achievement of the objectives set out in Article 8, Member States shall ensure that national regulatory authorities take the utmost account of those recommendations in carrying out their tasks. Where a national regulatory authority chooses not to follow a recommendation, it shall inform the Commission giving the reasoning for its position.

2.   Where the Commission finds that divergence at national level in regulations aimed at implementing Article 10(4) creates a barrier to the single market, the Commission may, acting in accordance with the procedure referred to in Article 22(3), take the appropriate technical implementing measures.

Article 20

Dispute resolution between undertakings

1.   In the event of a dispute arising in connection with obligations arising under this Directive or the Specific Directives between undertakings providing electronic communications networks or services in a Member State, the national regulatory authority concerned shall, at the request of either party, and without prejudice to the provisions of paragraph 2, issue a binding decision to resolve the dispute in the shortest possible time frame and in any case within four months except in exceptional circumstances. The Member State concerned shall require that all parties cooperate fully with the national regulatory authority.

2.   Member States may make provision for national regulatory authorities to decline to resolve a dispute through a binding decision where other mechanisms, including mediation, exist and would better contribute to resolution of the dispute in a timely manner in accordance with the provisions of Article 8. The national regulatory authority shall inform the parties without delay. If after four months the dispute is not resolved, and if the dispute has not been brought before the courts by the party seeking redress, the national regulatory authority shall issue, at the request of either party, a binding decision to resolve the dispute in the shortest possible time frame and in any case within four months.

3.   In resolving a dispute, the national regulatory authority shall take decisions aimed at achieving the objectives set out in Article 8. Any obligations imposed on an undertaking by the national regulatory authority in resolving a dispute shall respect the provisions of this Directive or the Specific Directives.

4.   The decision of the national regulatory authority shall be made available to the public, having regard to the requirements of business confidentiality. The parties concerned shall be given a full statement of the reasons on which it is based.

5.   The procedure referred to in paragraphs 1, 3 and 4 shall not preclude either party from bringing an action before the courts.

Article 21

Resolution of cross-border disputes

1.   In the event of a cross-border dispute arising under this Directive or the Specific Directives between parties in different

Member States, where the dispute lies within the competence of national regulatory authorities from more than one Member State, the procedure set out in paragraphs 2, 3 and 4 shall be applicable.

2. Any party may refer the dispute to the national regulatory authorities concerned. The national regulatory authorities shall coordinate their efforts in order to bring about a resolution of the dispute, in accordance with the objectives set out in Article 8. Any obligations imposed on an undertaking by the national regulatory authority in resolving a dispute shall respect the provisions of this Directive or the Specific Directives.

3. Member States may make provision for national regulatory authorities jointly to decline to resolve a dispute where other mechanisms, including mediation, exist and would better contribute to resolution of the dispute in a timely manner in accordance with the provisions of Article 8. They shall inform the parties without delay. If after four months the dispute is not resolved, if the dispute has not been brought before the courts by the party seeking redress, and if either party requests it, the national regulatory authorities shall coordinate their efforts in order to bring about a resolution of the dispute, in accordance with the provisions set out in Article 8.

4. The procedure referred to in paragraph 2 shall not preclude either party from bringing an action before the courts.

Article 22

Committee

1. The Commission shall be assisted by a Committee ('the Communications Committee').

2. Where reference is made to this paragraph, Articles 3 and 7 of Decision 1999/468/EC shall apply, having regard to the provisions of Article 8 thereof.

3. Where reference is made to this paragraph, Articles 5 and 7 of Decision 1999/468/EC shall apply, having regard to the provisions of Article 8 thereof.

The period laid down in Article 5(6) of Decision 1999/468/EC shall be three months.

4. The Committee shall adopt its rules of procedure.

Article 23

Exchange of information

1. The Commission shall provide all relevant information to the Communications Committee on the outcome of regular consultations with the representatives of network operators, service providers, users, consumers, manufacturers and trade unions, as well as third countries and international organisations.

2. The Communications Committee shall, taking account of the Community's electronic communications policy, foster the exchange of information between the Member States and between the Member States and the Commission on the situation and the development of regulatory activities regarding electronic communications networks and services.

Article 24

Publication of information

1. Member States shall ensure that up-to-date information pertaining to the application of this Directive and the Specific Directives is made publicly available in a manner that guarantees all interested parties easy access to that information. They shall publish a notice in their national official gazette describing how and where the information is published. The first such notice shall be published before the date of application referred to in Article 28(1), second subparagraph, and thereafter a notice shall be published whenever there is any change in the information contained therein.

2. Member States shall send to the Commission a copy of all such notices at the time of publication. The Commission shall distribute the information to the Communications Committee as appropriate.

Article 25

Review procedures

1. The Commission shall periodically review the functioning of this Directive and report to the European Parliament and to the Council, on the first occasion not later than three years after the date of application referred to in Article 28(1), second subparagraph. For this purpose, the Commission may request information from the Member States, which shall be supplied without undue delay.

CHAPTER V

FINAL PROVISIONS

Article 26

Repeal

The following Directives and Decisions are hereby repealed with effect from the date of application referred to in Article 28(1), second subparagraph:

— Directive 90/387/EEC,

— Council Decision 91/396/EEC of 29 July 1991 on the introduction of a single European emergency call number ([1]),

— Council Directive 92/44/EEC of 5 June 1992 on the application of open network provision to leased lines ([2]),

— Council Decision 92/264/EEC of 11 May 1992 on the introduction of a standard international telephone access code in the Community ([3]),

— Directive 95/47/EC,

— Directive 97/13/EC,

— Directive 97/33/EC,

— Directive 98/10/EC of the European Parliament and of the Council of 26 February 1998 on the application of open network provision (ONP) to voice telephony and on universal service for telecommunications in a competitive environment ([4]).

Article 27

Transitional measures

Member States shall maintain all obligations under national law referred to in Article 7 of Directive 2002/19/EC (Access Directive) and Article 16 of Directive 2002/22/EC (Universal Service Directive) until such time as a determination is made in respect of those obligations by a national regulatory authority in accordance with Article 16 of this Directive.

Operators of fixed public telephone networks that were designated by their national regulatory authority as having significant market power in the provision of fixed public telephone networks and services under Annex I, Part 1 of Directive 97/33/EC or Directive 98/10/EC shall continue to be considered 'notified operators' for the purposes of Regulation (EC) No 2887/2000 until such a time as the market analysis procedure referred to in Article 16 has been completed. Thereafter they shall cease to be considered 'notified operators' for the purposes of the Regulation.

Article 28

Transposition

1.   Member States shall adopt and publish the laws, regulations and administrative provisions necessary to comply with this Directive not later than 24 July 2003. They shall forthwith inform the Commission thereof.

They shall apply those measures from 25 July 2003.

2.   When Member States adopt these measures, they shall contain a reference to this Directive or be accompanied by such a reference on the occasion of their official publication. The methods of making such a reference shall be laid down by the Member States.

3.   Member States shall communicate to the Commission the text of the provisions of national law which they adopt in the field governed by this Directive and of any subsequent amendments to those provisions.

Article 29

Entry into force

This Directive shall enter into force on the day of its publication in the *Official Journal of the European Communities*.

Article 30

Addressees

This Directive is addressed to the Member States.

Done at Brussels, 7 March 2002.

For the European Parliament	*For the Council*
The President	*The President*
P. COX	J. C. APARICIO

([1]) OJ L 217, 6.8.1991, p. 31.
([2]) OJ L 165, 19.6.1992, p. 27. Directive as last amended by Commission Decision 98/80/EC (OJ L 14, 20.1.1998, p. 27).
([3]) OJ L 137, 20.5.1992, p. 21.
([4]) OJ L 101, 1.4.1998, p. 24.

ANNEX I

List of markets to be included in the initial Commission recommendation on relevant product and service markets referred to in Article 15

1. *Markets referred to in Directive 2002/22/EC (Universal Service Directive)*

   Article 16 — Markets defined under the former regulatory framework, where obligations should be reviewed.

   The provision of connection to and use of the public telephone network at fixed locations.

   The provision of leased lines to end users.

2. *Markets referred to in Directive 2002/19/EC (Access Directive)*

   Article 7 — Markets defined under the former regulatory framework, where obligations should be reviewed.

   Interconnection (Directive 97/33/EC)

   > call origination in the fixed public telephone network

   > call termination in the fixed public telephone network

   > transit services in the fixed public telephone network

   > call origination on public mobile telephone networks

   > call termination on public mobile telephone networks

   > leased line interconnection (interconnection of part circuits)

   Network access and special network access (Directive 97/33/EC, Directive 98/10/EC)

   > access to the fixed public telephone network, including unbundled access to the local loop

   > access to public mobile telephone networks, including carrier selection

   Wholesale leased line capacity (Directive 92/44/EEC)

   > wholesale provision of leased line capacity to other suppliers of electronic communications networks or services

3. *Markets referred to in Regulation (EC) No 2887/2000*

   Services provided over unbundled (twisted metallic pair) loops.

4. *Additional markets*

   The national market for international roaming services on public mobile telephone networks.

———

ANNEX II

Criteria to be used by national regulatory authorities in making an assessment of joint dominance in accordance with Article 14(2), second subparagraph

Two or more undertakings can be found to be in a joint dominant position within the meaning of Article 14 if, even in the absence of structural or other links between them, they operate in a market the structure of which is considered to be conducive to coordinated effects. Without prejudice to the case law of the Court of Justice on joint dominance, this is likely to be the case where the market satisfies a number of appropriate characteristics, in particular in terms of market concentration, transparency and other characteristics mentioned below:

— mature market,

— stagnant or moderate growth on the demand side,

— low elasticity of demand,

— homogeneous product,

— similar cost structures,

— similar market shares,

— lack of technical innovation, mature technology,

— absence of excess capacity,

— high barriers to entry,

— lack of countervailing buying power,

— lack of potential competition,

— various kinds of informal or other links between the undertakings concerned,

— retaliatory mechanisms,

— lack or reduced scope for price competition.

The above is not an exhaustive list, nor are the criteria cumulative. Rather, the list is intended to illustrate only the sorts of evidence that could be used to support assertions concerning the existence of joint dominance.

———————

I

(Acts whose publication is obligatory)

REGULATION (EC) No 2887/2000 OF THE EUROPEAN PARLIAMENT AND OF THE COUNCIL

of 18 December 2000

on unbundled access to the local loop

(Text with EEA relevance)

THE EUROPEAN PARLIAMENT AND THE COUNCIL OF THE EUROPEAN UNION,

Having regard to the Treaty establishing the European Community, and in particular Article 95 thereof,

Having regard to the proposal from the Commission,

Having regard to the opinion of the Economic and Social Committee (¹),

Acting in accordance with the procedure laid down in Article 251 of the Treaty (²),

Whereas:

(1) The conclusions of the European Council of Lisbon of 23 and 24 March 2000 note that, for Europe to fully seize the growth and job potential of the digital, knowledge-based economy, businesses and citizens must have access to an inexpensive, world-class communications infrastructure and a wide range of services. The Member States, together with the Commission, are called upon to work towards introducing greater competition in local access networks before the end of 2000 and unbundling the local loop, in order to help bring about a substantial reduction in the costs of using the Internet. The Feira European Council of 20 June 2000 endorsed the proposed 'e-Europe' Action Plan which identifies unbundled access to the local loop as a short-term priority.

(2) Local loop unbundling should complement the existing provisions in Community law guaranteeing universal service and affordable access for all citizens by enhancing competition, ensuring economic efficiency and bringing maximum benefit to users.

(3) The 'local loop' is the physical twisted metallic pair circuit in the fixed public telephone network connecting the network termination point at the subscriber's premises to the main distribution frame or equivalent facility. As noted in the Commission's Fifth Report on the implementation of the telecommunications regulatory package, the local access network remains one of the least competitive segments of the liberalised telecommunications market. New entrants do not have widespread alternative network infrastructures and are unable, with traditional technologies, to match the economies of scale and the coverage of operators designated as having significant market power in the fixed public telephone network market. This results from the fact that these operators rolled out their metallic local access infrastructures over significant periods of time protected by exclusive rights and were able to fund investment costs through monopoly rents.

(4) The European Parliament Resolution of 13 June 2000 on the Commission communication on the 1999 Communications review stresses the importance of enabling the sector to develop infrastructures which promote the growth of electronic communications and e-commerce and the importance of regulating in a way that supports this growth. It notes that the unbundling of the local loop currently concerns mainly the metallic infrastructure of a dominant entity and that investment in alternative infrastructures must have the possibility of ensuring a reasonable rate of return, since that might facilitate the expansion of these infrastructures in areas where their penetration is still low.

(5) The provision of new loops with high capacity optical fibre directly to major users is a specific market that is developing under competitive conditions with new investments. This Regulation therefore addresses access to metallic local loops, without prejudice to national obligations regarding other types of access to local infrastructures.

(¹) Opinion delivered on 19 October 2000 (not yet published in the Official Journal).
(²) Opinion of the European Parliament of 26 October 2000 (not yet published in the Official Journal) and Decision of the Council of 5 December 2000.

Reproduced from the Official Journal of the European Communities: L 336, 30/12/2000 P. 0004–0008

237

(6) It would not be economically viable for new entrants to duplicate the incumbent's metallic local access infrastructure in its entirety within a reasonable time. Alternative infrastructures such as cable television, satellite, wireless local loops do not generally offer the same functionality or ubiquity for the time being, though situations in Member States may differ.

(7) Unbundled access to the local loop allows new entrants to compete with notified operators in offering high bit-rate data transmission services for continuous Internet access and for multimedia applications based on digital subscriber line (DSL) technology as well as voice telephony services. A reasonable request for unbundled access implies that the access is necessary for the provision of the services of the beneficiary, and that refusal of the request would prevent, restrict or distort competition in this sector.

(8) This Regulation mandates unbundled access to the metallic local loops only of notified operators that have been designated by their national regulatory authorities as having significant market power in the fixed public telephone network supply market under the relevant Community provisions (hereinafter referred to as 'notified operators'). Member States have already notified to the Commission the names of those fixed public network operators which have significant market power under Annex I, Part 1, of Directive 97/33/EC of the European Parliament and of the Council of 30 June 1997 on interconnection in telecommunications with regard to ensuring universal service and interoperability through application of the principles of open network provision (ONP) ([1]), and Directive 98/10/EC of the European Parliament and of the Council of 26 February 1998 on the application of open network provision to voice telephony and on universal service for telecommunications in a competitive environment ([2]).

(9) A notified operator cannot be required to provide types of access which are not within its powers to provide, for example where fulfilment of a request would cause a violation of the legal rights of an independent third party. The obligation to provide unbundled access to the local loop does not imply that notified operators have to install entirely new local network infrastructure specifically to meet beneficiaries' requests.

(10) Although commercial negotiation is the preferred method for reaching agreement on technical and pricing issues for local loop access, experience shows that in most cases regulatory intervention is necessary due to imbalance in negotiating power between the new entrant and the notified operator, and lack of other alternatives. In certain circumstances the national regula-

tory authority may, in accordance with Community law, intervene on its own initiative in order to ensure fair competition, economic efficiency and maximum benefit for end-users. Failure of the notified operator to meet lead times should entitle the beneficiary to receive compensation.

(11) Costing and pricing rules for local loops and related facilities should be transparent, non-discriminatory and objective to ensure fairness. Pricing rules should ensure that the local loop provider is able to cover its appropriate costs in this regard plus a reasonable return, in order to ensure the long term development and upgrade of local access infrastructure. Pricing rules for local loops should foster fair and sustainable competition, bearing in mind the need for investment in alternative infrastructures, and ensure that there is no distortion of competition, in particular no margin squeeze between prices of wholesale and retail services of the notified operator. In this regard, it is considered important that competition authorities be consulted.

(12) Notified operators should provide information and unbundled access to third parties under the same conditions and of the same quality as they provide for their own services or to their associated companies. To this end, the publication by the notified operator of an adequate reference offer for unbundled access to the local loop, within a short time-frame and ideally on the Internet, and under the supervisory control of the national regulatory authority, would contribute to the creation of transparent and non-discriminatory market conditions.

(13) In its Recommendation 2000/417/EC of 25 May 2000 on unbundled access to the local loop enabling the competitive provision of a full range of electronic communications services including broadband multimedia and high-speed Internet ([3]) and its Communication of 26 April 2000 ([4]), the Commission set out detailed guidance to assist national regulatory authorities on the fair regulation of different forms of unbundled access to the local loop.

(14) In accordance with the principle of subsidiarity as set out in Article 5 of the Treaty, the objective of achieving a harmonised framework for unbundled access to the local loop in order to enable the competitive provision of an inexpensive, world-class communications infrastructure and a wide range of services for all businesses and citizens in the Community cannot be achieved by the Member States in a secure, harmonised and timely manner and can therefore be better achieved by the Community. In accordance with the principle of proportionality as set out in that Article, the provisions of this

---

([1]) OJ L 199, 26.7.1997, p. 32. Directive as amended by Directive 98/61/EC (OJ L 268, 3.10.1998, p. 37).
([2]) OJ L 101, 1.4.1998, p. 24.

([3]) OJ L 156, 29.6.2000, p. 44.
([4]) OJ C 272, 23.9.2000, p. 55.

Regulation do not go beyond what is necessary in order to achieve this objective for that purpose. They are adopted without prejudice to national provisions complying with Community law which set out more detailed measures, for example dealing with virtual collocation.

(15) This Regulation complements the regulatory framework for telecommunications, in particular Directives 97/33/EC and 98/10/EC. The new regulatory framework for electronic communications should include appropriate provisions to replace this Regulation,

HAVE ADOPTED THIS REGULATION:

Article 1

Aim and Scope

1. This Regulation aims at intensifying competition and stimulating technological innovation on the local access market, through the setting of harmonised conditions for unbundled access to the local loop, to foster the competitive provision of a wide range of electronic communications services.

2. This Regulation shall apply to unbundled access to the local loops and related facilities of notified operators as defined in Article 2(a).

3. This Regulation shall apply without prejudice to the obligations for notified operators to comply with the principle of non-discrimination, when using the fixed public telephone network in order to provide high speed access and transmission services to third parties in the same manner as they provide for their own services or to their associated companies, in accordance with Community provisions.

4. This Regulation is without prejudice to the rights of Member States to maintain or introduce measures in conformity with Community law which contain more detailed provisions than those set out in this Regulation and/or are outside the scope of this Regulation *inter alia* with respect to other types of access to local infrastructures.

Article 2

Definitions

For the purposes of this Regulation the following definitions apply:

(a) 'notified operator' means operators of fixed public telephone networks that have been designated by their national regulatory authority as having significant market power in the provision of fixed public telephone networks

and services under Annex I, Part 1, of Directive 97/33/EC or Directive 98/10/EC;

(b) 'beneficiary' means a third party duly authorised in accordance with Directive 97/13/EC [1] or entitled to provide communications services under national legislation, and which is eligible for unbundled access to a local loop;

(c) 'local loop' means the physical twisted metallic pair circuit connecting the network termination point at the subscriber's premises to the main distribution frame or equivalent facility in the fixed public telephone network;

(d) 'local sub-loop' means a partial local loop connecting the network termination point at the subscriber's premises to a concentration point or a specified intermediate access point in the fixed public telephone network;

(e) 'unbundled access to the local loop' means full unbundled access to the local loop and shared access to the local loop; it does not entail a change in ownership of the local loop;

(f) 'full unbundled access to the local loop' means the provision to a beneficiary of access to the local loop or local sub loop of the notified operator authorising the use of the full frequency spectrum of the twisted metallic pair;

(g) 'shared access to the local loop' means the provision to a beneficiary of access to the local loop or local sub loop of the notified operator, authorising the use of the non-voice band frequency spectrum of the twisted metallic pair; the local loop continues to be used by the notified operator to provide the telephone service to the public;

(h) 'collocation' means the provision of physical space and technical facilities necessary to reasonably accommodate and connect the relevant equipment of a beneficiary, as mentioned in Section B of the Annex;

(i) 'related facilities' means the facilities associated with the provision of unbundled access to the local loop, notably collocation, cable connections and relevant information technology systems, access to which is necessary for a beneficiary to provide services on a competitive and fair basis.

Article 3

Provision of unbundled access

1. Notified operators shall publish from 31 December 2000, and keep updated, a reference offer for unbundled access to their local loops and related facilities, which shall include at least the items listed in the Annex. The offer shall be sufficiently unbundled so that the beneficiary does not have to pay for network elements or facilities which are not necessary for the supply of its services, and shall contain a description of the components of the offer, associated terms and conditions, including charges.

[1] Directive 97/13/EC of the European Parliament and of the Council of 10 April 1997 on a common framework for general authorisations and individual licences in the field of telecommunications services (OJ L 117, 7.5.1997, p. 15).

2. Notified operators shall from 31 December 2000 meet reasonable requests from beneficiaries for unbundled access to their local loops and related facilities, under transparent, fair and non-discriminatory conditions. Requests shall only be refused on the basis of objective criteria, relating to technical feasibility or the need to maintain network integrity. Where access is refused, the aggrieved party may submit the case to the dispute resolution procedure referred to in Article 4(5). Notified operators shall provide beneficiaries with facilities equivalent to those provided for their own services or to their associated companies, and with the same conditions and time-scales.

3. Without prejudice to Article 4(4), notified operators shall charge prices for unbundled access to the local loop and related facilities set on the basis of cost-orientation.

Article 4

Supervision by the national regulatory authority

1. The national regulatory authority shall ensure that charging for unbundled access to the local loop fosters fair and sustainable competition.

2. The national regulatory authority shall have the power to:

(a) impose changes on the reference offer for unbundled access to the local loop and related facilities, including prices, where such changes are justified; and

(b) require notified operators to supply information relevant for the implementation of this Regulation.

3. The national regulatory authority may, where justified, intervene on its own initiative in order to ensure non-discrimination, fair competition, economic efficiency and maximum benefit for users.

4. When the national regulatory authority determines that the local access market is sufficiently competitive, it shall relieve the notified operators of the obligation laid down in Article 3(3) for prices to be set on the basis of cost-orientation.

5. Disputes between undertakings concerning issues included in this Regulation shall be subject to the national dispute resolution procedures established in conformity with Directive 97/33/EC and shall be handled promptly, fairly and transparently.

Article 5

Entry into force

This Regulation shall enter into force on the third day following that of its publication in the *Official Journal of the European Communities*.

This Regulation shall be binding in its entirety and directly applicable in all Member States.

Done at Brussels, 18 December 2000.

<table>
<tr><td>*For the European Parliament*</td><td>*For the Council*</td></tr>
<tr><td>*The President*</td><td>*The President*</td></tr>
<tr><td>N. FONTAINE</td><td>D. VOYNET</td></tr>
</table>

ANNEX

MINIMUM LIST OF ITEMS TO BE INCLUDED IN A REFERENCE OFFER FOR UNBUNDLED ACCESS TO THE LOCAL LOOP TO BE PUBLISHED BY NOTIFIED OPERATORS

A. Conditions for unbundled access to the local loop

  1. Network elements to which access is offered covering in particular the following elements:

  (a) access to local loops;

  (b) access to non-voice band frequency spectrum of a local loop, in the case of shared access to the local loop;

  2. Information concerning the locations of physical access sites (¹), availability of local loops in specific parts of the access network;

  3. Technical conditions related to access and use of local loops, including the technical characteristics of the twisted metallic pair in the local loop;

  4. Ordering and provisioning procedures, usage restrictions.

B. Collocation services

  1. Information on the notified operator's relevant sites (¹);

  2. Collocation options at the sites indicated under point 1 (including physical collocation and, as appropriate, distant collocation and virtual collocation);

  3. Equipment characteristics: restrictions, if any, on equipment that can be collocated;

  4. Security issues: measures put in place by notified operators to ensure the security of their locations;

  5. Access conditions for staff of competitive operators;

  6. Safety standards;

  7. Rules for the allocation of space where collocation space is limited;

  8. Conditions for beneficiaries to inspect the locations at which physical collocation is available, or sites where collocation has been refused on grounds of lack of capacity.

C. Information systems

  Conditions for access to notified operator's operational support systems, information systems or databases for pre-ordering, provisioning, ordering, maintenance and repair requests and billing.

D. Supply conditions

  1. Lead time for responding to requests for supply of services and facilities; service level agreements, fault resolution, procedures to return to a normal level of service and quality of service parameters;

  2. Standard contract terms, including, where appropriate, compensation provided for failure to meet lead times;

  3. Prices or pricing formulae for each feature, function and facility listed above.

(¹) Availability of this information may be restricted to interested parties only, in order to avoid public security concerns.

DIRECTIVE 2002/22/EC OF THE EUROPEAN PARLIAMENT AND OF THE COUNCIL

of 7 March 2002

on universal service and users' rights relating to electronic communications networks and services (Universal Service Directive)

THE EUROPEAN PARLIAMENT AND THE COUNCIL OF THE EUROPEAN UNION,

Having regard to the Treaty establishing the European Community, and in particular Article 95 thereof,

Having regard to the proposal from the Commission ([1]),

Having regard to the opinion of the Economic and Social Committee ([2]),

Having regard to the opinion of the Committee of the Regions ([3]),

Acting in accordance with the procedure laid down in Article 251 of the Treaty ([4]),

Whereas:

(1) The liberalisation of the telecommunications sector and increasing competition and choice for communications services go hand in hand with parallel action to create a harmonised regulatory framework which secures the delivery of universal service. The concept of universal service should evolve to reflect advances in technology, market developments and changes in user demand. The regulatory framework established for the full liberalisation of the telecommunications market in 1998 in the Community defined the minimum scope of universal service obligations and established rules for its costing and financing.

(2) Under Article 153 of the Treaty, the Community is to contribute to the protection of consumers.

(3) The Community and its Member States have undertaken commitments on the regulatory framework of telecommunications networks and services in the context of the World Trade Organisation (WTO) agreement on basic telecommunications. Any member of the WTO has the right to define the kind of universal service obligation it wishes to maintain. Such obligations will not be regarded as anti-competitive per se, provided they are administered in a transparent, non-discriminatory and competitively neutral manner and are not more burdensome than necessary for the kind of universal service defined by the member.

(4) Ensuring universal service (that is to say, the provision of a defined minimum set of services to all end-users at an affordable price) may involve the provision of some services to some end-users at prices that depart from those resulting from normal market conditions. However, compensating undertakings designated to provide such services in such circumstances need not result in any distortion of competition, provided that designated undertakings are compensated for the specific net cost involved and provided that the net cost burden is recovered in a competitively neutral way.

(5) In a competitive market, certain obligations should apply to all undertakings providing publicly available telephone services at fixed locations and others should apply only to undertakings enjoying significant market power or which have been designated as a universal service operator.

(6) The network termination point represents a boundary for regulatory purposes between the regulatory framework for electronic communication networks and services and the regulation of telecommunication terminal equipment. Defining the location of the network termination point is the responsibility of the national regulatory authority, where necessary on the basis of a proposal by the relevant undertakings.

(7) Member States should continue to ensure that the services set out in Chapter II are made available with the quality specified to all end-users in their territory, irrespective of their geographical location, and, in the light of specific national conditions, at an affordable price. Member States may, in the context of universal service obligations and in the light of national conditions, take specific measures for consumers in rural or geographically isolated areas to ensure their access to the services set out in the Chapter II and the affordability of those services, as well as ensure under

([1]) OJ C 365 E, 19.12.2000, p. 238 and OJ C 332 E, 27.11.2001, p. 292.
([2]) OJ C 139, 11.5.2001, p. 15.
([3]) OJ C 144, 16.5.2001, p. 60.
([4]) Opinion of the European Parliament of 13 June 2001 (not yet published in the Official Journal), Council Common Position of 17 September 2001 (OJ C 337, 30.11.2001, p. 55) and Decision of the European Parliament of 12 December 2001 (not yet published in the Official Journal). Council Decision of 14 February 2002.

the same conditions this access, in particular for the elderly, the disabled and for people with special social needs. Such measures may also include measures directly targeted at consumers with special social needs providing support to identified consumers, for example by means of specific measures, taken after the examination of individual requests, such as the paying off of debts.

(8) A fundamental requirement of universal service is to provide users on request with a connection to the public telephone network at a fixed location, at an affordable price. The requirement is limited to a single narrowband network connection, the provision of which may be restricted by Member States to the end-user's primary location/residence, and does not extend to the Integrated Services Digital Network (ISDN) which provides two or more connections capable of being used simultaneously. There should be no constraints on the technical means by which the connection is provided, allowing for wired or wireless technologies, nor any constraints on which operators provide part or all of universal service obligations. Connections to the public telephone network at a fixed location should be capable of supporting speech and data communications at rates sufficient for access to online services such as those provided via the public Internet. The speed of Internet access experienced by a given user may depend on a number of factors including the provider(s) of Internet connectivity as well as the given application for which a connection is being used. The data rate that can be supported by a single narrowband connection to the public telephone network depends on the capabilities of the subscriber's terminal equipment as well as the connection. For this reason it is not appropriate to mandate a specific data or bit rate at Community level. Currently available voice band modems typically offer a data rate of 56 kbit/s and employ automatic data rate adaptation to cater for variable line quality, with the result that the achieved data rate may be lower than 56 kbit/s. Flexibility is required on the one hand to allow Member States to take measures where necessary to ensure that connections are capable of supporting such a data rate, and on the other hand to allow Member States where relevant to permit data rates below this upper limit of 56 kbits/s in order, for example, to exploit the capabilities of wireless technologies (including cellular wireless networks) to deliver universal service to a higher proportion of the population. This may be of particular importance in some accession countries where household penetration of traditional telephone connections remains relatively low. In specific cases where the connection to the public telephony network at a fixed location is clearly insufficient to support satisfactory Internet access, Member States should be able to require the connection to be brought up to the level enjoyed by the majority of subscribers so that it supports data rates sufficient for access to the Internet. Where such specific measures produce a net cost burden for those consumers concerned, the net effect may be included in any net cost calculation of universal service obligations.

(9) The provisions of this Directive do not preclude Member States from designating different undertakings to provide the network and service elements of universal service. Designated undertakings providing network elements may be required to ensure such construction and maintenance as are necessary and proportionate to meet all reasonable requests for connection at a fixed location to the public telephone network and for access to publicly available telephone services at a fixed location.

(10) Affordable price means a price defined by Member States at national level in the light of specific national conditions, and may involve setting common tariffs irrespective of location or special tariff options to deal with the needs of low-income users. Affordability for individual consumers is related to their ability to monitor and control their expenditure.

(11) Directory information and a directory enquiry service constitute an essential access tool for publicly available telephone services and form part of the universal service obligation. Users and consumers desire comprehensive directories and a directory enquiry service covering all listed telephone subscribers and their numbers (including fixed and mobile numbers) and want this information to be presented in a non-preferential fashion. Directive 97/66/EC of the European Parliament and of the Council of 15 December 1997 concerning the processing of personal data and the protection of privacy in the telecommunications sector (^{1}) ensures the subscribers' right to privacy with regard to the inclusion of their personal information in a public directory.

(12) For the citizen, it is important for there to be adequate provision of public pay telephones, and for users to be able to call emergency telephone numbers and, in particular, the single European emergency call number ('112') free of charge from any telephone, including public pay telephones, without the use of any means of

---

(^{1}) OJ L 24, 30.1.1998, p. 1.

payment. Insufficient information about the existence of '112' deprives citizens of the additional safety ensured by the existence of this number at European level especially during their travel in other Member States.

(13) Member States should take suitable measures in order to guarantee access to and affordability of all publicly available telephone services at a fixed location for disabled users and users with special social needs. Specific measures for disabled users could include, as appropriate, making available accessible public telephones, public text telephones or equivalent measures for deaf or speech-impaired people, providing services such as directory enquiry services or equivalent measures free of charge for blind or partially sighted people, and providing itemised bills in alternative format on request for blind or partially sighted people. Specific measures may also need to be taken to enable disabled users and users with special social needs to access emergency services '112' and to give them a similar possibility to choose between different operators or service providers as other consumers. Quality of service standards have been developed for a range of parameters to assess the quality of services received by subscribers and how well undertakings designated with universal service obligations perform in achieving these standards. Quality of service standards do not yet exist in respect of disabled users. Performance standards and relevant parameters should be developed for disabled users and are provided for in Article 11 of this Directive. Moreover, national regulatory authorities should be enabled to require publication of quality of service performance data if and when such standards and parameters are developed. The provider of universal service should not take measures to prevent users from benefiting fully from services offered by different operators or service providers, in combination with its own services offered as part of universal service.

(14) The importance of access to and use of the public telephone network at a fixed location is such that it should be available to anyone reasonably requesting it. In accordance with the principle of subsidiarity, it is for Member States to decide on the basis of objective criteria which undertakings have universal service obligations for the purposes of this Directive, where appropriate taking into account the ability and the willingness of undertakings to accept all or part of the universal service obligations. It is important that universal service obligations are fulfilled in the most efficient fashion so that users generally pay prices that correspond to efficient cost provision. It is likewise important that universal service operators maintain the integrity of the network as well as service continuity and quality. The development of greater competition

and choice provide more possibilities for all or part of the universal service obligations to be provided by undertakings other than those with significant market power. Therefore, universal service obligations could in some cases be allocated to operators demonstrating the most cost-effective means of delivering access and services, including by competitive or comparative selection procedures. Corresponding obligations could be included as conditions in authorisations to provide publicly available services.

(15) Member States should monitor the situation of consumers with respect to their use of publicly available telephone services and in particular with respect to affordability. The affordability of telephone service is related to the information which users receive regarding telephone usage expenses as well as the relative cost of telephone usage compared to other services, and is also related to their ability to control expenditure. Affordability therefore means giving power to consumers through obligations imposed on undertakings designated as having universal service obligations. These obligations include a specified level of itemised billing, the possibility for consumers selectively to block certain calls (such as high-priced calls to premium services), the possibility for consumers to control expenditure via pre-payment means and the possibility for consumers to offset up-front connection fees. Such measures may need to be reviewed and changed in the light of market developments. Current conditions do not warrant a requirement for operators with universal service obligations to alert subscribers where a predetermined limit of expenditure is exceeded or an abnormal calling pattern occurs. Review of the relevant legislative provisions in future should consider whether there is a possible need to alert subscribers for these reasons.

(16) Except in cases of persistent late payment or non-payment of bills, consumers should be protected from immediate disconnection from the network on the grounds of an unpaid bill and, particularly in the case of disputes over high bills for premium rate services, should continue to have access to essential telephone services pending resolution of the dispute. Member States may decide that such access may continue to be provided only if the subscriber continues to pay line rental charges.

(17) Quality and price are key factors in a competitive market and national regulatory authorities should be able to monitor achieved quality of service for undertakings which have been designated as having universal service obligations. In relation to the quality of service attained by such undertakings, national

regulatory authorities should be able to take appropriate measures where they deem it necessary. National regulatory authorities should also be able to monitor the achieved quality of services of other undertakings providing public telephone networks and/or publicly available telephone services to users at fixed locations.

(18) Member States should, where necessary, establish mechanisms for financing the net cost of universal service obligations in cases where it is demonstrated that the obligations can only be provided at a loss or at a net cost which falls outside normal commercial standards. It is important to ensure that the net cost of universal service obligations is properly calculated and that any financing is undertaken with minimum distortion to the market and to undertakings, and is compatible with the provisions of Articles 87 and 88 of the Treaty.

(19) Any calculation of the net cost of universal service should take due account of costs and revenues, as well as the intangible benefits resulting from providing universal service, but should not hinder the general aim of ensuring that pricing structures reflect costs. Any net costs of universal service obligations should be calculated on the basis of transparent procedures.

(20) Taking into account intangible benefits means that an estimate in monetary terms, of the indirect benefits that an undertaking derives by virtue of its position as provider of universal service, should be deducted from the direct net cost of universal service obligations in order to determine the overall cost burden.

(21) When a universal service obligation represents an unfair burden on an undertaking, it is appropriate to allow Member States to establish mechanisms for efficiently recovering net costs. Recovery via public funds constitutes one method of recovering the net costs of universal service obligations. It is also reasonable for established net costs to be recovered from all users in a transparent fashion by means of levies on undertakings. Member States should be able to finance the net costs of different elements of universal service through different mechanisms, and/or to finance the net costs of some or all elements from either of the mechanisms or a combination of both. In the case of cost recovery by means of levies on undertakings, Member States should ensure that that the method of allocation amongst them is based on objective and non-discriminatory criteria and is in accordance with the principle of proportionality. This principle does not prevent Member States from exempting new entrants which have not yet achieved any significant market presence. Any funding mechanism should ensure that market participants only contribute to the financing of universal service

obligations and not to other activities which are not directly linked to the provision of the universal service obligations. Recovery mechanisms should in all cases respect the principles of Community law, and in particular in the case of sharing mechanisms those of non-discrimination and proportionality. Any funding mechanism should ensure that users in one Member State do not contribute to universal service costs in another Member State, for example when making calls from one Member State to another.

(22) Where Member States decide to finance the net cost of universal service obligations from public funds, this should be understood to comprise funding from general government budgets including other public financing sources such as state lotteries.

(23) The net cost of universal service obligations may be shared between all or certain specified classes of undertaking. Member States should ensure that the sharing mechanism respects the principles of transparency, least market distortion, non-discrimination and proportionality. Least market distortion means that contributions should be recovered in a way that as far as possible minimises the impact of the financial burden falling on end-users, for example by spreading contributions as widely as possible.

(24) National regulatory authorities should satisfy themselves that those undertakings benefiting from universal service funding provide a sufficient level of detail of the specific elements requiring such funding in order to justify their request. Member States' schemes for the costing and financing of universal service obligations should be communicated to the Commission for verification of compatibility with the Treaty. There are incentives for designated operators to raise the assessed net cost of universal service obligations. Therefore Member States should ensure effective transparency and control of amounts charged to finance universal service obligations.

(25) Communications markets continue to evolve in terms of the services used and the technical means used to deliver them to users. The universal service obligations, which are defined at a Community level, should be periodically reviewed with a view to proposing that the scope be changed or redefined. Such a review should take account of evolving social, commercial and technological conditions and the fact that any change of scope should be subject to the twin test of services that become available to a substantial majority of the

population, with a consequent risk of social exclusion for those who can not afford them. Care should be taken in any change of the scope of universal service obligations to ensure that certain technological choices are not artificially promoted above others, that a disproportionate financial burden is not imposed on sector undertakings (thereby endangering market developments and innovation) and that any financing burden does not fall unfairly on consumers with lower incomes. Any change of scope automatically means that any net cost can be financed via the methods permitted in this Directive. Member States are not permitted to impose on market players financial contributions which relate to measures which are not part of universal service obligations. Individual Member States remain free to impose special measures (outside the scope of universal service obligations) and finance them in conformity with Community law but not by means of contributions from market players.

(26) More effective competition across all access and service markets will give greater choice for users. The extent of effective competition and choice varies across the Community and varies within Member States between geographical areas and between access and service markets. Some users may be entirely dependent on the provision of access and services by an undertaking with significant market power. In general, for reasons of efficiency and to encourage effective competition, it is important that the services provided by an undertaking with significant market power reflect costs. For reasons of efficiency and social reasons, end-user tariffs should reflect demand conditions as well as cost conditions, provided that this does not result in distortions of competition. There is a risk that an undertaking with significant market power may act in various ways to inhibit entry or distort competition, for example by charging excessive prices, setting predatory prices, compulsory bundling of retail services or showing undue preference to certain customers. Therefore, national regulatory authorities should have powers to impose, as a last resort and after due consideration, retail regulation on an undertaking with significant market power. Price cap regulation, geographical averaging or similar instruments, as well as non-regulatory measures such as publicly available comparisons of retail tariffs, may be used to achieve the twin objectives of promoting effective competition whilst pursuing public interest needs, such as maintaining the affordability of publicly available telephone services for some consumers. Access to appropriate cost accounting information is necessary, in order for national regulatory authorities to fulfil their regulatory duties in this area, including the imposition of any tariff controls. However, regulatory controls on retail services should only be imposed where national regulatory authorities consider that relevant wholesale measures or measures regarding carrier selection or

pre-selection would fail to achieve the objective of ensuring effective competition and public interest.

(27) Where a national regulatory authority imposes obligations to implement a cost accounting system in order to support price controls, it may itself undertake an annual audit to ensure compliance with that cost accounting system, provided that it has the necessary qualified staff, or it may require the audit to be carried out by another qualified body, independent of the operator concerned.

(28) It is considered necessary to ensure the continued application of the existing provisions relating to the minimum set of leased line services in Community telecommunications legislation, in particular in Council Directive 92/44/EEC of 5 June 1992 on the application of open network provision to leased lines [1], until such time as national regulatory authorities determine, in accordance with the market analysis procedures laid down in Directive 2002/21/EC of the European Parliament and of the Council of 7 March 2002 on a common regulatory framework for electronic communications networks and services (Framework Directive) [2], that such provisions are no longer needed because a sufficiently competitive market has developed in their territory. The degree of competition is likely to vary between different markets of leased lines in the minimum set, and in different parts of the territory. In undertaking the market analysis, national regulatory authorities should make separate assessments for each market of leased lines in the minimum set, taking into account their geographic dimension. Leased lines services constitute mandatory services to be provided without recourse to any compensation mechanisms. The provision of leased lines outside of the minimum set of leased lines should be covered by general retail regulatory provisions rather than specific requirements covering the supply of the minimum set.

(29) National regulatory authorities may also, in the light of an analysis of the relevant market, require mobile operators with significant market power to enable their subscribers to access the services of any interconnected provider of publicly available telephone services on a call-by-call basis or by means of pre-selection.

---

[1] OJ L 165, 19.6.1992, p. 27. Directive as last amended by Commission Decision No 98/80/EC (OJ L 14, 20.1.1998, p. 27).
[2] See page 33 of this Official Journal.

(30) Contracts are an important tool for users and consumers to ensure a minimum level of transparency of information and legal security. Most service providers in a competitive environment will conclude contracts with their customers for reasons of commercial desirability. In addition to the provisions of this Directive, the requirements of existing Community consumer protection legislation relating to contracts, in particular Council Directive 93/13/EEC of 5 April 1993 on unfair terms in consumer contracts (¹) and Directive 97/7/EC of the European Parliament and of the Council of 20 May 1997 on the protection of consumers in respect of distance contracts (²), apply to consumer transactions relating to electronic networks and services. Specifically, consumers should enjoy a minimum level of legal certainty in respect of their contractual relations with their direct telephone service provider, such that the contractual terms, conditions, quality of service, condition for termination of the contract and the service, compensation measures and dispute resolution are specified in their contracts. Where service providers other than direct telephone service providers conclude contracts with consumers, the same information should be included in those contracts as well. The measures to ensure transparency on prices, tariffs, terms and conditions will increase the ability of consumers to optimise their choices and thus to benefit fully from competition.

(31) End-users should have access to publicly available information on communications services. Member States should be able to monitor the quality of services which are offered in their territories. National regulatory authorities should be able systematically to collect information on the quality of services offered in their territories on the basis of criteria which allow comparability between service providers and between Member States. Undertakings providing communications services, operating in a competitive environment, are likely to make adequate and up-to-date information on their services publicly available for reasons of commercial advantage. National regulatory authorities should nonetheless be able to require publication of such information where it is demonstrated that such information is not effectively available to the public.

(32) End-users should be able to enjoy a guarantee of interoperability in respect of all equipment sold in the Community for the reception of digital television. Member States should be able to require minimum harmonised standards in respect of such equipment. Such standards could be adapted from time to time in the light of technological and market developments.

(33) It is desirable to enable consumers to achieve the fullest connectivity possible to digital television sets. Interoperability is an evolving concept in dynamic markets. Standards bodies should do their utmost to ensure that appropriate standards evolve along with the technologies concerned. It is likewise important to ensure that connectors are available on television sets that are capable of passing all the necessary elements of a digital signal, including the audio and video streams, conditional access information, service information, application program interface (API) information and copy protection information. This Directive therefore ensures that the functionality of the open interface for digital television sets is not limited by network operators, service providers or equipment manufacturers and continues to evolve in line with technological developments. For display and presentation of digital interactive television services, the realisation of a common standard through a market-driven mechanism is recognised as a consumer benefit. Member States and the Commission may take policy initiatives, consistent with the Treaty, to encourage this development.

(34) All end-users should continue to enjoy access to operator assistance services whatever organisation provides access to the public telephone network.

(35) The provision of directory enquiry services and directories is already open to competition. The provisions of this Directive complement the provisions of Directive 97/66/EC by giving subscribers a right to have their personal data included in a printed or electronic directory. All service providers which assign telephone numbers to their subscribers are obliged to make relevant information available in a fair, cost-oriented and non-discriminatory manner.

(36) It is important that users should be able to call the single European emergency number '112', and any other national emergency telephone numbers, free of charge, from any telephone, including public pay telephones, without the use of any means of payment. Member States should have already made the necessary organisational arrangements best suited to the national organisation of the emergency systems, in order to ensure that calls to this number are adequately answered and handled. Caller location information, to be made available to the emergency services, will improve the level of protection and the security of users of '112' services and assist the emergency services, to the extent technically feasible, in the discharge of their duties, provided that the transfer of calls and associated data to the emergency services concerned is guaranteed. The reception and use of such information should comply with relevant Community law on the processing of personal data. Steady information technology

(¹) OJ L 95, 21.4.1993, p. 29.
(²) OJ L 144, 4.6.1997, p. 19.

improvements will progressively support the simultaneous handling of several languages over the networks at a reasonable cost. This in turn will ensure additional safety for European citizens using the '112' emergency call number.

(37) Easy access to international telephone services is vital for European citizens and European businesses. '00' has already been established as the standard international telephone access code for the Community. Special arrangements for making calls between adjacent locations across borders between Member States may be established or continued. The ITU has assigned, in accordance with ITU Recommendation E.164, code '3883' to the European Telephony Numbering Space (ETNS). In order to ensure connection of calls to the ETNS, undertakings operating public telephone networks should ensure that calls using '3883' are directly or indirectly interconnected to ETNS serving networks specified in the relevant European Telecommunications Standards Institute (ETSI) standards. Such interconnection arrangements should be governed by the provisions of Directive 2002/19/EC of the European Parliament and of the Council of 7 March 2002 on access to, and interconnection of, electronic communications networks and associated facilities (Access Directive) (¹).

(38) Access by end-users to all numbering resources in the Community is a vital pre-condition for a single market. It should include freephone, premium rate, and other non-geographic numbers, except where the called subscriber has chosen, for commercial reasons, to limit access from certain geographical areas. Tariffs charged to parties calling from outside the Member State concerned need not be the same as for those parties calling from inside that Member State.

(39) Tone dialling and calling line identification facilities are normally available on modern telephone exchanges and can therefore increasingly be provided at little or no expense. Tone dialling is increasingly being used for user interaction with special services and facilities, including value added services, and the absence of this facility can prevent the user from making use of these services. Member States are not required to impose obligations to provide these facilities when they are already available. Directive 97/66/EC safeguards the privacy of users with regard to itemised billing, by giving them the means to protect their right to privacy when calling line identification is implemented. The development of these services on a pan-European basis would benefit consumers and is encouraged by this Directive.

(40) Number portability is a key facilitator of consumer choice and effective competition in a competitive telecommunications environment such that end-users who so request should be able to retain their number(s) on the public telephone network independently of the organisation providing service. The provision of this facility between connections to the public telephone network at fixed and non-fixed locations is not covered by this Directive. However, Member States may apply provisions for porting numbers between networks providing services at a fixed location and mobile networks.

(41) The impact of number portability is considerably strengthened when there is transparent tariff information, both for end-users who port their numbers and also for end-users who call those who have ported their numbers. National regulatory authorities should, where feasible, facilitate appropriate tariff transparency as part of the implementation of number portability.

(42) When ensuring that pricing for interconnection related to the provision of number portability is cost-oriented, national regulatory authorities may also take account of prices available in comparable markets.

(43) Currently, Member States impose certain 'must carry' obligations on networks for the distribution of radio or television broadcasts to the public. Member States should be able to lay down proportionate obligations on undertakings under their jurisdiction, in the interest of legitimate public policy considerations, but such obligations should only be imposed where they are necessary to meet general interest objectives clearly defined by Member States in conformity with Community law and should be proportionate, transparent and subject to periodical review. 'Must carry' obligations imposed by Member States should be reasonable, that is they should be proportionate and transparent in the light of clearly defined general interest objectives, and could, where appropriate, entail a provision for proportionate remuneration. Such 'must carry' obligations may include the transmission of services specifically designed to enable appropriate access by disabled users.

(44) Networks used for the distribution of radio or television broadcasts to the public include cable, satellite and terrestrial broadcasting networks. They might also include other networks to the extent that a significant number of end-users use such networks as their principal means to receive radio and television broadcasts.

(¹) See page 7 of this Official Journal.

(45) Services providing content such as the offer for sale of a package of sound or television broadcasting content are not covered by the common regulatory framework for electronic communications networks and services. Providers of such services should not be subject to universal service obligations in respect of these activities. This Directive is without prejudice to measures taken at national level, in compliance with Community law, in respect of such services.

(46) Where a Member State seeks to ensure the provision of other specific services throughout its national territory, such obligations should be implemented on a cost efficient basis and outside the scope of universal service obligations. Accordingly, Member States may undertake additional measures (such as facilitating the development of infrastructure or services in circumstances where the market does not satisfactorily address the requirements of end-users or consumers), in conformity with Community law. As a reaction to the Commission's e-Europe initiative, the Lisbon European Council of 23 and 24 March 2000 called on Member States to ensure that all schools have access to the Internet and to multimedia resources.

(47) In the context of a competitive environment, the views of interested parties, including users and consumers, should be taken into account by national regulatory authorities when dealing with issues related to end-users' rights. Effective procedures should be available to deal with disputes between consumers, on the one hand, and undertakings providing publicly available communications services, on the other. Member States should take full account of Commission Recommendation 98/257/EC of 30 March 1998 on the principles applicable to the bodies responsible for out-of-court settlement of consumer disputes (¹).

(48) Co-regulation could be an appropriate way of stimulating enhanced quality standards and improved service performance. Co-regulation should be guided by the same principles as formal regulation, i.e. it should be objective, justified, proportional, non-discriminatory and transparent.

(49) This Directive should provide for elements of consumer protection, including clear contract terms and dispute resolution, and tariff transparency for consumers. It should also encourage the extension of such benefits to other categories of end-users, in particular small and medium-sized enterprises.

(50) The provisions of this Directive do not prevent a Member State from taking measures justified on grounds set out in Articles 30 and 46 of the Treaty, and in particular on grounds of public security, public policy and public morality.

(51) Since the objectives of the proposed action, namely setting a common level of universal service for telecommunications for all European users and of harmonising conditions for access to and use of public telephone networks at a fixed location and related publicly available telephone services and also achieving a harmonised framework for the regulation of electronic communications services, electronic communications networks and associated facilities, cannot be sufficiently achieved by the Member States and can therefore by reason of the scale or effects of the action be better achieved at Community level, the Community may adopt measures in accordance with the principles of subsidiarity as set out in Article 5 of the Treaty. In accordance with the principle of proportionality, as set out in that Article, this Directive does not go beyond what is necessary in order to achieve those objectives.

(52) The measures necessary for the implementation of this Directive should be adopted in accordance with Council Decision 1999/468/EC of 28 June 1999 laying down the procedures for the exercise of implementing powers conferred on the Commission (²),

HAVE ADOPTED THIS DIRECTIVE:

CHAPTER I

SCOPE, AIMS AND DEFINITIONS

Article 1

Scope and aims

1. Within the framework of Directive 2002/21/EC (Framework Directive), this Directive concerns the provision of electronic communications networks and services to end-users. The aim is to ensure the availability throughout the Community of good quality publicly available services through effective competition and choice and to deal with circumstances in which the needs of end-users are not satisfactorily met by the market.

2. This Directive establishes the rights of end-users and the corresponding obligations on undertakings providing publicly available electronic communications networks and services. With regard to ensuring provision of universal service within an environment of open and competitive markets, this Directive defines the minimum set of services of specified quality to which all end-users have access, at an affordable

(¹) OJ L 115, 17.4.1998, p. 31.

(²) OJ L 184, 17.7.1999, p. 23.

price in the light of specific national conditions, without distorting competition. This Directive also sets out obligations with regard to the provision of certain mandatory services such as the retail provision of leased lines.

Article 2

Definitions

For the purposes of this Directive, the definitions set out in Article 2 of Directive 2002/21/EC (Framework Directive) shall apply.

The following definitions shall also apply:

(a) 'public pay telephone' means a telephone available to the general public, for the use of which the means of payment may include coins and/or credit/debit cards and/or pre-payment cards, including cards for use with dialling codes;

(b) 'public telephone network' means an electronic communications network which is used to provide publicly available telephone services; it supports the transfer between network termination points of speech communications, and also other forms of communication, such as facsimile and data;

(c) 'publicly available telephone service' means a service available to the public for originating and receiving national and international calls and access to emergency services through a number or numbers in a national or international telephone numbering plan, and in addition may, where relevant, include one or more of the following services: the provision of operator assistance, directory enquiry services, directories, provision of public pay phones, provision of service under special terms, provision of special facilities for customers with disabilities or with special social needs and/or the provision of non-geographic services;

(d) 'geographic number' means a number from the national numbering plan where part of its digit structure contains geographic significance used for routing calls to the physical location of the network termination point (NTP);

(e) 'network termination point' (NTP) means the physical point at which a subscriber is provided with access to a public communications network; in the case of networks involving switching or routing, the NTP is identified by means of a specific network address, which may be linked to a subscriber number or name;

(f) 'non-geographic numbers' means a number from the national numbering plan that is not a geographic number.

It includes *inter alia* mobile, freephone and premium rate numbers.

CHAPTER II

UNIVERSAL SERVICE OBLIGATIONS INCLUDING SOCIAL OBLIGATIONS

Article 3

Availability of universal service

1.   Member States shall ensure that the services set out in this Chapter are made available at the quality specified to all end-users in their territory, independently of geographical location, and, in the light of specific national conditions, at an affordable price.

2.   Member States shall determine the most efficient and appropriate approach for ensuring the implementation of universal service, whilst respecting the principles of objectivity, transparency, non-discrimination and proportionality. They shall seek to minimise market distortions, in particular the provision of services at prices or subject to other terms and conditions which depart from normal commercial conditions, whilst safeguarding the public interest.

Article 4

Provision of access at a fixed location

1.   Member States shall ensure that all reasonable requests for connection at a fixed location to the public telephone network and for access to publicly available telephone services at a fixed location are met by at least one undertaking.

2.   The connection provided shall be capable of allowing end-users to make and receive local, national and international telephone calls, facsimile communications and data communications, at data rates that are sufficient to permit functional Internet access, taking into account prevailing technologies used by the majority of subscribers and technological feasibility.

Article 5

Directory enquiry services and directories

1.   Member States shall ensure that:

(a) at least one comprehensive directory is available to end-users in a form approved by the relevant authority, whether printed or electronic, or both, and is updated on a regular basis, and at least once a year;

(b) at least one comprehensive telephone directory enquiry service is available to all end-users, including users of public pay telephones.

2.   The directories in paragraph 1 shall comprise, subject to the provisions of Article 11 of Directive 97/66/EC, all subscribers of publicly available telephone services.

3.   Member States shall ensure that the undertaking(s) providing the services referred to in paragraph 1 apply the principle of non-discrimination to the treatment of information that has been provided to them by other undertakings.

Article 6

Public pay telephones

1.   Member States shall ensure that national regulatory authorities can impose obligations on undertakings in order to ensure that public pay telephones are provided to meet the reasonable needs of end-users in terms of the geographical coverage, the number of telephones, the accessibility of such telephones to disabled users and the quality of services.

2.   A Member State shall ensure that its national regulatory authority can decide not to impose obligations under paragraph 1 in all or part of its territory, if it is satisfied that these facilities or comparable services are widely available, on the basis of a consultation of interested parties as referred to in Article 33.

3.   Member States shall ensure that it is possible to make emergency calls from public pay telephones using the single European emergency call number '112' and other national emergency numbers, all free of charge and without having to use any means of payment.

Article 7

Special measures for disabled users

1.   Member States shall, where appropriate, take specific measures for disabled end-users in order to ensure access to and affordability of publicly available telephone services, including access to emergency services, directory enquiry services and directories, equivalent to that enjoyed by other end-users.

2.   Member States may take specific measures, in the light of national conditions, to ensure that disabled end-users can also take advantage of the choice of undertakings and service providers available to the majority of end-users.

Article 8

Designation of undertakings

1.   Member States may designate one or more undertakings to guarantee the provision of universal service as identified in Articles 4, 5, 6 and 7 and, where applicable, Article 9(2) so that the whole of the national territory can be covered. Member States may designate different undertakings or sets of undertakings to provide different elements of universal service and/or to cover different parts of the national territory.

2.   When Member States designate undertakings in part or all of the national territory as having universal service obligations, they shall do so using an efficient, objective, transparent and non-discriminatory designation mechanism, whereby no undertaking is a priori excluded from being designated. Such designation methods shall ensure that universal service is provided in a cost-effective manner and may be used as a means of determining the net cost of the universal service obligation in accordance with Article 12.

Article 9

Affordability of tariffs

1.   National regulatory authorities shall monitor the evolution and level of retail tariffs of the services identified in Articles 4, 5, 6 and 7 as falling under the universal service obligations and provided by designated undertakings, in particular in relation to national consumer prices and income.

2.   Member States may, in the light of national conditions, require that designated undertakings provide tariff options or packages to consumers which depart from those provided under normal commercial conditions, in particular to ensure that those on low incomes or with special social needs are not prevented from accessing or using the publicly available telephone service.

3.   Member States may, besides any provision for designated undertakings to provide special tariff options or to comply with price caps or geographical averaging or other similar schemes, ensure that support is provided to consumers identified as having low incomes or special social needs.

4.   Member States may require undertakings with obligations under Articles 4, 5, 6 and 7 to apply common tariffs, including geographical averaging, throughout the territory, in the light of national conditions or to comply with price caps.

5.   National regulatory authorities shall ensure that, where a designated undertaking has an obligation to provide special

tariff options, common tariffs, including geographical averaging, or to comply with price caps, the conditions are fully transparent and are published and applied in accordance with the principle of non-discrimination. National regulatory authorities may require that specific schemes be modified or withdrawn.

Article 10

Control of expenditure

1. Member States shall ensure that designated undertakings, in providing facilities and services additional to those referred to in Articles 4, 5, 6, 7 and 9(2), establish terms and conditions in such a way that the subscriber is not obliged to pay for facilities or services which are not necessary or not required for the service requested.

2. Member States shall ensure that designated undertakings with obligations under Articles 4, 5, 6, 7 and 9(2) provide the specific facilities and services set out in Annex I, Part A, in order that subscribers can monitor and control expenditure and avoid unwarranted disconnection of service.

3. Member States shall ensure that the relevant authority is able to waive the requirements of paragraph 2 in all or part of its national territory if it is satisfied that the facility is widely available.

Article 11

Quality of service of designated undertakings

1. National regulatory authorities shall ensure that all designated undertakings with obligations under Articles 4, 5, 6, 7 and 9(2) publish adequate and up-to-date information concerning their performance in the provision of universal service, based on the quality of service parameters, definitions and measurement methods set out in Annex III. The published information shall also be supplied to the national regulatory authority.

2. National regulatory authorities may specify, *inter alia*, additional quality of service standards, where relevant parameters have been developed, to assess the performance of undertakings in the provision of services to disabled end-users and disabled consumers. National regulatory authorities shall ensure that information concerning the performance of undertakings in relation to these parameters is also published and made available to the national regulatory authority.

3. National regulatory authorities may, in addition, specify the content, form and manner of information to be published, in order to ensure that end-users and consumers have access to comprehensive, comparable and user-friendly information.

4. National regulatory authorities shall be able to set performance targets for those undertakings with universal service obligations at least under Article 4. In so doing, national regulatory authorities shall take account of views of interested parties, in particular as referred to in Article 33.

5. Member States shall ensure that national regulatory authorities are able to monitor compliance with these performance targets by designated undertakings.

6. Persistent failure by an undertaking to meet performance targets may result in specific measures being taken in accordance with Directive 2002/20/EC of the European Parliament and of the Council of 7 March 2002 on the authorisation of electronic communications networks and services (Authorisation Directive) ([1]). National regulatory authorities shall be able to order independent audits or similar reviews of the performance data, paid for by the undertaking concerned, in order to ensure the accuracy and comparability of the data made available by undertakings with universal service obligations.

Article 12

Costing of universal service obligations

1. Where national regulatory authorities consider that the provision of universal service as set out in Articles 3 to 10 may represent an unfair burden on undertakings designated to provide universal service, they shall calculate the net costs of its provision.

For that purpose, national regulatory authorities shall:

(a) calculate the net cost of the universal service obligation, taking into account any market benefit which accrues to an undertaking designated to provide universal service, in accordance with Annex IV, Part A; or

(b) make use of the net costs of providing universal service identified by a designation mechanism in accordance with Article 8(2).

2. The accounts and/or other information serving as the basis for the calculation of the net cost of universal service obligations under paragraph 1(a) shall be audited or verified by

---

([1]) See page 21 of this Official Journal.

the national regulatory authority or a body independent of the relevant parties and approved by the national regulatory authority. The results of the cost calculation and the conclusions of the audit shall be publicly available.

Article 13

Financing of universal service obligations

1. Where, on the basis of the net cost calculation referred to in Article 12, national regulatory authorities find that an undertaking is subject to an unfair burden, Member States shall, upon request from a designated undertaking, decide:

(a) to introduce a mechanism to compensate that undertaking for the determined net costs under transparent conditions from public funds; and/or

(b) to share the net cost of universal service obligations between providers of electronic communications networks and services.

2. Where the net cost is shared under paragraph 1(b), Member States shall establish a sharing mechanism administered by the national regulatory authority or a body independent from the beneficiaries under the supervision of the national regulatory authority. Only the net cost, as determined in accordance with Article 12, of the obligations laid down in Articles 3 to 10 may be financed.

3. A sharing mechanism shall respect the principles of transparency, least market distortion, non-discrimination and proportionality, in accordance with the principles of Annex IV, Part B. Member States may choose not to require contributions from undertakings whose national turnover is less than a set limit.

4. Any charges related to the sharing of the cost of universal service obligations shall be unbundled and identified separately for each undertaking. Such charges shall not be imposed or collected from undertakings that are not providing services in the territory of the Member State that has established the sharing mechanism.

Article 14

Transparency

1. Where a mechanism for sharing the net cost of universal service obligations as referred to in Article 13 is established, national regulatory authorities shall ensure that the principles for cost sharing, and details of the mechanism used, are publicly available.

2. Subject to Community and national rules on business confidentiality, national regulatory authorities shall ensure that an annual report is published giving the calculated cost of universal service obligations, identifying the contributions made by all the undertakings involved, and identifying any market benefits, that may have accrued to the undertaking(s) designated to provide universal service, where a fund is actually in place and working.

Article 15

Review of the scope of universal service

1. The Commission shall periodically review the scope of universal service, in particular with a view to proposing to the European Parliament and the Council that the scope be changed or redefined. A review shall be carried out, on the first occasion within two years after the date of application referred to in Article 38(1), second subparagraph, and subsequently every three years.

2. This review shall be undertaken in the light of social, economic and technological developments, taking into account, *inter alia*, mobility and data rates in the light of the prevailing technologies used by the majority of subscribers. The review process shall be undertaken in accordance with Annex V. The Commission shall submit a report to the European Parliament and the Council regarding the outcome of the review.

CHAPTER III

REGULATORY CONTROLS ON UNDERTAKINGS WITH SIGNIFICANT MARKET POWER IN SPECIFIC MARKETS

Article 16

Review of obligations

1. Member States shall maintain all obligations relating to:

(a) retail tariffs for the provision of access to and use of the public telephone network, imposed under Article 17 of Directive 98/10/EC of the European Parliament and of the Council of 26 February 1998 on the application of open network provision (ONP) to voice telephony and on universal service for telecommunications in a competitive environment (^{1});

(b) carrier selection or pre-selection, imposed under Directive 97/33/EC of the European Parliament and of the Council of 30 June 1997 on interconnection in telecommunications with regard to ensuring universal

---

(^{1}) OJ L 101, 1.4.1998, p. 24.

service and interoperability through application of the principles of open network provision (ONP) (¹);

(c) leased lines, imposed under Articles 3, 4, 6, 7, 8 and 10 of Directive 92/44/EEC,

until a review has been carried out and a determination made in accordance with the procedure in paragraph 3 of this Article.

2.   The Commission shall indicate relevant markets for the obligations relating to retail markets in the initial recommendation on relevant product and service markets and the Decision identifying transnational markets to be adopted in accordance with Article 15 of Directive 2002/21/EC (Framework Directive).

3.   Member States shall ensure that, as soon as possible after the entry into force of this Directive, and periodically thereafter, national regulatory authorities undertake a market analysis, in accordance with the procedure set out in Article 16 of Directive 2002/21/EC (Framework Directive) to determine whether to maintain, amend or withdraw the obligations relating to retail markets. Measures taken shall be subject to the procedure referred to in Article 7 of Directive 2002/21/EC (Framework Directive).

Article 17

Regulatory controls on retail services

1.   Member States shall ensure that, where:

(a) as a result of a market analysis carried out in accordance with Article 16(3) a national regulatory authority determines that a given retail market identified in accordance with Article 15 of Directive 2002/21/EC (Framework Directive) is not effectively competitive, and

(b) the national regulatory authority concludes that obligations imposed under Directive 2002/19/EC (Access Directive), or Article 19 of this Directive would not result in the achievement of the objectives set out in Article 8 of Directive 2002/21/EC (Framework Directive),

national regulatory authorities shall impose appropriate regulatory obligations on undertakings identified as having significant market power on a given retail market in accordance with Article 14 of Directive 2002/21/EC (Framework Directive).

2.   Obligations imposed under paragraph 1 shall be based on the nature of the problem identified and be proportionate

---

(¹) OJ L 199, 26.7.1997, p. 32. Directive as amended by Directive 98/61/EC (OJ L 268, 3.10.1998, p. 37).

and justified in the light of the objectives laid down in Article 8 of Directive 2002/21/EC (Framework Directive). The obligations imposed may include requirements that the identified undertakings do not charge excessive prices, inhibit market entry or restrict competition by setting predatory prices, show undue preference to specific end-users or unreasonably bundle services. National regulatory authorities may apply to such undertakings appropriate retail price cap measures, measures to control individual tariffs, or measures to orient tariffs towards costs or prices on comparable markets, in order to protect end-user interests whilst promoting effective competition.

3.   National regulatory authorities shall, on request, submit information to the Commission concerning the retail controls applied and, where appropriate, the cost accounting systems used by the undertakings concerned.

4.   National regulatory authorities shall ensure that, where an undertaking is subject to retail tariff regulation or other relevant retail controls, the necessary and appropriate cost accounting systems are implemented. National regulatory authorities may specify the format and accounting methodology to be used. Compliance with the cost accounting system shall be verified by a qualified independent body. National regulatory authorities shall ensure that a statement concerning compliance is published annually.

5.   Without prejudice to Article 9(2) and Article 10, national regulatory authorities shall not apply retail control mechanisms under paragraph 1 of this Article to geographical or user markets where they are satisfied that there is effective competition.

Article 18

Regulatory controls on the minimum set of leased lines

1.   Where, as a result of the market analysis carried out in accordance with Article 16(3), a national regulatory authority determines that the market for the provision of part or all of the minimum set of leased lines is not effectively competitive, it shall identify undertakings with significant market power in the provision of those specific elements of the minimum set of leased lines services in all or part of its territory in accordance with Article 14 of Directive 2002/21/EC (Framework Directive). The national regulatory authority shall impose obligations regarding the provision of the minimum set of leased lines, as identified in the list of standards published in the *Official Journal of the European Communities* in accordance with Article 17 of Directive 2002/21/EC (Framework Directive), and the conditions for such provision set out in

Annex VII to this Directive, on such undertakings in relation to those specific leased line markets.

2. Where as a result of the market analysis carried out in accordance with Article 16(3), a national regulatory authority determines that a relevant market for the provision of leased lines in the minimum set is effectively competitive, it shall withdraw the obligations referred to in paragraph 1 in relation to this specific leased line market.

3. The minimum set of leased lines with harmonised characteristics, and associated standards, shall be published in the *Official Journal of the European Communities* as part of the list of standards referred to in Article 17 of Directive 2002/21/EC (Framework Directive). The Commission may adopt amendments necessary to adapt the minimum set of leased lines to new technical developments and to changes in market demand, including the possible deletion of certain types of leased line from the minimum set, acting in accordance with the procedure referred to in Article 37(2) of this Directive.

Article 19

Carrier selection and carrier pre-selection

1. National regulatory authorities shall require undertakings notified as having significant market power for the provision of connection to and use of the public telephone network at a fixed location in accordance with Article 16(3) to enable their subscribers to access the services of any interconnected provider of publicly available telephone services:

(a) on a call-by-call basis by dialling a carrier selection code; and

(b) by means of pre-selection, with a facility to override any pre-selected choice on a call-by-call basis by dialling a carrier selection code.

2. User requirements for these facilities to be implemented on other networks or in other ways shall be assessed in accordance with the market analysis procedure laid down in Article 16 of Directive 2002/21/EC (Framework Directive) and implemented in accordance with Article 12 of Directive 2002/19/EC (Access Directive).

3. National regulatory authorities shall ensure that pricing for access and interconnection related to the provision of the facilities in paragraph 1 is cost oriented and that direct charges to subscribers, if any, do not act as a disincentive for the use of these facilities.

CHAPTER IV

END-USER INTERESTS AND RIGHTS

Article 20

Contracts

1. Paragraphs 2, 3 and 4 apply without prejudice to Community rules on consumer protection, in particular Directives 97/7/EC and 93/13/EC, and national rules in conformity with Community law.

2. Member States shall ensure that, where subscribing to services providing connection and/or access to the public telephone network, consumers have a right to a contract with an undertaking or undertakings providing such services. The contract shall specify at least:

(a) the identity and address of the supplier;

(b) services provided, the service quality levels offered, as well as the time for the initial connection;

(c) the types of maintenance service offered;

(d) particulars of prices and tariffs and the means by which up-to-date information on all applicable tariffs and maintenance charges may be obtained;

(e) the duration of the contract, the conditions for renewal and termination of services and of the contract;

(f) any compensation and the refund arrangements which apply if contracted service quality levels are not met; and

(g) the method of initiating procedures for settlement of disputes in accordance with Article 34.

Member States may extend these obligations to cover other end-users.

3. Where contracts are concluded between consumers and electronic communications services providers other than those providing connection and/or access to the public telephone network, the information in paragraph 2 shall also be included in such contracts. Member States may extend this obligation to cover other end-users.

4. Subscribers shall have a right to withdraw from their contracts without penalty upon notice of proposed modifications in the contractual conditions. Subscribers shall be given adequate notice, not shorter than one month, ahead

of any such modifications and shall be informed at the same time of their right to withdraw, without penalty, from such contracts, if they do not accept the new conditions.

Article 21

Transparency and publication of information

1. Member States shall ensure that transparent and up-to-date information on applicable prices and tariffs, and on standard terms and conditions, in respect of access to and use of publicly available telephone services is available to end-users and consumers, in accordance with the provisions of Annex II.

2. National regulatory authorities shall encourage the provision of information to enable end-users, as far as appropriate, and consumers to make an independent evaluation of the cost of alternative usage patterns, by means of, for instance, interactive guides.

Article 22

Quality of service

1. Member States shall ensure that national regulatory authorities are, after taking account of the views of interested parties, able to require undertakings that provide publicly available electronic communications services to publish comparable, adequate and up-to-date information for end-users on the quality of their services. The information shall, on request, also be supplied to the national regulatory authority in advance of its publication.

2. National regulatory authorities may specify, *inter alia*, the quality of service parameters to be measured, and the content, form and manner of information to be published, in order to ensure that end-users have access to comprehensive, comparable and user-friendly information. Where appropriate, the parameters, definitions and measurement methods given in Annex III could be used.

Article 23

Integrity of the network

Member States shall take all necessary steps to ensure the integrity of the public telephone network at fixed locations and, in the event of catastrophic network breakdown or in cases of *force majeure*, the availability of the public telephone network and publicly available telephone services at fixed locations. Member States shall ensure that undertakings providing publicly available telephone services at fixed locations take all reasonable steps to ensure uninterrupted access to emergency services.

Article 24

Interoperability of consumer digital television equipment

In accordance with the provisions of Annex VI, Member States shall ensure the interoperability of the consumer digital television equipment referred to therein.

Article 25

Operator assistance and directory enquiry services

1. Member States shall ensure that subscribers to publicly available telephone services have the right to have an entry in the publicly available directory referred to in Article 5(1)(a).

2. Member States shall ensure that all undertakings which assign telephone numbers to subscribers meet all reasonable requests to make available, for the purposes of the provision of publicly available directory enquiry services and directories, the relevant information in an agreed format on terms which are fair, objective, cost oriented and non-discriminatory.

3. Member States shall ensure that all end-users provided with a connection to the public telephone network can access operator assistance services and directory enquiry services in accordance with Article 5(1)(b).

4. Member States shall not maintain any regulatory restrictions which prevent end-users in one Member State from accessing directly the directory enquiry service in another Member State.

5. Paragraphs 1, 2, 3 and 4 apply subject to the requirements of Community legislation on the protection of personal data and privacy and, in particular, Article 11 of Directive 97/66/EC.

Article 26

Single European emergency call number

1. Member States shall ensure that, in addition to any other national emergency call numbers specified by the national regulatory authorities, all end-users of publicly available telephone services, including users of public pay telephones, are able to call the emergency services free of charge, by using the single European emergency call number '112'.

2. Member States shall ensure that calls to the single European emergency call number '112' are appropriately answered and handled in a manner best suited to the national organisation of emergency systems and within the technological possibilities of the networks.

3. Member States shall ensure that undertakings which operate public telephone networks make caller location information available to authorities handling emergencies, to the extent technically feasible, for all calls to the single European emergency call number '112'.

4. Member States shall ensure that citizens are adequately informed about the existence and use of the single European emergency call number '112'.

Article 27

European telephone access codes

1. Member States shall ensure that the '00' code is the standard international access code. Special arrangements for making calls between adjacent locations across borders between Member States may be established or continued. The end-users of publicly available telephone services in the locations concerned shall be fully informed of such arrangements.

2. Member States shall ensure that all undertakings that operate public telephone networks handle all calls to the European telephony numbering space, without prejudice to the need for an undertaking that operates a public telephone network to recover the cost of the conveyance of calls on its network.

Article 28

Non-geographic numbers

Member States shall ensure that end-users from other Member States are able to access non-geographic numbers within their territory where technically and economically feasible, except where a called subscriber has chosen for commercial reasons to limit access by calling parties located in specific geographical areas.

Article 29

Provision of additional facilities

1. Member States shall ensure that national regulatory authorities are able to require all undertakings that operate public telephone networks to make available to end-users the facilities listed in Annex I, Part B, subject to technical feasibility and economic viability.

2. A Member State may decide to waive paragraph 1 in all or part of its territory if it considers, after taking into account the views of interested parties, that there is sufficient access to these facilities.

3. Without prejudice to Article 10(2), Member States may impose the obligations in Annex I, Part A, point (e), concerning disconnection as a general requirement on all undertakings.

Article 30

Number portability

1. Member States shall ensure that all subscribers of publicly available telephone services, including mobile services, who so request can retain their number(s) independently of the undertaking providing the service:

(a) in the case of geographic numbers, at a specific location; and

(b) in the case of non-geographic numbers, at any location.

This paragraph does not apply to the porting of numbers between networks providing services at a fixed location and mobile networks.

2. National regulatory authorities shall ensure that pricing for interconnection related to the provision of number portability is cost oriented and that direct charges to subscribers, if any, do not act as a disincentive for the use of these facilities.

3. National regulatory authorities shall not impose retail tariffs for the porting of numbers in a manner that would distort competition, such as by setting specific or common retail tariffs.

Article 31

'Must carry' obligations

1. Member States may impose reasonable 'must carry' obligations, for the transmission of specified radio and television broadcast channels and services, on undertakings under their jurisdiction providing electronic communications networks used for the distribution of radio or television broadcasts to the public where a significant number of end-users of such networks use them as their principal means to receive radio and television broadcasts. Such obligations shall only be imposed where they are necessary to meet clearly defined general interest objectives and shall be proportionate and transparent. The obligations shall be subject to periodical review.

2. Neither paragraph 1 of this Article nor Article 3(2) of Directive 2002/19/EC (Access Directive) shall prejudice the ability of Member States to determine appropriate remuneration, if any, in respect of measures taken in accordance with this Article while ensuring that, in similar

circumstances, there is no discrimination in the treatment of undertakings providing electronic communications networks. Where remuneration is provided for, Member States shall ensure that it is applied in a proportionate and transparent manner.

Article 32

Additional mandatory services

Member States may decide to make additional services, apart from services within the universal service obligations as defined in Chapter II, publicly available in its own territory but, in such circumstances, no compensation mechanism involving specific undertakings may be imposed.

Article 33

Consultation with interested parties

1.   Member States shall ensure as far as appropriate that national regulatory authorities take account of the views of end-users, and consumers (including, in particular, disabled users), manufacturers, undertakings that provide electronic communications networks and/or services on issues related to all end-user and consumer rights concerning publicly available electronic communications services, in particular where they have a significant impact on the market.

2.   Where appropriate, interested parties may develop, with the guidance of national regulatory authorities, mechanisms, involving consumers, user groups and service providers, to improve the general quality of service provision by, *inter alia*, developing and monitoring codes of conduct and operating standards.

Article 34

Out-of-court dispute resolution

1.   Member States shall ensure that transparent, simple and inexpensive out-of-court procedures are available for dealing with unresolved disputes, involving consumers, relating to issues covered by this Directive. Member States shall adopt measures to ensure that such procedures enable disputes to be

settled fairly and promptly and may, where warranted, adopt a system of reimbursement and/or compensation. Member States may extend these obligations to cover disputes involving other end-users.

2.   Member States shall ensure that their legislation does not hamper the establishment of complaints offices and the provision of on-line services at the appropriate territorial level to facilitate access to dispute resolution by consumers and end-users.

3.   Where such disputes involve parties in different Member States, Member States shall coordinate their efforts with a view to bringing about a resolution of the dispute.

4.   This Article is without prejudice to national court procedures.

Article 35

Technical adjustment

Amendments necessary to adapt Annexes I, II, III, VI and VII to technological developments or to changes in market demand shall be adopted by the Commission, acting in accordance with the procedure referred to in Article 37(2).

Article 36

Notification, monitoring and review procedures

1.   National regulatory authorities shall notify to the Commission by at the latest the date of application referred to in Article 38(1), second subparagraph, and immediately in the event of any change thereafter in the names of undertakings designated as having universal service obligations under Article 8(1).

The Commission shall make the information available in a readily accessible form, and shall distribute it to the Communications Committee referred to in Article 37.

2.   National regulatory authorities shall notify to the Commission the names of operators deemed to have significant market power for the purposes of this Directive, and the obligations imposed upon them under this Directive. Any changes affecting the obligations imposed upon undertakings or of the undertakings affected under the provisions of this Directive shall be notified to the Commission without delay.

3.   The Commission shall periodically review the functioning of this Directive and report to the European Parliament and to the Council, on the first occasion not later than three years

after the date of application referred to in Article 38(1), second subparagraph. The Member States and national regulatory authorities shall supply the necessary information to the Commission for this purpose.

Article 37

Committee

1. The Commission shall be assisted by the Communications Committee, set up by Article 22 of Directive 2002/21/EC (Framework Directive).

2. Where reference is made to this paragraph, Articles 5 and 7 of Decision 1999/468/EC shall apply, having regard to the provisions of Article 8 thereof.

The period laid down in Article 5(6) of Decision 1999/468/EC shall be three months.

3. The Committee shall adopt its rules of procedure.

Article 38

Transposition

1. Member States shall adopt and publish the laws, regulations and administrative provisions necessary to comply with this Directive by 24 July 2003 at the latest. They shall forthwith inform the Commission thereof.

They shall apply those measures from 25 July 2003.

2. When Member States adopt these measures, they shall contain a reference to this Directive or be accompanied by such a reference on the occasion of their official publication. The methods of making such a reference shall be laid down by the Member States.

3. Member States shall communicate to the Commission the text of the provisions of national law which they adopt in the field governed by this Directive and of any subsequent modifications to those provisions.

Article 39

Entry into force

This Directive shall enter into force on the day of its publication in the *Official Journal of the European Communities*.

Article 40

Addressees

This Directive is addressed to the Member States.

Done at Brussels, 7 March 2002.

For the European Parliament	*For the Council*
The President	*The President*
P. COX	J. C. APARICIO

ANNEX I

DESCRIPTION OF FACILITIES AND SERVICES REFERRED TO IN ARTICLE 10 (CONTROL OF EXPENDITURE) AND ARTICLE 29 (ADDITIONAL FACILITIES)

Part A: Facilities and services referred to in Article 10

(a) *Itemised billing*

Member States are to ensure that national regulatory authorities, subject to the requirements of relevant legislation on the protection of personal data and privacy, may lay down the basic level of itemised bills which are to be provided by designated undertakings (as established in Article 8) to consumers free of charge in order that they can:

(i) allow verification and control of the charges incurred in using the public telephone network at a fixed location and/or related publicly available telephone services, and

(ii) adequately monitor their usage and expenditure and thereby exercise a reasonable degree of control over their bills.

Where appropriate, additional levels of detail may be offered to subscribers at reasonable tariffs or at no charge.

Calls which are free of charge to the calling subscriber, including calls to helplines, are not to be identified in the calling subscriber's itemised bill.

(b) *Selective call barring for outgoing calls, free of charge*

I.e. the facility whereby the subscriber can, on request to the telephone service provider, bar outgoing calls of defined types or to defined types of numbers free of charge.

(c) *Pre-payment systems*

Member States are to ensure that national regulatory authorities may require designated undertakings to provide means for consumers to pay for access to the public telephone network and use of publicly available telephone services on pre-paid terms.

(d) *Phased payment of connection fees*

Member States are to ensure that national regulatory authorities may require designated undertakings to allow consumers to pay for connection to the public telephone network on the basis of payments phased over time.

(e) *Non-payment of bills*

Member States are to authorise specified measures, which are to be proportionate, non-discriminatory and published, to cover non-payment of telephone bills for use of the public telephone network at fixed locations. These measures are to ensure that due warning of any consequent service interruption or disconnection is given to the subscriber beforehand. Except in cases of fraud, persistent late payment or non-payment, these measures are to ensure, as far as is technically feasible, that any service interruption is confined to the service concerned. Disconnection for non-payment of bills should take place only after due warning is given to the subscriber. Member States may allow a period of limited service prior to complete disconnection, during which only calls that do not incur a charge to the subscriber (e.g. '112' calls) are permitted.

Part B: List of facilities referred to in Article 29

(a) *Tone dialling or DTMF (dual-tone multi-frequency operation)*

I.e. the public telephone network supports the use of DTMF tones as defined in ETSI ETR 207 for end-to-end signalling throughout the network both within a Member State and between Member States.

(b) *Calling-line identification*

I.e. the calling party's number is presented to the called party prior to the call being established.

This facility should be provided in accordance with relevant legislation on protection of personal data and privacy, in particular Directive 97/66/EC.

To the extent technically feasible, operators should provide data and signals to facilitate the offering of calling-line identity and tone dialling across Member State boundaries.

———

INFORMATION TO BE PUBLISHED IN ACCORDANCE WITH ARTICLE 21
(TRANSPARENCY AND PUBLICATION OF INFORMATION)

The national regulatory authority has a responsibility to ensure that the information in this Annex is published, in accordance with Article 21. It is for the national regulatory authority to decide which information is to be published by the undertakings providing public telephone networks and/or publicly available telephone services and which information is to be published by the national regulatory authority itself, so as to ensure that consumers are able to make informed choices.

1.   Name(s) and address(es) of undertaking(s)

        I.e. names and head office addresses of undertakings providing public telephone networks and/or publicly available telephone services.

2.   Publicly available telephone services offered

2.1.   Scope of the publicly available telephone service

        Description of the publicly available telephone services offered, indicating what is included in the subscription charge and the periodic rental charge (e.g. operator services, directories, directory enquiry services, selective call barring, itemised billing, maintenance, etc.).

2.2.   Standard tariffs covering access, all types of usage charges, maintenance, and including details of standard discounts applied and special and targeted tariff schemes.

2.3.   Compensation/refund policy, including specific details of any compensation/refund schemes offered.

2.4.   Types of maintenance service offered.

2.5.   Standard contract conditions, including any minimum contractual period, if relevant.

3.   Dispute settlement mechanisms including those developed by the undertaking.

4.   Information about rights as regards universal service, including the facilities and services mentioned in Annex I.

———

ANNEX III

ANNEX III

QUALITY OF SERVICE PARAMETERS

Supply-time and quality-of-service parameters, definitions and measurement methods referred to Articles 11 and 22

Parameter (¹)	Definition	Measurement method
Supply time for initial connection	ETSI EG 201 769-1	ETSI EG 201 769-1
Fault rate per access line	ETSI EG 201 769-1	ETSI EG 201 769-1
Fault repair time	ETSI EG 201 769-1	ETSI EG 201 769-1
Unsuccessful call ratio (²)	ETSI EG 201 769-1	ETSI EG 201 769-1
Call set up time (²)	ETSI EG 201 769-1	ETSI EG 201 769-1
Response times for operator services	ETSI EG 201 769-1	ETSI EG 201 769-1
Response times for directory enquiry services	ETSI EG 201 769-1	ETSI EG 201 769-1
Proportion of coin and card operated public pay telephones in working order	ETSI EG 201 769-1	ETSI EG 201 769-1
Bill correctness complaints	ETSI EG 201 769-1	ETSI EG 201 769-1

(¹) Parameters should allow for performance to be analysed at a regional level (i.e. no less than Level 2 in the Nomenclature of Territorial Units for Statistics (NUTS) established by Eurostat).
(²) Member States may decide not to require that up-to-date information concerning the performance for these two parameters be kept, if evidence is available to show that performance in these two areas is satisfactory.

Note: Version number of ETSI EG 201 769-1 is 1.1.1 (April 2000).

CALCULATING THE NET COST, IF ANY, OF UNIVERSAL SERVICE OBLIGATIONS AND ESTABLISHING ANY RECOVERY OR SHARING MECHANISM IN ACCORDANCE WITH ARTICLES 12 AND 13

Part A: Calculation of net cost

Universal service obligations refer to those obligations placed upon an undertaking by a Member State which concern the provision of a network and service throughout a specified geographical area, including, where required, averaged prices in that geographical area for the provision of that service or provision of specific tariff options for consumers with low incomes or with special social needs.

National regulatory authorities are to consider all means to ensure appropriate incentives for undertakings (designated or not) to provide universal service obligations cost efficiently. In undertaking a calculation exercise, the net cost of universal service obligations is to be calculated as the difference between the net cost for a designated undertaking of operating with the universal service obligations and operating without the universal service obligations. This applies whether the network in a particular Member State is fully developed or is still undergoing development and expansion. Due attention is to be given to correctly assessing the costs that any designated undertaking would have chosen to avoid had there been no universal service obligation. The net cost calculation should assess the benefits, including intangible benefits, to the universal service operator.

The calculation is to be based upon the costs attributable to:

(i) elements of the identified services which can only be provided at a loss or provided under cost conditions falling outside normal commercial standards.

This category may include service elements such as access to emergency telephone services, provision of certain public pay telephones, provision of certain services or equipment for disabled people, etc;

(ii) specific end-users or groups of end-users who, taking into account the cost of providing the specified network and service, the revenue generated and any geographical averaging of prices imposed by the Member State, can only be served at a loss or under cost conditions falling outside normal commercial standards.

This category includes those end-users or groups of end-users which would not be served by a commercial operator which did not have an obligation to provide universal service.

The calculation of the net cost of specific aspects of universal service obligations is to be made separately and so as to avoid the double counting of any direct or indirect benefits and costs. The overall net cost of universal service obligations to any undertaking is to be calculated as the sum of the net costs arising from the specific components of universal service obligations, taking account of any intangible benefits. The responsibility for verifying the net cost lies with the national regulatory authority.

Part B: Recovery of any net costs of universal service obligations

The recovery or financing of any net costs of universal service obligations requires designated undertakings with universal service obligations to be compensated for the services they provide under non-commercial conditions. Because such a compensation involves financial transfers, Member States are to ensure that these are undertaken in an objective, transparent, non-discriminatory and proportionate manner. This means that the transfers result in the least distortion to competition and to user demand.

In accordance with Article 13(3), a sharing mechanism based on a fund should use a transparent and neutral means for collecting contributions that avoids the danger of a double imposition of contributions falling on both outputs and inputs of undertakings.

The independent body administering the fund is to be responsible for collecting contributions from undertakings which are assessed as liable to contribute to the net cost of universal service obligations in the Member State and is to oversee the transfer of sums due and/or administrative payments to the undertakings entitled to receive payments from the fund.

———

PROCESS FOR REVIEWING THE SCOPE OF UNIVERSAL SERVICE IN ACCORDANCE WITH ARTICLE 15

In considering whether a review of the scope of universal service obligations should be undertaken, the Commission is to take into consideration the following elements:

— social and market developments in terms of the services used by consumers,

— social and market developments in terms of the availability and choice of services to consumers,

— technological developments in terms of the way services are provided to consumers.

In considering whether the scope of universal service obligations be changed or redefined, the Commission is to take into consideration the following elements:

— are specific services available to and used by a majority of consumers and does the lack of availability or non-use by a minority of consumers result in social exclusion, and

— does the availability and use of specific services convey a general net benefit to all consumers such that public intervention is warranted in circumstances where the specific services are not provided to the public under normal commercial circumstances?

———

INTEROPERABILITY OF DIGITAL CONSUMER EQUIPMENT REFERRED TO IN ARTICLE 24

1. *The common scrambling algorithm and free-to-air reception*

   All consumer equipment intended for the reception of digital television signals, for sale or rent or otherwise made available in the Community, capable of descrambling digital television signals, is to possess the capability to:

   — allow the descrambling of such signals according to the common European scrambling algorithm as administered by a recognised European standards organisation, currently ETSI;

   — display signals that have been transmitted in clear provided that, in the event that such equipment is rented, the rentee is in compliance with the relevant rental agreement.

2. *Interoperability for analogue and digital television sets*

   Any analogue television set with an integral screen of visible diagonal greater than 42 cm which is put on the market for sale or rent in the Community is to be fitted with at least one open interface socket, as standardised by a recognised European standards organisation, e.g. as given in the CENELEC EN 50 049-1:1997 standard, permitting simple connection of peripherals, especially additional decoders and digital receivers.

   Any digital television set with an integral screen of visible diagonal greater than 30 cm which is put on the market for sale or rent in the Community is to be fitted with at least one open interface socket (either standardised by, or conforming to a standard adopted by, a recognised European standards organisation, or conforming to an industry-wide specification) e.g. the DVB common interface connector, permitting simple connection of peripherals, and able to pass all the elements of a digital television signal, including information relating to interactive and conditionally accessed services.

CONDITIONS FOR THE MINIMUM SET OF LEASED LINES REFERRED TO IN ARTICLE 18

Note: In accordance with the procedure in Article 18, provision of the minimum set of leased lines under the conditions established by Directive 92/44/EC should continue until such time as the national regulatory authority determines that there is effective competition in the relevant leased lines market.

National regulatory authorities are to ensure that provision of the minimum set of leased lines referred to in Article 18 follows the basic principles of non-discrimination, cost orientation and transparency.

1.   *Non discrimination*

National regulatory authorities are to ensure that the organisations identified as having significant market power pursuant to Article 18(1) adhere to the principle of non-discrimination when providing leased lines referred to in Article 18. Those organisations are to apply similar conditions in similar circumstances to organisations providing similar services, and are to provide leased lines to others under the same conditions and of the same quality as they provide for their own services, or those of their subsidiaries or partners, where applicable.

2.   *Cost orientation*

National regulatory authorities are, where appropriate, to ensure that tariffs for leased lines referred to in Article 18 follow the basic principles of cost orientation.

To this end, national regulatory authorities are to ensure that undertakings identified as having significant market power pursuant to Article 18(1) formulate and put in practice a suitable cost accounting system.

National regulatory authorities are to keep available, with an adequate level of detail, information on the cost accounting systems applied by such undertakings. They are to submit this information to the Commission on request.

3.   *Transparency*

National regulatory authorities are to ensure that the following information in respect of the minimum set of leased lines referred to in Article 18 is published in an easily accessible form.

3.1.   Technical characteristics, including the physical and electrical characteristics as well as the detailed technical and performance specifications which apply at the network termination point.

3.2.   Tariffs, including the initial connection charges, the periodic rental charges and other charges. Where tariffs are differentiated, this must be indicated.

Where, in response to a particular request, an organisation identified as having significant market power pursuant to Article 18(1) considers it unreasonable to provide a leased line in the minimum set under its published tariffs and supply conditions, it must seek the agreement of the national regulatory authority to vary those conditions in that case.

3.3.   Supply conditions, including at least the following elements:

— information concerning the ordering procedure,

— the typical delivery period, which is the period, counted from the date when the user has made a firm request for a leased line, in which 95 % of all leased lines of the same type have been put through to the customers.

This period will be established on the basis of the actual delivery periods of leased lines during a recent time interval of reasonable duration. The calculation must not include cases where late delivery periods were requested by users,

— the contractual period, which includes the period which is in general laid down in the contract and the minimum contractual period which the user is obliged to accept,

— the typical repair time, which is the period, counted from the time when a failure message has been given to the responsible unit within the undertaking identified as having significant market power pursuant to Article 18(1) up to the moment in which 80 % of all leased lines of the same type have been re-established and in appropriate cases notified back in operation to the users. Where different classes of quality of repair are offered for the same type of leased lines, the different typical repair times shall be published,

— any refund procedure.

In addition where a Member State considers that the achieved performance for the provision of the minimum set of leased lines does not meet users' needs, it may define appropriate targets for the supply conditions listed above.

Index